The Best Places to Meet Good Men

ELLEN LEDERMAN

Keep an eye on this book. Shar might steal it!

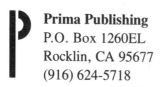

Prima Publishing
P.O. Box 1260EL
Rocklin, CA 95677
(916) 624-5718

Typography by Dharma Enterprises
Production by Carol Dondrea, Bookman Productions
Copyediting by Anne Montague
Interior design by Renee Deprey
Cover design by The Dunlavey Studio
Chapter opening art by Elizabeth Morales-Denney

Prima Publishing

Library of Congress Cataloging-in-Publication Data

Lederman, Ellen, 1954–
    Best places to meet good men : the single women's yellow pages / Ellen Lederman.
        p.   cm.
    Includes index.
    ISBN 1-55958-106-9
        1. Dating (Social customs)—Directories.   2. Mate selection—United States—Directories.   3. Societies—United States—Directories.   I. Title.
HQ801.L37   1991
646.7'7'025--dc20   91-20746
                                              CIP

91 92 93 94 RRD 10 9 8 7 6 5 4 3 2 1
Printed in the United States of America

A special note to Canadian readers:
Opportunities for meeting men are not limited to the United States. You will be able to use the ideas in this book to develop your own strategies and plans for connecting in Canada with the type of men you prefer. The organizations and associations profiled throughout the book will be happy to provide you with the addresses and phone numbers of their Canadian counterparts.

How to Order:
Quantity discounts are available from Prima Publishing, P.O. Box 1260EL, Rocklin, CA 95677; telephone (916) 624-5718. On your letterhead include information concerning the intended use of the books and the number of books you wish to purchase.
U.S. Bookstores and Libraries: Please submit all orders to St. Martin's Press, 175 Fifth Avenue, New York, NY 10010; telephone (212) 674-5151.

C O N T E N T S

CHAPTER 3   *Volunteer, Political, and Civic Work*   **98**
              Service Clubs   **98**

ACKNOWLEDGMENTS

THIS BOOK WAS MADE POSSIBLE by the assistance of numerous individuals. Representatives from the various organizations and associations were extremely helpful in providing statistics, descriptions, and other information. The Fulton County (Georgia) library system provided the resources and personnel to facilitate information gathering. Patti Breitman's insightful editing improved the original manuscript. Candice Fuhrman recognized that Prima would be the ideal publisher for the book and facilitated its acceptance. Andrew Lederman's computer expertise eliminated many would-be and actual computer glitches. Many thanks to all concerned.

INTRODUCTION

WHERE ARE ALL THE GOOD (AVAILABLE, INTERESTING, ATTRACTIVE, SEXY, HEALTHY, FINANCIALLY STABLE) MEN?

This is the question single women most often ask themselves. Bemoaning the difficulty they have meeting men (or the right type of men), they suspect and hope that "Mr. Right" is out there, but have no idea how to find him.

The problem is really not as complex as it might appear. There *are* men out there . . . millions of them! And with a little knowledge, effort, and imagination, you can meet an impressive number of quality males. This book will arm you with the information you need. If you're willing to get involved in just a few of the many activities, organizations, and experiences profiled on these pages, you will significantly expand your man-meeting opportunities.

If, like so many other women, you have the desire to meet men but hate the idea of leaving yourself open to rejection or openly admitting that you're looking to connect with someone, don't despair. This is the first book to focus exclusively on ways to meet men that go beyond the typical singles scene. You won't find any mention of singles bars or dances, video or computer dating, or personal ads. These work sometimes for some women, but the game playing and artificial situations can be uncomfortable and even offensive to many.

The Best Places to Meet Good Men offers a different way of connecting with men. The key is active involvement in activities that interest *you*. All of the groups in the listings that follow are interesting and worthwhile in their own right. Although they enable you to meet men, that's not their reason for existence. You should become involved in them not just to meet someone but because they will:

- broaden your horizons
- improve your intellect
- increase your physical fitness
- make a contribution to your community or to the world
- enhance your leisure time

- allow you to make better use of your community's resources
- add interest and variety to your life
- develop your network of friends and acquaintances (both male and female)

Chances are excellent that you'll meet men by pursuing the suggestions in this book. But even if you don't, you won't have lost anything. Unlike the more contrived man-meeting methods such as bars, video/computer dating, and personal ads, where you're likely to feel that you wasted your time or money if you don't connect with someone, the opportunities in this book won't make you feel this way. Because whether or not you meet Mr. Right, you will still have done something meaningful with your time, money, and energy. Whether it's coaching a Little League team, learning to water-ski, cycling through New England, studying psychology, attending an ethnic festival, breeding show cats, or making more use of your public library, you will have enjoyed yourself and gained something from the experience— quite apart from your success in meeting a man.

Had this book been written three or four decades ago, it would have advised you to simply go wherever the men were without considering your own interests. Even if you loathed football or thought chess was the most boring game in the world, you would have been told to pursue these activities because of their appeal to men. But in our time, such advice would be inappropriate. You need to be honest when picking activities and experiences from the book. Choose only those that have some attraction for you. (If you get involved in stickball, for example, only because it's a predominantly male sport, you're setting yourself up for a major disappointment if you're not successful in meeting someone.) You will be more likely to attract men when you are genuinely interested and enthusiastic about an activity. Pretending to like something just to meet a man is dishonest, and it may backfire if the man eventually learns that your interest was feigned. He may feel he could never trust you about anything else. Remember that the men in these activities and organizations really care about what they're involved in. Don't insult them (or yourself) by being insincere.

The old adage about being able to lead a horse to water but not to make it drink applies here as well. This book provides you with the tools to meet men but it cannot make sure you take advantage of the possibilities. If you shelve the book without following any of the suggestions, your reading will have been in vain. Make a resolution—and keep it—to try a few of the options in each chapter. If these don't work out, then try some different ones. Keep going until you find some activities *and* some men you like!

CHAPTER 1

Sports and Fitness

BEING A COUCH POTATO WON'T do much for your physical, mental, or social well-being. If you want to stay in shape, increase your energy, and meet men, it's imperative that you turn off the TV, stop lounging on the sofa, and plunge into some sort of physical activity. Whether it's a vigorous sport like lacrosse or a more genteel pastime like croquet, the main thing is to find an activity you enjoy.

Ideally, for fitness you should select several activities from this chapter to ensure that you get the best possible workout. For example, yoga is great for flexibility, but you should also look for an activity that offers aerobic challenges (such as tennis or cycling). You also need some outdoor activities that take advantage of good weather as well as some that can be performed indoors in inclement weather. While you may want to consider some sports that you used to be involved with but haven't done since high school or college, also try some new ones to expand your abilities and skills. Choose as well a couple of activities that may not necessarily increase your stamina, strength, or cardiovascular functioning, but are just plain fun. Hot-air ballooning or rock climbing, polo or flying disc games, stickball or orienteering . . . your choices are virtually unlimited if you are willing to discover new activities and mingle with the men who pursue them.

Archery

Archery is one of the oldest sports known to man. The bow and arrow have been used for more than 35,000 years as both weapons and sports equipment.

Target archery generally consists of a round of 36 arrows shot from four distances (30, 50, 60, and 70 meters for women; 30, 50, 70, and 90 meters for men) at a single target. Field archery has a 28-target course laid out in wooded and open areas. Shooting positions range from 15 feet to 80 yards. Field archery also encompasses bow hunting for game animals and bow fishing.

Some 7 million people in the United States own bows. Both men and women participate in the sport, although there appears to be much more male participation (perhaps twice as much).

Archers generally have a quiet strength. They may not be the most verbal or social people around, but their well-developed powers of concentration and sizing up a situation allow them to make informed decisions that ensure their success in life. Bow hunters often exhibit a more macho and somewhat less sensitive way of relating to women than archers who limit their shooting to inanimate objects.

There are more than 94 National Archery Association clubs in the United States. The NAA can direct you to the club nearest you.

National Archery Association
1750 East Boulder Street
Colorado Springs, CO 80909-5774
(719) 578-4576

Arm Wrestling

Sylvester Stallone's film *Over the Top* brought national prominence to the sport of arm wrestling. But you don't have to be a muscle-bound male to partake in this activity. If you feel you might enjoy the challenge of matching the strength of your arm against an opponent's, all you need to become proficient at this sport is to practice.

Although much arm wrestling occurs informally in bars and gyms, actual competitions on regional, national, and international levels are held in hotel ballrooms. About 80 percent of arm wrestlers are men, but both men and women compete in the four weight classes.

Typically, women compete against other women, but some men may be willing to wrestle with you, especially if you develop substantial strength and skill. As for the kind of men you'll meet, they'll tend to be strong, silent types. They want to prove themselves and prefer to do it as individuals rather than as part of a team. Classifying them all as uneducated blue-collar workers would be unfair and untrue, but you're not likely to find many highly cultured sophisticates, either. If you want a man who enjoys a night at the opera, an arm wrestler may not be right for you. But if you're interested in a man who knows what he wants in life and takes a straightforward approach to getting it, you may do very well with one of these men.

The American Armwrestling Association (AAA) has 5,000 members and about 40 state directors who manage local and regional events. Contact this organization for the name of your state chairman so that you can get involved in local practice and competitions.

American Armwrestling Association
P.O. Box 132
Scranton, PA 18504-0132
(717) 342-4984

Badminton

You may think you're familiar with badminton if you're one of the millions of people who have played the game at a picnic or barbecue. But the real sport of competitive badminton is a different game entirely. Competitive badminton is always played indoors, by two to four people on a rectangular court with light racquets that are used to volley a shuttlecock over a high net. While the serve is similar to the one used in tennis, badminton is actually a faster-paced game. Because the shuttlecock is in play much more than the ball is in a tennis match, badminton offers a superior aerobics workout.

Currently the United States Badminton Association has fewer than 2,000 members (although thousands more play the game without belonging to the USBA). Membership should continue to grow as a result of badminton becoming an Olympic sport in 1992. Membership in the USBA in both the adult (19 to 39 years) and senior (40-plus) divisions is composed of twice as many men as women.

You'll find men in this sport to be intense and committed to everything they're involved in. They are fiercely competitive, but they want to win more by their intellectual prowess than by brute strength. Self-confident by nature, they aren't preoccupied with status and prestige. These men are secure with who they are and don't need to continually prove themselves or to be accepted by conforming.

The USBA can put you in touch with one of the 70 clubs located throughout the country.

U.S. Badminton Association
501 West Sixth Street
Papillion, NE 68046
(402) 592-7309

Ballooning

No other sport offers better scenic views than hot-air ballooning. Give it a try as a crew member and see if you don't become hooked. After you become comfortable as one of the three or four members of the crew, you can consider learning to pilot the balloon and eventually obtain your FAA license.

The Balloon Federation of America (BFA) currently has about 4,300 members. Men outnumber women 3 to 1. All ages participate in the sport, although pilots have to be at least 16 to become licensed. Ballooning takes place all over the country, in both densely populated and rural areas. A cross-section of the population is involved in ballooning. You can find everyone from truck drivers and cabbies to business tycoons up in a balloon. But many balloon owners tend to be on the wealthy side, as the sport involves a large investment of capital.

What sort of man might you meet through involvement in ballooning? Most have a keen interest in the world around them. These are not people who live for sitcom reruns. They have a sense of romance and an appreciation for beauty.

To get involved in the sport, you may be able to join a crew by finding a local balloonist via the Yellow Pages. Or obtain the phone number of your local club by contacting the BFA.

Balloon Federation of America
P.O. Box 891
King of Prussia, PA 19406

Basketball

You don't have to be seven feet tall to enjoy playing basketball. All it takes is some mental alertness and a little eye-hand coordination. Shooting hoops presents an athletic challenge with moderate physical demands. You may not have played the game since junior high P.E., but why not give it a try and discover why it retains its appeal for so many adults?

Most nonprofessional basketball is played on an informal, nonorganized level. It is therefore difficult to determine how many thousands of people play each year. The vast majority of players in pickup games are men.

Men who play basketball are usually well-balanced individuals who are capable of moving fast but know when to slow down and take things easy. Most are positive thinkers and optimists. Get involved in basketball by locating some courts either indoors or out (at health clubs, Y's, schools, parks). Call the director to ask when pickup games are usually played.

Bicycle Polo

If you feel more comfortable on a bike than a horse or you've written off polo because you'll never be able to afford a string of polo ponies, try this low-rent version instead. Players hit plastic balls toward a goal while riding bikes. To play the game, all you'll need is a bicycle (any type will do, although smaller ones are easiest to maneuver and it's best if they don't have hand brakes or five speeds to worry about), a protective helmet, and a mallet (shorter than a regular polo mallet: 36 inches or less). Two teams of six players compete against each other, but only four on each team play at any one time on the 100-by-45-foot field. Matches consist of six periods of play of 7½ minutes each.

Only a few hundred people regularly play bike polo, but the United States Bicycle Polo Association is working to promote the sport and increase its popularity. Currently teams are located in San Francisco, Denver, Chicago, Toronto, New York, and Montreal. The bicycle polo season begins in August and lasts until the cold weather in November, then goes south to Texas and Florida.

Though the players aren't exclusively men, men do predominate. Participants tend to be young professionals such as stockbrokers, lawyers, and advertising executives. The sport can be aggressive and action-packed, so it attracts men who play hard and fast. These are not laid-back types. They have enthusiasm, energy, and guts. These qualities which enable them to do well at bicycle polo also ensure their success in the business world and in other areas of their lives.

U.S. Bicycle Polo Association
c/o Ron Kraut
Becker Spielvogel Bates Inc.
The Chrysler Building
405 Lexington Avenue
New York, NY 10174
(212) 297-8551

Boomerangs

These aerodynamic wonders present a unique challenge for throwing and catching. Proper handling of a boomerang requires considerable skill. This sport is affordable and convenient to pursue. All you need is a boomerang or two and an open outdoor area that offers enough space to comfortably and safely practice your throws and catches. The sport can be played on an individual or team basis.

It's estimated that tens of thousands of people throw "booms" on a casual recreational basis. About 600 people are active members of the United States Boomerang Association (USBA). Ninety percent of boom chuckers are men between the ages of 20 and 45. They're highly educated (college or beyond) with moderate incomes. Throwers seem to be concentrated in Ohio, Maryland, Virginia, New York, Washington State, Oregon, Colorado, and the Midwest, but local enthusiasts can be found in every part of the country.

Boomeranging is not a mainstream sport, so expect its enthusiasts to be a little different as well. Men in this sport are usually not conformists. They're secure in their individuality and enjoy things that are somewhat off the beaten track. If you're tired of men who seem to have sprung from the same predictable mold, a boom chucker can be a refreshing change.

To find throwers in your area and learn more about the sport, contact:

U.S. Boomerang Association
P.O. Box 182
Delaware, OH 43015

Bowling

Bowling is one of those activities that you probably enjoyed immensely the last time you did it, but now it's been ages since you even thought about it. This is unfortunate, because bowling is an affordable, year-round, safe yet challenging sport that provides a great deal of camaraderie. It's one of the most social activities around. Instead of being cutthroat and intense like many other sports, it provides an outlet for relaxation while demanding your best eye-hand coordination.

Although *you* may not have been bowling recently, lots of other people have been enjoying the sport. There are 68 million bowlers who visit their neighborhood bowling centers each year. Seven million adults regularly participate by belonging to a league. Most leagues bowl once a week during the regular season (September–May) or summer season (June–August).

Bowlers constitute a broad demographic spectrum. The biggest percentage are in the 24-to-34 age group, but there are also sizable numbers in the 18-to-24, 35-to-49, 50-to-64, and even 65-plus categories. Although bowling has sometimes been stereotyped as a blue-collar sport, 75 percent of bowlers are actually white-collar workers. Over half have a college background; 39 percent have annual incomes over $35,000. About 11 percent are single.

Most men you'll meet in this sport are successful in their careers but they're not workaholics. They do their jobs and they do them well, but they also know how and when to relax. Human relationships are ultimately more important to them than any financial or other quantifiable goal. If you want a man who is more concerned about people (and maybe eventually you!) than his rung on the career ladder, a bowler may be just the type of man you're looking for.

Getting involved in the sport is as easy as dropping by your local bowling center. Bowl a few games on your own or with friends, and ask if there is a league with an opening. Even mid-season, many leagues need substitutes or replacements for regular bowlers. Ask at the desk of your local lanes.

Combined Training

If you love to ride horses and want a real challenge, combined training is the perfect sport for you. It consists of three equestrian disciplines:

1. Dressage: Performing required movements at a specific level of competition on the flat.
2. Cross-country: Galloping and jumping over varying terrain and solid obstacles at a speed and fence height appropriate to that level of competition.
3. Stadium jumping: Jumping a course of other than natural obstacles that can be knocked down.

A "combined" score is obtained by taking the penalty points recorded for the three phases. The horse and rider compete in a horse trial (often called "an event") for a combined low score which attests to an overall balance in their training.

The sport is not dangerous when horses and riders use proper conditioning, training, and riding techniques. Beginners start with simple tests in all three phases with slow speeds and uncomplicated fences.

The United States Combined Training Association has more than 9,000 members. About three-quarters of the members are females between 14 and 35, but males of all ages also participate. These are horse lovers who ride because they truly enjoy it, not because they want to impress people by being part of the "horsey" set. They're true athletes rather than dilettantes who just like the way they look in riding clothes. They are hard workers and friendly people who are always willing to lend a hand to help someone else.

The Combined Training Association suggests that you go to a USCTA Registered Horse Trial near you and explain to members that you would like to learn what goes on and to help out. They can advise you about any nearby events.

U.S. Combined Training Association
292 Bridge Street
South Hamilton, MA 01982-1497
(508) 468-7133

Croquet

Croquet, anyone? Thousands of people in recent years have been answering affirmatively and enjoying a sport that combines the strategy of chess with the eye-hand coordination of billiards and golf. The object of the game is to race your opponent(s) around the course of six wickets twice and hit the finishing stake before they do. Wooden balls are knocked through the wickets using wooden mallets. The game can be played by either two or four people.

Because players are not under any time constraints, they can plot their strategy and execute their moves at a leisurely pace. Few players ever work up a sweat or experience any injuries while playing this game. Croquet courts are perfectly manicured lawns always situated in beautiful surroundings. A highly social sport, it allows players to sip champagne and nibble caviar while waiting for their turn.

Croquet is becoming more accessible to the general public. Clubs and resorts are allowing people to rent the courts and equipment at an affordable price. Nonetheless, the demographics of active croquet players are impressive. Many wealthy and powerful people play croquet. One-quarter of all players have a net worth of $1 million or more. The average income is $150,000, and 42 percent make more than $200,000. Three-quarters have attended college; 88 percent are in professional/managerial jobs. Fifty-seven

In her book *Taking a Chance on Love* (New York: Schocken, 1984), Emily Marlin notes that the people who find love most easily are those who are really open. To get what you want and need, she suggests that you "open yourself to a variety of new experiences and go after life actively." Pick as many new experiences from this book as you can, and see if a more active lifestyle doesn't improve your love life.

percent are male; 28 percent are single. The average age is 43. More than half the players are between 35 and 64. Forty-two percent of all players live in Florida, California, and New York, but the game is played in 48 states.

Men who play croquet are a quality lot. They have a quiet self-confidence and inner strength. They don't feel the need to prove themselves by brute strength; they would much prefer to use their minds. Most favor a more civilized and refined approach to life than the current norm. A sense of romance is evident in many.

If you're serious about learning the game (and meeting men as well), you shouldn't play croquet in your backyard. The real game is played on professionally maintained courts at private croquet clubs; country, golf, tennis, and sports clubs; some real estate developments; and hotels, resorts, and inns. To find out about the more than 300 croquet clubs representing more than 3,500 members (and new clubs which continue to join at an average rate of one a week), contact:

U.S. Croquet Association
500 Avenue of Champions
Palm Beach, FL 33418
(407) 627-3999

Curling

Don't get the wrong idea here. Standing in front of your mirror every morning and winding your hair around an electric wand is *not* a sport. Curling is a legitimate and unique sport played on a narrow sheet of ice. Two teams of four try to shoot a specially contoured granite stone into a predetermined place or to move another team's rock. Each player shoots two stones alternately with an opponent from the other team. Twisting the wrist while releasing the stone makes the stone "curl" (curve) as it slides across the ice. While one player shoots, two sweep the ice with a specially made broom or brush to polish the ice so the stone travels farther.

Games last about two hours. During this time, a curler walks about two miles. In addition to the exercise, the game requires strategy and eye-hand coordination. It also offers a great deal of camaraderie. Curlers join local teams much as they would a bowling league. Tournaments called "bonspiels" offer curlers the opportunity to meet athletes from elsewhere in the state, nation, or world.

Worldwide there are 2 million curlers. Twenty thousand people in the United States curl; 60 percent are men. Over half have college degrees. Curling takes place primarily in the northern United States (October through March). States with the largest participation are Wisconsin, Minnesota, North Dakota, Illinois, New York, and Massachusetts. The game attracts a cross-section of professions and occupations: Attorneys, bankers, iron miners, entrepreneurs, insurance executives, and educators all curl.

The game of curling is a proud, 400-year-old tradition that originated in Scotland. Sportsmanship is an integral feature. A curler would never deliberately break a rule of the game or distract an opponent to prevent him or her from playing his or her best. If you want a man with integrity, curling is a good place to find one. These men won't take advantage of you. They truly believe in the golden rule of treating people (including women) the way they would want to be treated.

U.S. Curling Association
1100 Center Point Drive, Box 971
Stevens Point, WI 54481
(715) 344-1199

Cycling

If your cycling is limited to a boring 20 minutes three times a week on a stationary exercise bike, you will find that you get just as much exercise (if not more) and enjoy the experience much more on a regular bicycle. Instead of looking at the same four walls by yourself, hop on a bike, experience the great outdoors, and discover the fun of being part of a cycling club.

While it isn't necessary to join a club, belonging to one will allow you to participate in touring or racing and will hook you up with fellow enthusiasts who might be interested in a cycling vacation. There are more than 1,100 cycling clubs around the country; one of them is bound to be convenient for you.

You'll find plenty of company in this sport. It's estimated that one of every four Americans rides a bicycle. Just a little under half the cyclists are men. The greatest concentration of recreational cyclists are between 25 and 34 years old, college graduates, professionals or managers, and have incomes of $30,000 or more. Slightly fewer than half are single.

Men in this sport are multitalented. They've been born with or have worked hard to achieve strength, stamina, speed, and smarts. Essentially they're up for any challenge. But they're usually not workaholics. They exert a lot of effort to achieve their goals, but they know how to relax as well.

For the bicycle club nearest you and information about the sport, write or call:

U.S. Cycling Federation
1750 East Boulder Street
Colorado Springs, CO 80909-5774
(719) 578-4581

Disc Sports (Frisbees)

You may have tossed around a Frisbee or two on the beach just for fun, but many people are fiercely competitive about this sport. Throwing a flying disc (Frisbees are the most commonly used, but other brands are available as well) can be a more complex and demanding activity than you may think. Skilled players don't just pass the disc back and forth to each other. Com-

---

The odds are probably a million to one that you'll meet someone special just sitting at home. Sure, there's the (extremely remote) possibility that the washing machine repairman will turn out to be the man of your dreams. But if your appliances are working well or the repairman turns out to be married, staying at home won't offer you many opportunities to meet the type of man you want. So get out of the house and do something! No matter what activity you choose, you'll increase your odds tremendously.

petitive events include the game of Ultimate (profiled under its own heading in this chapter), distance throwing, double-disc court (two discs are used in a space-age tennis game, played as doubles), disc-off golf (teeing off from the tee area, players try to aim into a series of baskets), freestyle (difficult moves, choreographed to music), self-caught flight (like the standard beach game, players attempt to aim for the maximum in the air and then catch it).

There are 125 clubs nationwide with 5,000 registered members in United States Disc Sports. Thousands more play informally, without belonging to an organization or club. The sport attracts a preponderance of males, estimated at a 4 to 1 ratio; 70 percent are single. The predominant age category is the early twenties, but there are senior competitions for the over-35 and over-55 age groups.

Disc sportsmen are an enthusiastic lot who go for the gusto, even in the small and relatively unimportant parts of their lives. Whatever they do, they want to have fun at it and do their best. Not easily discouraged, these people bounce right back after a defeat and try again.

U.S. Disc Sports
1144 East Garfield
Davenport, IA 52803

Diving

Olympic athletes make it look so easy, but in reality diving is anything but. It's as demanding as gymnastics, requiring excellent strength and coordination of every body part. If you are in top-notch shape, you may want to try to achieve the power and grace associated with diving. You'll probably never win a medal, but you will have the satisfaction of acquiring a modest repertoire of dives.

As with gymnastics, most competitive and recreational divers are in their teens and twenties. However, the United States Diving organization does have a master's program for divers 21 and older. Local meets and indoor/outdoor national championships are held annually. But even if you never get to this level, you can still enjoy practice sessions at your neighborhood pool.

Half of all divers are men, so you stand a good chance of meeting a man while perfecting your form. These are men who combine strength with graceful agility. Masculine but not macho, they want to know and control as much in their lives as possible, but they can also cope with the unexpected and improvise as they go along.

You can learn to dive at your local pool. Contact United States Diving for more information about the sport.

U.S. Diving
Pan American Plaza
201 South Capitol Avenue, Suite 430
Indianapolis, IN 46225

Fencing

Most people's experience with the sport of fencing is limited to whatever they've seen in movies about medieval times. But for a small group of individuals, fencing is an activity pursued with passion. You, too, might find that you enjoy this challenging sport. Don't worry about safety. Weapons such as épées, sabers, and foils are used, but you are protected by gloves, a face mask, and a jacket. Fencing demands good sportsmanship and an etiquette all its own. The objective is to score points by touching the legal target area (the entire body or just the upper torso) of the opponent, but the proper protocol must be followed at all times.

About 75 percent of fencers are men. The sport is most popular in the Northeast, but fencers live all over the United States. At least 90 percent have gone to or are currently enrolled in college. About 40 percent are professionals (doctors, dentists, lawyers, accountants); many are students working toward a professional career. Although the predominant age group is 16 to 20 (reflecting the college population), 33 percent are over 30.

Most male fencers enjoy the sport because it appeals to their romantic side. It transports them to earlier times when chivalry was the order of the day. They're imaginative dreamers who have some wild fantasies and like to act them out.

Your best bet for learning fencing is to check with a nearby college's physical education department. The United States Fencing Association can provide further information about the sport and let you know of fencing activities in your community.

U.S. Fencing Association
1750 East Boulder Street
Colorado Springs, CO 80909-5774

Footbag

No, this is not a typo. There really is a sport called footbag. You may not have heard of it, but more than 12,000 people in 22 countries have, and they belong to the World Footbag Association. Footbags (such as the well-known Hacky Sack) are constructed of leather, weigh a little more than an ounce, and are about two inches in diameter. To keep the footbag airborne, basic standard and advanced freestyle kicks are used. The game can be played solo or as part of a team. In addition to the aerobic challenge of just keeping the footbag in the air for as long as possible, variations can include footbag golf (kicking the footbag through and around various hazards and finally into a designated area) and footbag net (combining basic and fancy footwork with the scoring rules of volleyball and the playing rules of tennis).

Footbag develops eye-foot coordination, balance, and agility. It serves as a warm-up and off-season conditioner for other sports, although many players enjoy it for its own sake.

Eighty percent of the players are men. Ages range from 3 to 74, with the largest concentration in the 12-to-27 category. Many players are college-educated. Instead of showing an extreme right- or left-brained dominance like so many other men, footbag players use both sides and seem to have the best of both worlds. Many are highly creative, as evidenced by their ability to develop and choreograph their own kicks. But rather than being eccentric and unstructured to the point of disorganization, footbag players need to be (and are) alert, disciplined, and methodical.

World Footbag Association
1317 Washington Avenue, Suite 7
Golden, CO 80401
(303) 278-9797

Golf

Even if you've never played the game, you still know what golf is all about. If you've watched it as a spectator, you may have been less than enthralled with the sport and wondered why so many people are devoted to it. But you shouldn't write off golf until you actually play it. Once you swing the club yourself, you may discover why it has so many (about 20 million) fans.

You're also wrong if you think that most men who play golf are retirees. In reality, only 10 percent of golfers are 65 years or older. The highest percentage (26 percent) are in the 20-to-29 category, closely followed by 22 percent in the 30-to-39 range. Another 25 percent are between 40 and 59. More than 77 percent of golfers are men. Most are college graduates who are employed in a professional or managerial capacity. The largest number of golfers are on the East Coast, but there are golfers throughout the United States.

Male golfers are patient and introspective. They like to think through a situation and size it up before taking action. Recklessness is not their style. A slow, steady approach works best for them. You can depend on a golfer to be even-tempered and reliable. He knows who he is and how he functions best, and he doesn't always need to experiment.

Getting involved in the game is as easy as taking lessons at your local golf course. Further information can be obtained from the United States Golf Association or the National Golf Foundation.

U.S. Golf Association
Golf House, P.O. Box 708
Far Hills, NJ 07931-0708
(800) 223-0041
(201) 234-2300 in New Jersey

National Golf Foundation
1150 South U.S. Highway One
Jupiter, FL 33477

Gymnastics

If you're no longer a teenager, it's too late for you to become seriously involved in gymnastics. This sport is definitely designed for young people in superior shape. But even though you won't be able to compete professionally, you may still want to try out some gymnastic equipment in a gym (with a trainer or, at the very least, a spotter) to gain flexibility and strength. Be sure that you're in adequate physical condition before you attempt the balance beam, rings, parallel bars, or vaulting.

The vast majority of active competitive gymnasts are in their preteen to teenage years, but you'll also see some college men practicing their routines. A few older (as in middle twenties to thirties) people may be using the equipment as well. In general, however, there are about six females for every male gymnast.

If you've ever admired the physiques of the male gymnasts in the Olympics, you've already developed an appreciation of the sport. You may not meet an Olympian at your local gym, but you can still find some talented men who keep themselves in terrific shape. Gymnasts are typically very clean-cut, dedicated, and poised. They're self-confident and will work hard to achieve their goals.

For information about local opportunities in gymnastics and joining the 166,000 gymnasts who belong to their national organization, contact:

U.S. Gymnastics Federation
Pan American Plaza, Suite 300
201 South Capitol Avenue
Indianapolis, IN 46225
(800) 345-4719
(317) 237-5066 in Indiana

Handball

This fast-paced game is played by two, three, or four players, typically on a four-wall court, although variations of the game are played on one, two, or three walls. Instead of a racquet, the gloved hand or fist is used to serve and return the ball. The objective is to serve or return the ball in a way that prevents the opponent from keeping it in play. A serve or rally is won when a side is unable to return the ball to the front wall before it touches the floor twice. The game is played with both hands and demands the mastery of as many as 250 possible shots.

Of the estimated 2.5 million handball players, 97 percent are men; 14 percent are single. Graduate degrees are common. Most players are professionals. The majority are from 31 to 50 years old. A small percentage are in their twenties and many players are over 50.

You'll find the men involved in the sport to be dynamic individuals who play as hard as they work. Although they're college-educated and professionally employed, there's a ruggedness to them. They don't like life to get too "soft" or easy; they prefer to be continually stimulated and challenged. Although they relate well to others, they're most comfortable being independent and not having to rely on anyone (or anything else) to succeed.

You can get involved with the sport by joining one of the more than 2,000 private sports facilities and 1,000 public facilities across the country. For further information:

U.S. Handball Association
930 North Benton Avenue
Tucson, AZ 85711
(602) 795-0434

Hang Gliding

Here is a sport guaranteed to give you a lift! You, too, can follow in the footsteps of the Wright brothers by learning this adventurous sport, which combines the freedom of parachuting with the challenge of piloting a glider. Hang gliding can be dangerous, so be sure to take lessons only from a certified instructor.

Thousands of people hang glide. The United States Hang Gliding Association currently has 15,000 members. Fewer than 4 percent are female. Ages range from 15 to 71. Almost half are single. The majority are college graduates with an average salary of $40,000 and with some members earning salaries of $380,000. There are about 100 local chapters and clubs throughout the country.

Male hang gliders are gutsy risk takers. They're not interested in playing it safe. If you decide to take up hang gliding, you'll be guaranteed thrills in the air . . . and maybe a few on the ground, if you get involved with one of these daring types!

U.S. Hang Gliding Association
P.O. Box 8300
Colorado Springs, CO 80933
(719) 632-8300

Hiking

For toning your legs and enjoying great scenery, you can't beat hiking. Traipsing through a forest or park is guaranteed to give you a sense of inner peace as you commune with nature. Best of all, it doesn't require any special talent or skill. If you can walk, you can hike. As a beginner, you may have to start with fairly short distances and level surfaces, but as you build endurance, you'll be able to go for more challenging hikes.

It is estimated that 100 million people go on hikes. About 16 million are regular and dedicated hikers. Men slightly outnumber women. Hikers range in age from 4 to over 80. Male hikers have a quiet strength. They're capable and independent. Some are loners at heart, but those who join a hiking club also enjoy being around other people and sharing with them.

You can get outfitted for hiking at your local outdoor equipment or sporting goods store. For safety's sake as well as men-meeting opportunities, don't hike alone. Ask for the names of local clubs where you buy your gear or contact the American Hiking Society for clubs in your area.

American Hiking Society
1015 31st Street NW, 4th floor
Washington, DC 20007-4490
(202) 385-3252

Hockey

You're probably quite familiar with field hockey from your high school days
and ice hockey from televised games. You know that they both involve two
teams who use hockey sticks to hit a puck (ice hockey) or ball (field hockey)
into the netted goal at each end (field hockey) or the opponent's cage (ice
hockey). Ice hockey has 6 players per team, field hockey has 11. Both ice
and field hockey can be rough games. This doesn't deter people from playing
them; to the contrary, the potential risk, fast pace, and aggressive play add
to the excitement and thrill. If you're tired of ladylike sports where you're
too busy being polite to really get engrossed in the game, try hockey.

Hockey is largely a young person's game, but an estimated 30,000
adults play. Most (95 percent) are men. The majority are 18 to 30 years old,
but there are also teams exclusively for players over 30. Watching men
playing the sport may lead you to the conclusion that they're aggressive to
the point of being vicious and dangerous. But in actuality, male hockey
players are apt to be calm and gentle off the field. Hockey enables them to
work out their frustrations and hostilities so that they can be relaxed and
even-tempered when they put down the hockey stick.

More information can be obtained from:

Amateur Hockey Association
2997 Broadmoor Valley Road
Colorado Springs, CO 80906
(719) 576-4990

Horseshoes

In the days of the Roman Empire soldiers pitched horseshoes discarded from
the horses that pulled their chariots. The game is now played all over the
world and by such luminaries as President George Bush, who considers it
his number one hobby and had a new horseshoe court built at the White
House. The sport's popularity can be attributed to its simplicity, economy,

challenge, and safety. The game can be played on indoor or outdoor courts. Points are given for horseshoes that come to rest encircling or resting within six inches of the stake. The pitching distance is 30 feet for women and 40 feet for men.

It is estimated that there are more than 30 million horseshoe pitchers. Sixteen thousand are avid enough enthusiasts to belong to the National Horseshoe Pitchers Association (NHPA); 90 percent are male. The average age is 46. Pitchers tend to live in cities and are above the norm in income and education. There are 59 local clubs throughout the country, but if one is not within your vicinity, the NHPA can provide a brochure on starting a local league. Sanctioned tournaments are available on the regional, national, and international levels.

You'll meet men who are competitive in a quiet, nonaggressive manner. They live full but sensible lives, partaking in challenge, but without undue risk. Horseshoe pitching is an ideal place to meet men with balanced personalities.

For further information:

National Horseshoe Pitchers Association
Box 278
Munroe Falls, OH 44262

Ice Skating

When was the last time you were at an ice skating rink? It's probably an activity you enjoyed as a child but forgot about as you got older. Maybe it's time to try it again. Picture visiting your local rink during those hot summer days, cooling off and getting exercise at the same time. It can be as exhilarating or relaxing as you want it to be. Further challenges are available by learning to figure skate.

The United States Figure Skating Association sponsors basic ice skating instruction at rinks throughout the country with its "Skate with U.S." basic skills program. Offered at a nominal charge and taught by qualified coaches, the program is based on a sequential step-by-step developmental approach where you can advance at your own pace. Basic skating skills are learned while coordination, balance, and overall physical fitness are improved. Advanced study is available in specialties such as freestyle, hockey, precision skating (teams of 12 or more skaters perform precise maneuvers with speed and synchronization to music), ice dancing, or figures.

It's estimated that thousands of people of all ages skate. A little more than half are female. The majority are children and teenagers, but you'll find men in their twenties to fifties who have always skated or are rediscovering the sport. Men who skate are independent types, but they can be quietly gregarious and have a good sense of humor.

You can get into skating by participating at your local rink. For information on the competitive aspects of figure skating or the "Skate with U.S." basic skills program, contact:

U.S. Figure Skating Association
20 First Street
Colorado Springs, CO 80906
(719) 635-5200

Korfball

If you hate being just one of the crowd, here's a sport that is unique and not known or practiced by many people. Korfball is a Dutch sport that resembles basketball. Eight players (four men and four women) are divided equally into offensive and defensive positions and placed on opposite sides of a half court. The goal is to make a basket, but players can't block, dribble, or run with the ball.

Only 75 people belong to the U.S. Korfball Association (although many play it in the Netherlands). Due to the makeup of the teams, the ratio of male to female is 50-50. Members range in age from 16 to 45. Occupations include students, geologists, salespeople, engineers, managers, teachers, counselors, and construction workers. Currently, players can be found in Tulsa, Houston, Southern California, and Portland, Oregon. If you don't live in one of these four places, think about starting your own team.

As a child, you may have loved fairy tales, but you need to put them aside now that you're an adult. Sleeping Beauty fell asleep waiting for Mr. Right to appear, while Cinderella stayed home waiting for her prince to come. These are not role models you want to emulate! You need to make love happen, not wait for it to happen to you.

Men in this sport really do like women. Unlike some other men who use sports as a way to escape from the opposite sex, these men choose to play a sport where women are equally represented. Definitely a refreshing change, isn't it?

U.S. Korfball Association
11017 Bel Air
Oklahoma City, OK 74104

Lacrosse

If you played lacrosse in high school or college, you know it's an action-packed game demanding power, precision, courage, and endurance. It has been said that it's the fastest game on two feet, and few people who have been involved in this sport would disagree.

The object of the game is simple enough. Players try to score by causing a 5¼-ounce solid rubber ball to enter a 6-by-6-foot goal while preventing the opponent from securing the ball and scoring. The ball is kept in play by being carried, thrown, or batted with the crosse (lacrosse stick), rolled or kicked. Two teams composed of 10 (in men's lacrosse) or 12 (in women's lacrosse) compete against each other.

The majority of lacrosse players are men. While the largest percentage of players are of high school and college age, over 12,000 players are 23–30 years old and about 6,000 are over 30. Most have at least a college education and annual incomes of over $50,000.

Tired of men who can't make a decision about anything? You'll find a lacrosse player to be a change in the right direction. The game demands mental agility. Decisions have to be made and strategies mapped out quickly. A lacrosse man will be assertive but not aggressive and self-confident without being egotistical.

Teams are usually segregated by sex, but you can meet men before and after the games if you use the same field.

For information about lacrosse, contact:

Lacrosse Foundation
Newton H. White Athletic Center, Homewood
Baltimore, MD 21218
(301) 235-6882

Specific information about women's lacrosse can be provided by:

U.S. Women's Lacrosse Association
20 East Sunset Avenue
Philadelphia, PA 19118
(215) 248-3771

Lifesaving

If you've ever worked as a lifeguard or if you have always wanted to be certified in lifesaving, consider getting yourself in shape through lifesaving training. Once you pass the 56-hour open-water training, you can join the United States Lifesaving Association. You may not want to actually work as a lifeguard, but if you enjoy the water and physical fitness activities you'll probably also enjoy the rigorous competitions sponsored by the 271 local and national chapters.

Competitive activities include the surf rescue team race (in which a rescuer must run 10 meters to the waterline, swim out to the "victim," and pull him or her back to shore), the 3K beach run on the wet sand of the beach, the 1,000-meter surf swim, the 1,000-meter surf ski race (involving paddling out 500 meters around buoys and paddling back to shore), the landline rescue team relay (two team members stationed at the landline pull the victim and rescuer to the beach), the 1,000-meter board race (running to the water, mounting rescue boards, paddling out 500 meters and back, running up to the finish line with the board), dory race (a dory team consists of two oarsmen doing two 1,000-meter laps), and beach flags (in the soft sand, competitors race to obtain a flag).

The United States Lifesaving Association has about 11,000 members. Most are in their early twenties to thirties. Men outnumber women by more

To train yourself to be more open to meeting new people, initiate one conversation a day with someone you know slightly or not at all. The conversation can take place in a waiting room, elevator, the grocery store checkout line, a health club, or the gas station pumps. What you say doesn't have to be original or profound; your goal is only to improve your ability to connect with people, even if only in a small way. Your enhanced communication skills can help you connect with the right man when you find him.

than 2 to 1. You'll find that males in this sport thrive under pressure. They like the adrenaline rush that's a by-product of competition. But they're not foolhardy excitement junkies. They're reasonable and rational. People and the environment are extremely important to them and they'll go out of their way to protect them.

U.S. Lifesaving Association
425 East McFetridge Drive
Chicago, IL 60605

Martial Arts

Millions of Americans are learning what used to be an exclusively Asian practice. The martial arts are becoming increasingly popular for physical and mental exercise and self-defense. Each martial art provides a unique mental and physical challenge.

Karate. As a system of balanced exercise, it increases agility, endurance, reflexes, and coordination. Originating in China and further developed in Japan, it emphasizes a series of blocks and counterattacks.

Tae-Kwon-Do. This Korean style of empty-hand combat is similar to the older form of karate. Both hand and foot techniques are utilized, along with form and breathing exercises.

Aikido. Based on ancient samurai techniques, this discipline emphasizes internal and external harmony with nature (*ai*) through control of spiritual energy (*ki*) along the right path (*do*). Aikido is more closely related to dance than the other varieties of martial arts are, since its leverage holds and throws are performed with circular, fluid movements.

Jujitsu. This predates aikido as a form of armed and unarmed combat. It focuses on the art of striking through kicking, kneeing, joint-locking, throwing, and choking techniques.

Judo. Unarmed techniques are emphasized here, along with the philosophies of maximum effect with minimum effort, and respect for one's opponent.

Several million people practice the martial arts in the United States each year. Over two-thirds are male. Ages range from 5 to 60.

Men who are into martial arts are courteous and respectful (to both males and females). They enjoy keeping their minds and bodies active. While they can be assertive, they're never aggressive. Most are self-confident and centered.

The best way to become involved in the sport is to choose a martial arts school from the Yellow Pages. Once you've attended some classes, you can investigate clubs and organizations in your area.

Orienteering

Don't feel bad if you've never heard of this sport. It doesn't receive much publicity or fanfare. Nonetheless, there are thousands of people who pursue orienteering with gusto. As far as they're concerned, it's one of the few real "thinking sports," combining physical endurance and speed with intellectual abilities and navigational skills. Using a detailed topographical map and a compass, orienteers find their way from one point to another in a forest or parkland setting. Orienteers can find their "control flags" or "objective stations" only if they read their maps accurately. Once they find each destination, they record pertinent information to prove they were there. In competitive orienteering, participants try to move through the course as quickly as possible; wayfaring is the noncompetitive version, which requires the same skills but allows them to be used at a more leisurely pace. Orienteering is usually done on foot, but it can also be done on horseback, cross-country skis, or in canoes.

More than 31,000 people participate in orienteering each year. Two-thirds are men. Over half are 34 or older and have graduate degrees. The sport is enjoyed all over the country in about 35 states, but it is most popular in the Northeast.

You can expect men in this sport to thoroughly enjoy intellectual stimulation. But these are not men who want to escape from the world by burying their noses in books. They want to be out and about, experiencing the world and all it offers. They're up for any challenge in life, be it physical or mental.

U.S. Orienteering Federation
P.O. Box 1444
Forest Park, GA 30051

National Association of
   Competitive Mountain
   Orienteering
Route 2, Box 290
Ogilvie, MN 56358

According to author Tracy Cabot in *Marrying Later, Marrying Smarter* (New York: McGraw-Hill, 1990): ". . . a real man with imperfections can beat a fantasy perfect man—if you just give him a chance" (p. 145).

Paddle Tennis

Paddle tennis has some similarities to regular tennis (the ball is hit over a net in both games), but there are also quite a few differences. Instead of a long-handled racquet, paddle tennis uses short-handled paddles. And it uses a standard tennis ball punctured to deaden its bounce. The court is smaller than that for tennis (20 by 50 feet for paddle tennis vs. 36 by 78 feet). But paddle tennis can be just as challenging as its better-known cousin. The fast returns and smashes combined with lightning-speed footwork make it an invigorating sport.

Statistics on the number of paddle tennis players are not available, but the game continues to grow in popularity. It is believed to be fairly equally divided between males and females. Ages range from children to senior adults.

Paddle tennis players are similar in many respects to tennis players. They're both energetic and assertive. But paddle tennis players seem to place less emphasis on prestige and status. Instead, they're more concerned with just being and enjoying. They also tend to be determined and committed, even in the face of adversity. Whereas other men might crumble when things aren't going smoothly, paddle tennis players are undaunted.

U.S. Paddle Tennis Association
P.O. Box 30
Culver City, CA 90232

Polo

Polo has a certain mystique and romance not found in any other competitive sport. Although it's actually quite fast, rough, and dangerous, it also exudes gentility and refinement (perhaps due to its aristocratic origins). The sport combines horsemanship with challenges of eye-hand coordination. Two teams of four players each race down a ten-acre grass field on thoroughbred horses. The object of the game is to move the ball downfield with the side of a mallet, with the ultimate aim of getting it through the goal for a score.

The United States Polo Association (USPA) has 3,000 registered players. Eight times as many men as women play. Many of the men who play polo in the United States are from foreign countries, but more American men are gradually developing interest in the sport. The game has long been associated with money and social position, but not everyone involved in the sport is fabulously wealthy and prominent. Some play polo professionally to make a living, whereas others participate simply because they're horse lovers who enjoy the challenges of the sport. Anyone with sufficient skill can play polo, but only those with lots of money can actually afford to own a horse.

The men you'll find in polo definitely are special. They do tend to come from privileged backgrounds and are extremely self-confident and secure. They're open to taking risks; in fact, they're too busy living and enjoying life to worry about what calamities may occur. Polo players are also skilled communicators. Their teamwork is not limited to the other players, but also encompasses an implicit understanding between horse and player. Consequently, polo players can be highly intuitive and perceptive.

Contact the USPA for more information about becoming involved with an amateur team.

U.S. Polo Association
4059 Iron Works Pike
Lexington, KY 40511
(606) 255-0593

River Sports

You're in an enviable position if you live near a river. You can take up the exciting sports of canoeing, kayaking, or rafting. Whitewater crafts are inexpensive compared to other types of boats and the paddling offers a great workout amid beautiful scenery. For safety's sake, don't just purchase a kayak or raft and think you're ready to go. It is strongly recommended that you enroll in a whitewater school to learn the basic techniques of the different strokes as well as how to cope with dangerous conditions.

Whitewater enthusiasts number in the tens of thousands. Some do not live close enough to a river to participate on a regular basis, but others try to do it every weekend. Exact gender ratios are unknown, but it has been observed that men dominate the sport. Kayaking is the most popular of the river sports. Male whitewater enthusiasts are outdoorsy and active. They have the courage and determination to master whatever they set out to accomplish.

National Organization for River Sports
314 North 20th Street, Box 6847
Colorado Springs, CO 80904
(719) 473-2466

Rock Climbing

Climbing rocky surfaces can be physically and mentally challenging. But what if you live thousands of miles away from hills and mountains? Do you have to resign yourself to a stationary bicycle for your exercise? Fortunately, you don't. Even if you live somewhere as flat as Kansas, you can still participate in sport climbing. Also known as indoor/artificial rock climbing, this is one of the newest fitness activities around. Textured wall surfaces and grooves simulate the feel and challenge of real rock climbing. Walls can range from heights of 12 feet to 120 or more. They are usually indoors, but a few can be found outdoors.

The equipment used in artificial wall climbing is the same as that used for traditional climbing: sturdy harnesses, ropes, and special shoes. During the climb, instructor and student are attached by a rope that connects their nylon safety harnesses. When the student climbs, the instructor stays on the ground and controls the tension in the rope (which is also looped through a pulley system at the peak of the wall), preventing the climber from falling.

It's estimated that there are about 150,000 rock climbers nationwide; the sport of artificial wall climbing is too new to know exactly how many people participate in it. Slightly more men than women may be attracted to it. Men who do real rock climbing tend to be rugged individualists who truly love nature. Men who are into artificial rock climbing are apt to be trendy, upscale types who are quick to embrace whatever is new and hot at the moment.

To get involved in real rock climbing, find an outdoor club or hiking-travel company that can provide you with the proper equipment and supervision. For artificial climbing, inquire at your local health clubs, university physical education departments, and outdoor outfitter stores.

Roller Skating

Most people have roller-skated at least a few times in their lives. Typically, this roller skating experience occurred in childhood or adolescence, often as part of a birthday party. Participants would skate around the rink a few times and then stop for refreshments and socializing. But roller skating can be far more challenging than your previous exposure to the sport may have indicated. It can be highly competitive, invigorating, and aesthetically gratifying. Try one of the following skating specialties and see if you don't get hooked.

- Artistic skating. Categories include figures, singles, pairs, and dance skating.
- Roller hockey. Five-person teams use a hockey stick to try to score a goal.
- Speed skating. Includes both sprinting and distance racing.

Millions of adults roller-skate, indoors and outdoors. In competitive artistic skating, about 60 percent of participants are female. Speed skating runs about 50-50 male-female; 90 percent of roller hockey players are male. You'll find different types of men in each of the three specialty areas. Artistic skaters are sensitive, creative, and open to new ideas and experiences. Speed skaters are quick in actions and words; they get a lot accomplished but can be impatient and unhappy when anything slows them down. Hockey players can be aggressive in pursuing what they want out of life, but they're also loyal friends to those people who share their values and interests.

You can bone up on your roller skating skills at your nearest rink. Contact the United States Amateur Confederation of Roller Skating for more information.

U.S. Amateur Confederation of Roller Skating
P.O. Box 6579
Lincoln, NE 68506
(402) 483-7551

Rowing

There may be other sports that are just as exhilarating, but rowing has the added bonus of enabling you to enjoy scenic views while being out on the water. For a terrific upper-body workout, take up rowing as either a recreational or competitive sport. Rowing can be done as a single, pair, or in groups of four to eight. Consider joining a team if you can't afford to buy your own boat or if you just want the camaraderie. There are at least 500 rowing clubs and organizations in the United States; one of them is likely to be in a location convenient for you. Sixty-five percent of rowers are male. Eighty-one percent are between the ages of 18 and 45. Close to 100 percent have a college degree and over a third have graduate degrees. Most are professionals with incomes of $35,000–$100,000. Rowers who participate in the team version of the sport have excellent interpersonal skills. They know how to be part of a cooperative effort and have no difficulty pulling together to accomplish a goal. Singles rowers are more independent and not as skilled at the art of mutual support. But regardless of which type of rowing he undertakes, a man in this sport can be counted on to be energetic, determined, and capable.

For more information on both competitive and recreational rowing, contact:

U.S. Rowing Association
201 South Capitol Avenue, Suite 400
Indianapolis, IN 46225
(317) 237-5656

Rugby

This fast-moving game, which combines the skills of soccer, football, and basketball, is the one from which football originated. It uses two teams of 15 players each (8 forwards and 7 backs). Unlike soccer, it permits running with the ball, as well as kicking or carrying the ball or passing it backward. Runners can be tackled to prevent a score. If you like a highly active game that permits you to be aggressive, you'll like rugby.

An international sport played in more than 100 countries, it's gaining popularity in the United States. There are more than 100,000 players in more than 1,200 clubs in every state. Most are in urban areas. Half of all players are between 25 and 34, with another 18 percent between 35 and 49. More than 93 percent attended college. Half of all rugby participants earn more than $30,000. The majority are men. There are separate teams for women, but you might want to see if you can break the gender barrier, as have high school girls on their football teams.

Rugby-playing men are assertive and goal-oriented. They know what they want in life and they go after it enthusiastically (usually quite success-fully). Most are fairly sophisticated and worldly.

USA Rugby
830 N. Tejon, Suite 104B
Colorado Springs, CO 80903
(719) 632-1022

Running/Jogging

Even if you've never run as a fitness activity, you know what it's all about. Running results in a high that is almost addictive. It offers an intense aerobic workout as it tones the body (with the emphasis on the lower half) and controls weight.

Male runners outnumber females about 2.5 to 1. Most are in their twenties to forties. They're urban dwellers, suburbanites, and country folk. A majority are well-educated professionals, but there is also a substantial number of blue-collar types.

Men who run tend to be self-motivated and independent. They like to compete for external rewards (particularly in the business world), but they also care about doing well for its own sake. While many male runners may be on the quiet side, don't ever mistake this as a sign of apathy. Underneath that reticent exterior can be a passion and intensity just waiting to be unleashed.

Running can be a solitary physical activity, but many communities do have local running clubs. You can also meet runners through competitive

According to Miss Manners (a.k.a. Judith Martin) in *Miss Manners' Guide for the Turn of the Millennium* (New York: Pharos, 1989), if you had lived during Victorian times and wanted to show a man that you were interested, you would carry a fan in your right hand and hold it over the lower half of your face. She proposes using a book as a modern social prop, keeping it open on your lap and holding your head tilted upward. This indicates that you're available and willing to converse.

events or simply by making contact as you both run through the park, on a track and field course at a local school, or on the street.

Shooting Sports

Even if you're a pacifist by nature, you can still enjoy shooting sports. Marksmanship is a skill requiring a great deal of concentration and good eye-hand coordination. Among the many disciplines of shooting sports are bull's-eye pistol and rifle, trapshooting (in which clay pigeons are hurled into the air from a trap), and skeet shooting (a form of trapshooting using two traps; targets are hurled singly or in pairs at varying elevations and speeds in simulation of the flight patterns of game birds). In addition to the sport value of these activities, women find that firearms skills are valuable for self-protection.

The National Rifle Association has 3 million members in 12,000 clubs across the country. Millions more participate in shooting sports without belonging to an organization. Ninety-five percent are men. The majority are between 35 and 49 years of age, but there are plenty who are younger and older.

Male shooters tend to be on the traditional and conservative side. They may not be as outwardly feminist as some other men, but once a woman proves herself, she'll be treated as an equal.

You can develop your marksmanship at your local shooting range. If you want to join a gun club, ask a gun shop for some names and addresses. The National Rifle Association can put you in touch with the NRA-affiliated club that's closest to you.

National Rifle Association
1600 Rhode Island Avenue NW
Washington, DC 20036
(202) 828-6000

Skiing

It's no wonder that skiing has so many devotees. The sport is both exhilarating and relaxing. You don't have to be the world's most coordinated person to be able to enjoy it. And the after-ski activities and camaraderie add to the experience.

If you hate the summer because it means you have to give up skiing, consider sand skiing. You might meet some interesting people, such as the Moon Dune Loonies. This Colorado group skis with alpine equipment in the light of the full moon at Grand Sand Dunes Monument. You're guaranteed not to get frostbite; sand temperature on midsummer days reaches 140 degrees!

Millions of people ski each year. Some do it as an occasional winter weekend vacation, whereas others pursue it regularly and race competitively. It truly is a sport for all ages, so you'll find people in their twenties as well as some who are well past 60. Nordic/cross-country skiing attracts equal numbers of men and women, whereas men dominate in Alpine/downhill skiing.

Male skiers are individualists who want to do things their way without outside interference. They like to be in control and set their own pace.

All you have to do to get involved in the sport is take some lessons, buy or rent the right equipment, and find your nearest ski area. But if you want more information on the sport or on racing teams, contact:

U.S. Ski Association
P.O. Box 100
Park City, UT 84060
(801) 649-9090

Sledding

Remember how much you enjoyed sled riding as a child? You don't have to stop just because you grew up. Adults can and do ride sleds! About 300 grown-ups even do it on a competitive level. (You may have watched them in the Winter Olympics.) If cold weather doesn't bother you, and you can't get enough of the rides at amusement parks, you're a good candidate for sled riding and racing.

People all over the United States are into sledding. They're of all ages and occupations. The male-female ratio is 6 to 1. Men in this sport are fearless thrill seekers who see risk as something to be embraced rather than avoided.

For information on the United States Bobsled and Skeleton Federation's training camps for pushers and drivers, or for the names of sledders who may live close to you, contact:

U.S. Bobsled and Skeleton Federation
P.O. Box 828
Lake Placid, NY 12946
(518) 523-1842

Soccer

People all over the world enjoy this active game. It's also gaining increased popularity with Americans. Soccer is actually a form of football. Two teams of 11 players each try to advance the ball by kicking or bouncing it off any part of the body except the arms and hands. (The goalkeepers, or goalies, are the only players who can use their hands to catch, carry, throw, or stop the ball.) The fun and challenge of the game is the creative use of the body in forwarding the ball.

Three million adults (age 18 and over) play soccer each year; 63 percent are male. The men you'll meet in this sport are original and individualistic. They know how to be part of a team effort, but each one has his own unique style. Expect to be entertained and surprised by these dynamic men.

More information on hooking up with a soccer team can be obtained from:

U.S. Soccer Federation
1750 East Boulder Street
Colorado Springs, CO 80909
(719) 578-4662

Softball

You played softball when you were in grade school, of course. Why stop just because you've grown up? The fun of the game can still be yours. Softball continues to be the most popular team participant sport, and not just for kids. The Amateur Softball Association registers more than 180,000 adult teams each year (over four times as many as the youth teams).

More than 60 percent of softball players are male (playing on male or coed teams); 14 percent are single. Twenty percent are between 25 and 34;

An article in the June 1988 issue of *Cosmopolitan* quotes a 28-year-old personnel agent as recommending that women who want to meet men carry an odd object such as a saxophone or baseball mitt. The object has to reflect your personal interests or it will become nothing more than an artificial prop. But the right object may just provoke the right men into noticing you and starting up a conversation!

11 percent between 35 and 54. They earn moderate incomes (in the $20,000–$30,000 range). Thirty-two percent have a college or postgraduate degree; 24 percent have only a high school education.

According to a recent Gallup Poll, one in four men (18 and older) play softball. With this many involved in the sport, you'll find a great diversity. The one thing they all have in common is a love for this all-American sport. No matter what they do or how they act off the softball field, they're intensely enthusiastic when playing their game. This passion for the sport allows men of all ages, races, ethnic origins, educational levels, occupations, and interests to transcend their usual roles and become just human beings who thoroughly enjoy softball.

Openings on local community and corporate teams should be fairly easy to find via the newspaper, phone calls to community recreational centers, or networking with people on a company team. For further assistance, contact:

Amateur Softball Association
2801 NE 50th Street
Oklahoma City, OK 73111
(405) 424-5266

Squash/Racquetball

Squash and racquetball are similar racquet games played by two, three, or four players. Each rally is won by serving or returning the ball so the opponent is unable to keep it in play. When played vigorously, the games provide an aerobic workout and a real test of eye-hand coordination. These games can also work off the hostility and aggression you've been accumulating throughout the day!

There are half a million squash players and 10 million racquetball players in the United States. Ages range from children to 80-year-olds. Most racquetball players are in their twenties or thirties; squash players are typically in their thirties or forties. These sports are largely male-dominated; only 15 percent of squash players and 28 percent of racquetball players are female. Like handball players, they may have achieved success in their lives but want to continue to be mentally and physically challenged.

For more information:

U.S. Racquets Association
21 Ford Road
Bala-Cynwyd, PA 19004
(215) 667-4006

**American Amateur
Racquetball Association**
915 North Kentucky Avenue
Winter Park, FL 32789-4736
(407) 647-4298

**International Amateur
Racquetball Federation**
815 North Weber
Colorado Springs, CO 80903
(719) 635-5396

Stickball

If you didn't grow up in New York City, you may not be familiar with stickball. But more than 1,500 people love the sport and play it regularly. Stickball is a version of baseball that uses a lightweight ball and broomstick (although the growing popularity of the sport is leading to the introduction of new products such as aluminum bats). Each team has five players. The game, played in city streets, is actually more action-packed than regular baseball, since players don't have to cover as large a playing field.

Only a few players are women; 99.5 percent are male. The age range is 14 to 60, with most players in their twenties and thirties. Players are both

---

Being chosen by "Mr. Right" is a flattering concept, but it could take forever for him to find you. Instead, use your intelligence, personality, and energy to do the choosing. You have the abilities to empower yourself to make good things happen rather than just waiting for them to happen to you.

single and married, students and business people. Teams can be found in New York, New Jersey, Connecticut, Atlanta, Boston, and Philadelphia.

Men who play stickball are down-to-earth and unpretentious. They're definitely urbanites who are happier in city environments than they ever could be in the country. These men tend to have a good sense of humor and don't take themselves too seriously.

If you don't live in one of the areas with stickball teams, consider starting one in your own city. Contact:

U.S. Stickball League Inc.
P.O. Box 363
East Rockaway, NY 11518

Surfing

If you love the ocean but have never surfed, you've been depriving yourself of a highly enjoyable experience. Whether you use a hard board or soft, a long board or short, a single fin, double fin, or tri-fin board, and whether you surf standing, on your knees, or lying down, there's nothing like catching a great wave. Surfing is becoming more of a legitimate competitive sport rather than just a laid-back amateur pastime (although this kind of surfing is also available) and may even win a place in upcoming Olympic games.

No, you don't have to be a 16-year-old Californian with sunstreaked hair to partake in the sport. The United States Surfing Federation has 13,000 members and estimates that more than a million people surf. These surfers are all ages (even people in their late sixties compete) and from all walks of life (math teachers, gardeners, civil engineers). About 10 percent are women. It helps, of course, to have ready access to the water. There are regional groups on the East Coast, Texas, West Coast, and Hawaii (in addition to the National Scholastic Federation for college students, Women's International, and Christian surfing groups).

Male surfers are rugged individualists who like a challenge. They don't seek out soft or easy guarantees in life. They like to take chances and be in command of their own performance. Needless to say, they're also nature lovers and especially treasure the ocean.

For information about classes in surfing education, surfing camps, and championships, contact:

U.S. Surfing Federation
7104 Island Village Drive
Long Beach, CA 90803

Survival Game

The National Survival Game is an armed, trademarked version of the child's game of Capture the Flag. Two teams, ranging from 12 to 40 players, attempt to capture their opponents' flag placed on a tree about half a mile away and bring it back to home base without being "shot." All players wear camouflage clothes, with colored ribbons on one arm to identify which team they belong to, and carry an airgun which shoots pellets of water-based paint-filled gelatin balls. When "shot," the "dead" player puts on a bright orange "dead vest" and leaves the battlefield.

The game, which typically lasts about an hour, has some hazards. Goggles must be worn to protect the eyes from the paint pellets. Because the game is played in heavily wooded areas, players can be exposed to poison oak and rattlesnakes.

But these risks don't deter the 35,000 Survival Game aficionados from playing the game each weekend. Over a million people have played at least once. Ninety-five percent are men between the ages of 18 and 35. Participants have included stockbrokers, doctors, lawyers, computer programmers, carpenters, photographers, and cab drivers.

Don't think that all the men who play the game are bloodthirsty savages. Although it's fantasized murder, it's not much different from playing cops and robbers. Many of the men are actually pacifists who just enjoy the drama and humor of the game. They may not always lead the most exciting lives day-to-day, but they get an adrenaline rush from the game. By combining their adult capacities with childlike imagination and lack of inhibitions, they enjoy a unique experience.

The game is played in more than 200 locations in 45 states. For the name of the nearest playing field or league, contact:

National Survival Game
P.O. Box 1439
New London, NH 03257
(800) 225-7529

Swimming

Of course you're familiar with swimming. You probably enjoy it every summer. Splashing around in the water can be both relaxing and refreshing. But for a real challenge as well as the ultimate fitness activity, think about amateur competitive swimming. See if you can develop your butterfly, breaststroke, or backstroke to the point where you can successfully compete.

In both recreational and competitive swimming, the sexes are fairly equally represented. Men who enjoy swimming are usually very sensual. They know how to move fast and rush through life as well as the next person, but they try to savor the experience at the same time. If it's at all possible, they strive to make even the most mundane and utilitarian activities pleasurable.

For information on joining your local swimming committee or club and participating in events, contact:

U.S. Swimming Inc.
1750 East Boulder Street
Colorado Springs, CO 80909-5770
(719) 578-4578

Table Tennis

If you think tennis is the most popular of all the racquet sports, think again. Table tennis (possibly better known by the trade name Ping-Pong) is played more than any other racquet sport in the United States and the world. More than 21 million Americans play recreational table tennis, and 10 million annually participate in sanctioned tournaments. Although the sport began as a parlor game around the turn of the century, it has evolved into a highly competitive sport which was awarded full medal status in the 1988 Olympics.

Membership in the United States Table Tennis Association is about 90 percent male. More than half the membership is over 40. Most have above-average educations. Players are located all over the United States, but concentration is heaviest on the east and west coasts.

This sport is extremely fast-paced. Balls can move at speeds exceeding 100 miles an hour. Obviously, male table tennis players like to be on the go. They aren't men who enjoy just lazing around. On the other hand, they aren't

In *Love Tactics* (Garden City, N.Y.: Avery, 1988), Thomas W. McKnight and Robert H. Phillips write that most people are really looking for a lasting, permanent relationship—one that can't usually be found in bars. They propose the analogy of not settling for "table scraps" when you'd rather be feasting at "the banquet of true love."

necessarily adventurous types. Rather, they like a certain degree of predictability and familiarity in their environments. Exploring the great outdoors or the world at large isn't as appealing to them as sticking with what they know.

Anyone wishing to learn table tennis or to become involved in one of the more than 300 local clubs throughout the United States should contact:

U.S. Table Tennis Association
1750 East Boulder Street
Colorado Springs, CO 80909-5769
(719) 578-4583

Tennis

You may never compete at Wimbledon, but that shouldn't take anything away from your enjoyment of playing tennis. The United States Tennis Association estimates that more than 20 million people a year play the game. If you're not one of them, think about learning or relearning this sport. It provides you with an aerobic workout and is just plain fun besides.

Males slightly outnumber females in tennis. The men you'll meet on a tennis court are dynamic, success-driven individuals. They're self-confident and know they have the ability to handle life's challenges. They're not men who shy away from getting involved; they know they can deal with the demands of a relationship.

Locate your nearest courts or instructors in the phone book (check under "Tennis" and "Tennis Instruction" in the Yellow Pages) or contact your city's recreation department. The United States Tennis Association, the sport's governing body, can provide details about the game.

U.S. Tennis Association
1212 Avenue of the Americas
New York, NY 10036
(212) 302-3322

Touch Football

Touch football encompasses most of the fundamentals of football except for a few deviations. In blocking, the player must remain on both feet before, during, and after contact. Instead of tackling, the player makes a one-hand touch between the opponent's shoulders and knees. If you've ever lamented being barred from playing football because you're female, the touch version enables you to enjoy the challenge and action of football without the violence or potential for injury.

Because touch football is usually organized informally (for example, two teams of about seven players each, evolving and changing frequently), it is difficult to provide statistics as to the number of participants or their characteristics. A large number are men, but women are generally welcome to play.

Are you looking for a real macho man? You won't find one here. Touch football players are comfortable enough with their masculinity to allow themselves to be sensitive and gentle. They're not wimps, but they don't feel compelled to constantly prove how tough they are.

Look for touch football games in parks and other open areas around your community. Some businesses organize touch football leagues.

Ultimate

If you've ever enjoyed throwing a Frisbee disc but eventually found that it wasn't exciting enough to hold your interest, Ultimate may be the sport for you. Played with a Frisbee, it combines the passing and scoring of football, the cutting and guarding of basketball, and the field movement of hockey. Two seven-person teams attempt to pass the disc from teammate to teammate until a pass is caught in the opponent's end zone. Unlike football, running with the disc is not allowed; the player must stop running and establish a pivot foot before passing again. Each player acts as quarterback, receiver, and defender. But again, unlike football, no overt contact or tackling is allowed. Instead, the defending team tries to force a turnover by guarding the thrower and potential receivers or by playing a zone defense.

The disc sinks, floats, and curves, adding a suspenseful excitement to the game that isn't present in other sports. Another difference between Ultimate and regular sports is Ultimate's lack of referees. Because players on the field are responsible for their own foul and line calls, they're required to adhere to the highest standards of sportsmanship.

It's estimated that more than 25,000 individuals currently play regularly. Eighty percent are male. Eighty percent are single as well. The majority are college graduates. Over half are between 24 and 29 years old; 20 percent are 30 or older. Nationally there are at least 500 teams that participate annually in the Ultimate Players Association traditional championship. On a more informal level, it's played in co-ed community and corporate leagues throughout the United States.

With 80 percent male players, chances are good that you'll meet some interesting men if you become involved in the sport. You'll find them to be bright, energetic, and full of integrity. These are men who play fair and respect other people (including women!). Physically fit and mentally evolved, these men really are the ultimate as friends and lovers.

More information on the sport as well as local/regional/national tournaments can be obtained from:

Ultimate Players Association
P.O. Box 2331
Silver City, NM 88062

Underwater Sports

Splashing around in a pool is fine for some people, but others want more challenging aquatic adventures. If you love spending time in the water but are becoming bored with swimming, try an underwater sport. Snorkeling and scuba diving are the best known activities, but there's also:

- Underwater rugby. A breath-hold sport played in a pool with a weighted ball and underwater hoops. There are 15 players on a team, but only 6 are in the water at one time. The ball is passed from one player to another to be thrown into the goal.
- Fin swimming. Using crawl or butterfly strokes, swimmers wearing fins, as well as a mask or goggles and a snorkel, race one another in pools or open water.

- Underwater photography. Divers compete to obtain the best photos.
- Underwater hockey. Teams of six compete on the bottom of the swimming pool. Each player is equipped with mask, fins, snorkel, protective glove, and a short stick used to pass the metal puck along the bottom of the pool toward the opposing team's goal.
- Spear fishing. Divers drop into a school of very large fish and aim spears at the fish.

Thousands of individuals snorkel or scuba dive. About 1,000 participate in other water sports. Ages range from teens to middle-agers. The ratio of males to females is 3 to 1.

Men who favor underwater sports are independent and self-reliant. They like to be in control, but they also enjoy dealing with the unexpected.

Check with your local pool or aquatic center to see whether any of these sports is offered, or contact the Underwater Society of America for more information about the sports and about local, regional, and national competitions.

Underwater Society of America
P.O. Box 628
Daly City, CA 94017

Unicycling

For a change of pace from the four wheels of your car or the two wheels of your bicycle, try the challenge of riding one wheel. Unicycles have been

---

Should you meet your future husband while scuba diving, you might want to copy the wedding of Bill Barrow and Ruthie Schrenzel. They were married at Key Largo National Marine Sanctuary in Florida . . . underwater. As pictured in the May 16, 1988, issue of *People* magazine, the bride wore a one-piece pink diving suit with a matching mask, regulator, and fins. The groom wore a black tie with his scuba gear. They exchanged vows by passing a diving slate to each other and checking off the "I do" box. A notary public (who doubles as the diving center owner) performed the ceremony. Among the guests were several moray eels.

around for more than a hundred years, but are only now starting to catch on as a unique and fun means of recreation and transportation. Learning to ride isn't as difficult as it might appear. Once the basics are mastered, you can try riding backward, turning sharply, and spinning.

Although you probably don't personally know a unicyclist, they do exist! Some 600 are official members of the Unicycling Society of America. The membership is equally divided between men and women. Members range in age from 1 to 80 (and all ages in between). The local unicycle clubs enable members to mingle and hone their skills in practice meets, parades, and shows. They participate in a national meet each year, competing in racing, group and parade formations, and artistic skill riding.

Unicycling is not a mainstream sport, so don't expect its participants to be run-of-the-mill. Men attracted to this activity are interesting characters with unique personalities. A little bit quirky, maybe, but in the nicest possible way. A sense of humor and a good deal of creativity are also standard.

Intrigued? Contact:

Unicycling Society of America
P.O. Box 40534
Redford, MI 48240

Volleyball

If your image of a volleyball player is a high school boy making a halfhearted attempt to get the ball over the net while his P.E. teacher watches, think again. You'll also need to revise your perceptions if you think that most

---

Most couples don't get married on unicycles, but then again, most couples don't meet through unicycling. Unicycling was responsible for at least one couple's meeting and falling in love, however, so it was inevitable that they would have a unicycle wedding. When Teresa Hemminger and Sem Abrahams were married in 1988 in Redford, Michigan, they, the maid of honor, the best man, and the bride's father rode in on unicycles. Naturally, the first "dance" took place on unicycles. If you meet your husband-to-be on a unicycle, you might be tempted to have a unicycle wedding of your own!

volleyball players are Californians who play a few rounds on the beach while consuming an inordinate amount of beer and wine coolers.

The truth is that volleyball is actually an upscale sport played all over the country (but especially in the South), by males and females equally. Over 9 million participants are between 25 and 34, 4 million are 35 to 44, and 1.5 million are between 45 and 54. Many players have incomes of $35,000 to $50,000 or more. Quite a few of them take the game very seriously and even compete on teams in local, regional, and national events.

You'll find that male volleyball players are alert, energetic, and caring. They are sensitive to the needs of others, especially those they are closest to. Power trips aren't something they indulge in; they simply want to work hard and play fair without infringing on anyone else's rights or happiness.

You can hook up with a volleyball team in your community through your local Y, health club, physical education courses, or recreation department. For more information about the sport, contact:

U.S. Volleyball Association
1750 East Boulder Street
Colorado Springs, CO 80909-5766
(719) 578-4750

Walking

It may not be the most glamorous or exciting means of exercise. It can't compete with the thrill of skiing or the challenge of tennis. Nonetheless, walking is considered by many experts to be one of the best fitness activities around. It can be performed all year almost anywhere, with minimum expense (all you need are good walking shoes) and a negligible potential for injury. Small wonder that millions of people are choosing fitness/power walking as their main exercise regimen or as part of a cross-training approach.

According to the National Sporting Goods Association, at least 62 million Americans walk for exercise. Among walkers in their twenties to forties, women seem to outnumber men 1.5 to 1. For the 50-plus population, more men than women walk (perhaps as a result of their physicians' recommendations after a heart attack).

Male walkers are a solid bunch who can make loyal and faithful mates. They're not thrill seekers, continually looking for something new or risky. Once they make a commitment, they'll stick with it.

Most communities have walking clubs that encourage some socialization while exercising. Check your local listings in the outdoor section of the sports pages or in the entertainment section of your weekend newspaper. Also, athletic-shoe stores or sporting goods shops should be able to put you in touch with a walking group. Many shopping malls open their doors before business hours so that individual walkers or clubs can use their climate-controlled premises when they're not crowded; check with the mall management to find out more.

Water Polo

You may not personally be familiar with water polo, but the sport has a good number of fans. This game of skill, endurance, and swimming ability is played in water in an area 20 by 30 meters. Seven players (6 field players and 1 goalkeeper) play at any one time, although there are actually 13 players on a team. The object of the game is to shoot a rubber ball into a goal. The ball must be handled with only one hand and can be advanced by passing it or swimming ("dribbling") with it. Games consist of four seven-minute quarters.

Ten thousand people play the game actively enough to belong to United States Water Polo Inc. Players range in age from 12 to 55. The game is especially popular in California, but is played all over the country. Males outnumber females 10 to 1. The men in this sport are active, alert individuals who don't shy away from challenges. They like to experience all that life offers and want to succeed in all they do, but never at someone else's expense.

For local teams, contact:

U.S. Water Polo Inc.
1750 East Boulder Street
Colorado Springs, CO 80909
(719) 578-4549

Waterskiing

If you like snow skiing, chances are you'll also enjoy waterskiing. If you don't like being outside in cold weather, waterskiing will enable you to experience a thrill similar to downhill skiing, but without the frostbite.

(Sunburn, of course, is a distinct possibility.) Even if you've never tried any type of skiing, you can master the basics of waterskiing very quickly. About a million people between the ages of 25 and 35 learn the sport each year. Why not join them and discover its unique challenges for yourself?

Recreational waterskiing continues to grow in popularity, as does interest in tournament waterskiing. There are now more than 450 tournaments each season sanctioned by the American Water Ski Association. These range from local events for novices to national and world-record tournaments for experienced competitors. In addition to standard waterskiing, specialty skills include barefoot, kneeboard, slalom, jump, and trick skiing.

You'll be in good company if you take up waterskiing. Of the more than 13 million people who participate in waterskiing each year, 57 percent are male. The majority are 18 to 34 years old, but there are quite a few who are 35 to 54 and even some who are 55-plus. More than half of all participants have at least some college education. As for marital status, about half are single. A sizable proportion have incomes over $50,000 a year. Men who participate in this sport can be expected to be reasonably active, enjoy a challenge and moderate risk, and prefer to be in small group settings rather than large social functions.

For more information about the sport, including lists of ski schools, events, and the more than 400 American Water Ski Association–affiliated local clubs, contact:

American Water Ski Association
799 Overlook Drive
Winter Haven, FL 33884-1671
(813) 324-4341

Weight Lifting

Having bulging biceps might not appeal to you, but weight lifting doesn't necessarily have to lead to exaggerated muscle bulk. You can use this fitness activity as a way to gently tone and define your body. Weight lifting requires a combination of strength, speed, and coordination, and can be a challenging way to improve your general physical condition.

Millions of people lift weights on an informal basis. About 2,500 pursue it as a competitive activity and belong to the United States Weightlifting Federation. Fewer than 10 percent of weight lifters are female. Ages range from 13 to 84. Lifters hold jobs ranging from postal carrier to chiropractor to Wall Street analyst. Most of the men are intense, serious, and capable of deep concentration on whatever is important to them. They tend to be on the reticent side and can't always be counted on to be good conversationalists, but they can be good listeners.

You can begin a weight-lifting program at your local gym. For more information, contact:

U.S. Weightlifting Federation
1750 East Boulder Street
Colorado Springs, CO 80909-5764
(719) 578-4508

Windsurfing

Windsurfing (also known as board sailing or sailboarding) combines the best of surfing and sailing. It uses a 12-foot board similar to a surfboard with a free sail fastened to it by a universal joint. The mast (which is the only moving part) is the tiller. If the mast is tipped forward, the front of the board dips down into the water. If the mast is leaned backward, the back of the board is pushed downward and the windsurfer heads into the wind. It provides a similar sensation to snow skiing (in terms of gliding across a smooth surface) and waterskiing (balancing precariously). Windsurfing can be performed in fresh water as well as the sea.

The sport has continued to increase in popularity since it was included in the 1984 Olympics. Europe has the most devotees, but windsurfing is catching on in the United States. About 50,000 members belong to the 600 local groups of the International Windsurfers Class Association. Participants range from 9 to 63 years of age. Males and females are equally represented.

Because windsurfing requires more finesse than strength, you'll tend to meet less macho men than in other sports. The men who pursue this sport are usually sensitive, sensual, and self-reliant. They're not concerned with showing off or proving themselves to anyone else; they just want to enjoy life and all its experiences. Most are equally comfortable in relaxing or invigorating circumstances.

Windsurfing is easier to learn than surfing, since there's something to hold on to, and it can usually be learned in a three-hour course combining a pivotal land simulator and actual on-water practice. Contact your local surfing or boating centers (check your Yellow Pages) for more details.

International Windsurfers Class Association
2030 East Gladwick Street
Compton, CA 90220
(213) 608-1651

Yacht Racing

If you yearn to be on the sea but want to do something more challenging than just leisurely sailing, try yacht racing. The sport offers you extended time out in the ocean, camaraderie, and thrills.

It's estimated that 200,000 people race; 80 percent are men. They're typically in their early forties, college-educated, affluent ($95,000 annual income), and live all over the United States. Racers have well-balanced, mentally healthy outlooks on life. They like to combine hard work with pleasure and play. They're capable individuals who can fend for themselves, but they're also good communicators and team players.

For information on learning to sail, contact 1-800-336-BOAT. This computer-bank service can provide local contacts in most areas of the United States. To find out the name and address of your local sailing club or association, contact:

U.S. Yacht Racing Union
Box 209
Newport, RI 02840
(401) 849-5200

Yoga

Hatha yoga is a unique form of exercise that tones and relaxes the mind as well as the body. Meditation and breathing exercises are combined with stretching performed in standing, sitting, kneeling, prone, and supine positions. Ideally, yoga is practiced daily for maximum physical and mental well-being.

Estimating the number of people who practice yoga is difficult because of the vast number who do it in the privacy of their own homes without joining a class or organization. It is believed to be growing in popularity as people seek gentler activities that won't result in injuries but relieve stress. While some people do yoga in their twenties, most devotees are in their thirties to fifties. There appear to be twice as many women as men who are actively involved.

The men you'll meet in yoga classes and groups are less competitive and less aggressive than many men you'd meet elsewhere. They're more introspective and less social than most, but this doesn't preclude a meaningful, intimate relationship with a well-chosen individual.

Your best bet for learning yoga is to enroll in a class offered by your local Y, New Age center, community recreational center, adult education system, or at a health and fitness center.

Leisure Activities

NO MATTER HOW BUSY YOUR schedule, it's essential that you set aside some time just for yourself. This is not a time for work (volunteer or paid job), nor is it time for doing household chores or even getting yourself in shape through exercise. All you should concentrate on is having fun. Depending on your interests, this can range from playing bridge to gardening, collecting antique music boxes to raising West Highland terriers, carving wood to operating a ham radio.

Each of the following possibilities can lead to your meeting and connecting with a variety of men. Don't just stop with one activity; try a number of them and see which ones suit you best. An extensive repertoire of leisure skills will enrich your life and increase your man-meeting opportunities.

Aerobatics

If your adrenaline was pumping during *Top Gun* and you wished for a moment that you could learn to do all those stunts in an airplane, why not make your dream a reality? Take flying lessons, gain some proficiency, and then learn to do some fancy aerial stunts.

The International Aerobatic Club has 5,100 active members. About 90 percent are men. Most aerobats are well-educated (college or beyond) professional people in their forties and fifties. Since flying is an expensive activity, the majority are in the upper middle class, many with six-figure incomes. Expect many men who enjoy this pastime to be determined, fearless, take-charge individuals. Couch potatoes they're not!

Contact the International Aerobatic Club for more information on how to learn aerobatics and where the approximately 30 schools in the United States that teach aerobatics are located. The organization has 43 local chapters, many of which sponsor seminars and other activities that help members perfect their skills.

International Aerobatic Club
P.O. Box 3086
Oshkosh, WI 54903
(414) 426-4800

Antique Cars

If you love cars or history or both, you'd probably enjoy belonging to a club that preserves, restores, and maintains antique automobiles (25 years or older). You don't have to own an antique auto to participate in a club (although after seeing a 1929 Duesenberg, you may be sorely tempted!); all you need is a genuine interest in antique automobiles. Antique car meets, automobile touring on designated routes, workshops, and conferences are all available.

The Antique Automobile Club of America has about 55,000 members in 383 regions and chapters. Ages range from young adults to senior citizens. About 70 percent are men.

Men who care about antique autos are truly a special breed. They tend to have gentle, nurturing natures. More so than most men, they're sentimental and not afraid to show their softer side. You'll share the romance of the past as you restore and ride in an antique car with one of these special men.

Antique Automobile Club of America
501 West Governor Road
P.O. Box 417
Hershey, PA 17033
(717) 534-1910

Backgammon

Backgammon is a game that has experienced intermittent popularity over the years. But true backgammon fans don't care whether the game is in fashion or not. They enjoy the competition and challenge that this easy-to-learn game offers year after year.

You would have had to have been living in a cave not to have played or at least seen the game of backgammon. To refresh your memory, all it requires is two players and a board with two tables or parts. The pieces are moved in accordance with throws of the dice, so the game incorporates both luck and strategy.

It's impossible to pinpoint the number of backgammon players, since most people play informally without ever joining a club. If you'd like to play the game and be in a social situation where you can meet people (especially men), look for a backgammon club in your community. (Ask your recreation and parks department, or check in bars or game halls.) If you become sufficiently skilled and engrossed in the game, you can play in tournaments. The International Backgammon Association has 3,500 members and offers a dozen or more tournaments each year (in New York City, South Florida, Vermont, the West Coast, Canada, Mexico, and the Caribbean). Participants range in age from 21 to 90. Males predominate, 9 to 1.

While you'll meet some men who are almost fanatical about backgammon, most are well-rounded individuals who enjoy the game but also devote their time and energy to other interests. They may show some competitiveness and aggressiveness on the backgammon board but are usually mild-mannered in real life.

International Backgammon Association
1300 Citrus Isle
Fort Lauderdale, FL 33315

Beer Can Collecting

You probably just throw away empty beer cans without giving them a second thought, but thousands of people think beer cans are worth saving and collecting—current or obsolete, in various colors, and from a variety of breweries or locations. Other characteristics collectors focus on are the seams, bottoms, and tops. Collectors obtain cans by "dump hunting," buying, or trading through the mail, at local club meetings, and at regional/national "canventions."

At least 28,000 individuals have been members of the Beer Can Collectors of America Club at one time or another. Currently 4,500 belong to the organization and one of its 102 nationwide chapters. The average age is 35, but collectors do range from children to senior citizens. The ratio of males to females is 10 to 1.

Since collecting is most successful within a wide network of interested persons, you'll find beer can collectors to be outgoing and helpful. While many do enjoy beer (as does the general population), they're not necessarily heavy drinkers. The appeal of beer can collecting is not so much in the imbibing as in the chase and acquisition of cans that enhance one's collection.

Beer Can Collectors
of America
747 Merus Court
Fenton, MO 63026

Bonsai

If you're a nature lover, you will really enjoy bonsai, because it brings the outdoors inside your home. Started by the Chinese in about 202 B.C. and perfected by the Japanese, bonsai is the art of creating living trees in miniature. Through the techniques of bud pinching, root pruning, trimming, fertilizing, and watering, trees such as pines, spruces, juniper, maples, elms, flowering quinces, cherries, and crabapples can be reduced to a foot or less and maintained in a tray. No two people will shape the same tree in the same way; each bonsai practitioner interprets the tree according to his or her own vision and artistry.

More than 50,000 individuals practice bonsai in the United States. Almost 4,000 belong to the Bonsai Clubs International and one of the 331 local clubs. An equal number of men and women, usually in their thirties or older, participate in this living art form.

Male bonsai enthusiasts are patient, creative, nature-loving individualists. Instead of being totally goal-oriented like so many other men, they're into *process*. They enjoy the doing and being as much as (if not more than) just obtaining the desired end results.

Bonsai Clubs International
2636 West Mission Road #277
Tallahassee, FL 32304

Bridge

Skip bid, three hearts.

If these four words don't make any sense to you, you obviously are not a duplicate bridge player. Even if you generally don't like card games, it can be well worth your while to try this one. Bridge is an engrossing activity based on brains rather than luck. For an intellectual challenge as well as a fantastic social outlet, bridge clubs should be explored.

Bridge is too complicated a game to fully explain here, but it involves strategic bidding to accumulate the desired cards and score points. Competitive bridge can be a little different from the recreational bridge you may have seen your parents play. Competitive duplicate bridge compares the scores of many tables and awards masterpoints for those who place in the top third. Duplicate games are held daily in every big city in the United States and Canada. If you don't have a partner, one can be assigned. Instead of worrying about how the house looks, baking dessert, or searching for a fourth, you can leave your home and head for a bridge club where you pay to enter and have the benefit of a director who oversees the mechanics of the games, makes a ruling when an irregularity occurs, scores, and awards the masterpoints. Players move to a nearby table after the director calls the round, which increases the number of people you can meet. After the game is over, players typically discuss the game and analyze the strategies they used and problems they encountered.

Millions of people play bridge; 200,000 are committed enough to belong to the American Contract Bridge League. Sixty percent are women. The average age is 57, with a range from teens to octogenarians. Ninety percent have attended college, with 33 percent having postgraduate schooling. The average income is over $53,000. There are 4,200 clubs across the country. More than 1,000 tournaments (which attract younger people up to the mid-forties) are also sponsored by the American Contract Bridge League. There are no qualifications for membership. You can drop by a bridge club and find someone to teach you and play with you, even if you're an absolute beginner.

What kind of man might you meet over the bridge table? He will be intelligent and contemplative. Mental action rather than physical is his style. While he can be a good communicator, he's probably not especially long-winded or verbose. He's introverted to some extent but also enjoys being around other people.

Look in your phone book for bridge clubs or contact:

American Contract Bridge League
2200 Democrat Road
Memphis, TN 38132
(901) 332-5586

Cat Lovers' Groups

Abyssinian, American Shorthair, Balinese, Burmese, Devon Rex, Himalayan, Japanese Bobtail, Korat, Persian, Russian Blue, Siamese, Turkish Angora. If these names mean anything to you, you're probably a cat lover and would enjoy participating in a group that shares your fancy for felines.

Many of the people you'll meet in cat clubs are primarily interested in showing their cats. You'll find slightly more women than men, since women tend to be more partial to cats, but there will be plenty of men to meet, both in local clubs and national/international cat shows. Men who love cats are special people who appreciate beauty and who care about animals. Those who show cats tend to be detail-oriented, perfectionistic, and competitive. If you want a laid-back, easy-living type of guy, you should look elsewhere. But if you want a man who has high standards concerning everything in his life, you may want to get involved with a cat group or show.

American Cat Fanciers Association Inc.
P.O. Box 203
Point Lookout, MO 65726
(417) 334-5430

Checkers

Undoubtedly you played checkers as a child. You probably owned at least one cardboard checkerboard (with a backgammon board on the flip side).

Taking action and trying to achieve something in your life will make you feel good about yourself. But if you sit around doing nothing, just wishing that something would happen, both your confidence and your energy will plummet. Get involved with groups and activities for the sake of your physical and mental health, as well as your love life.

And you probably haven't played it since you turned 13. But checkers doesn't have to be a kid's game. There are unlimited strategies and moves to plot. In fact, top-level players plot 30 to 40 moves in advance (as compared to the 8 to 10 moves planned by expert chess players). It takes years of practice to become a really skilled checkers player.

Checkers is not a highly social game, but you do need people to compete against. You can find all the opponents you need at a local checkers club. There are about 100 clubs and 1,000 members affiliated with the American Checker Federation. Tournaments are offered throughout the year on district, state, national, and international levels.

The age of master players is in the sixties, but the rapidly growing revival of checkers among Russian immigrants and other younger people should cause the average age to drop to the twenties and thirties. Only about 1 percent of players in tournaments are female.

Checkers players can be mildly introverted, but they generally don't have difficulty in one-on-one relationships. They can establish intimacy. They're analytical and introspective, but not to the point where they're unable to take action and do whatever needs to be done. In fact, they can even be quietly aggressive when they go after what they want, both on and off the checkerboard.

American Checker Federation
P.O. Box 365
Petal, MS 39465

Chess

If your work isn't always as stimulating as you'd like and you sometimes wish you had something in your life that was intellectually challenging, you should try chess. You're probably familiar with the basics. Each player commands an army of 16 men by using strategic moves and jumps. People

---

"**N**othing ventured, nothing gained" is as true a maxim in love as it is in business or chess. Take a chance on love. There's so little to lose and an enormous amount to be gained. Don't be afraid to make the first move to meet someone who interests you. Both of you may discover that you're glad you did!

who get hooked on chess find it to be one of the most engrossing parts of their lives, offering challenges and satisfactions that aren't available through any other outlet.

Thousands of people play chess. Over 51,000 play the game seriously enough to belong to the United States Chess Federation and one of the 1,600 affiliated organizations and clubs. Chess is definitely a male-dominated game; only 4 percent of players are female. It will come as no surprise that chess players are brainy. If a man's mind is more important to you than his physique, you'll appreciate a chess player. He'll be analytical, thoughtful, and creative in his approach to life. Although they're not highly emotional or especially talkative, they do understand, respect, and appreciate another person's feelings and needs. These are men you can talk to; they'll really listen and try to relate to what you're experiencing.

To get involved in local clubs and tournaments, contact:

U.S. Chess Federation
186 Route 9W
New Windsor, NY 12550
(914) 562-8350

Clowning

Clowning is an irresistible hobby. After all, how many other leisure activities allow their participants to be as silly as they want and offer opportunities to bring a smile to a child's face? Clowning can be done on a volunteer basis (for example, in parades or pediatric hospitals) as well as for profit (at children's birthday parties or at retail store promotions).

It's estimated that about 11,000 people are active in clowning professionally or as a hobby. There are about 70 clown alleys (local organizations) throughout the country. About 40 percent are men. Most clowns are 40-plus, but a growing number of 25-to-40-year-olds are discovering clowning.

Any man you'll meet through clowning will obviously bring humor and whimsy into your life. He'll be a people lover who cares about making everyone happy. But don't think that clowns are always "on" and demanding to be the center of attention. Once they take off their makeup and costumes, they put away their clown personas.

By joining the Clowns of America International, you can meet male clowns in your local clown alleys and participate in educational programs, national/regional conventions, and competitions (such as makeup, skits, etc.).

Clowns of America International
P.O. Box 570
Lake Jackson, TX 77566
(713) 486-6623

Coin Collecting (Numismatics)

Money is fun to spend, but it can also be fun to collect. One of the oldest of all hobbies, coin collecting originated with the introduction of coinage in the mid-seventh century B.C. when owners saved coins as a means of storing wealth and began collecting them as miniature works of art. There's a special thrill when you are holding an old coin in your hand as you imagine who else might have held it or where it has traveled. Coin collecting doesn't have to be an expensive hobby; some pieces from the ancient Roman Empire can be purchased for as little as $5.

You can start a coin collection by saving the change in your pocket. You can try to collect specific dates or mint marks. You can also specialize in certain countries or types of coins, medals, or tokens. Coins can be bought through local dealers or mail-order outfits. But you really should join a coin club to meet and socialize with fellow collectors.

It's estimated that millions of people collect coins. The most serious collectors (34,000 throughout the world) belong to the American Numismatic Association (ANA), the world's largest organization for collectors of coins, tokens, medals, and paper money. The ANA currently has about 650 local clubs in the United States. Over half its members are male. The median age is 43 years, but there are members of every age. The majority hold a college degree and are employed in professional or managerial positions. While members live all over the world, the largest numbers reside in California, New York, Florida, Texas, Pennsylvania, Illinois, Ohio, New Jersey, Massachusetts, and Michigan.

In *Marrying Later, Marrying Smarter* (New York: McGraw-Hill, 1990), Tracy Cabot notes that women often know more about the new boots they're going to buy than the new man they want in their lives. Put some thought and effort into the type of man you want and go after him!

Coin collectors like to be in control and want to have direct involvement in everything that concerns them. They don't do well with uncertainty; they like to know exactly what to expect in their lives.

For information about local clubs, as well as discounts on purchases, coin grading services, and access to a unique reference library, contact:

American Numismatic Association
818 North Cascade Avenue
Colorado Springs, CO 80903-3279
(719) 632-2646

Collecting

Anything can be collected as a hobby. Postcards, political items, pencils, salt and pepper shakers, angels in any form, and Chinese snuff bottles are all fair game. This chapter includes in-depth profiles of some collecting activities (beer cans, stamps, coins, and miniatures), but space limitations do not permit inclusion of every possibility. For a comprehensive listing of all collecting organizations, refer to the *Encyclopedia of Associations,* available at your local library.

Computer Interactive Communication

Do you have a personal computer, a modem, a telephone, and communications software? If so, you can hook up with an information service that will connect you with people all over the country. Many of these services have interactive forums, bulletin and message boards, and mail systems that let members "talk" with each other via their computers.

CompuServe, one of the largest information services (over half a million members), offers more than 150 on-line forums where you can find people pursuing all kinds of interests and sharing information. Some of the special-interest forums include health and fitness, food and wine, photography, sailing, gardening, music, and personal investing. A CB simulator serves as the social center of CompuServe. The 72 channels of the CB are available for spontaneous conversation, prearranged meetings, and private discussion You can also play games ranging from space wars, war strategies, role-playing, trivia contests, electronic casino tables, word games, and spelling quizzes. Adults can meet and form opposing teams to answer questions.

As Nancy E. Schaumburger and Marcia Brinton note in *Finding, Loving, and Marrying Your Lifetime Partner* (Greensboro, N.C.: Tudor, 1988), mate-seeking singles can usually find enough partners for an active social and sexual life. The problem is finding the *right* partner. Instead of *chance* encounters, cultivate *choice* encounters by finding and choosing those situations most likely to put you in touch with the most suitable partners.

Obviously, the computer doesn't provide you with face-to-face contact. You'll be getting to know men without ever seeing what they look like. And you'll probably never meet most of them, since many will live far from you. But it's always possible that you'll find yourself communicating with someone who does live within a reasonable distance, and you can always fly out to meet someone or have him come to your neck of the woods. There's an infinite variety of men you can meet. Different special-interest groups will attract specific types. For example, a man interested in the wine forum will be entirely different from someone into health and fitness or games.

For more information, contact:

CompuServe Information Service
Dept. L, Box 477
P.O. Box 18161
Columbus, OH 43272-4630
(800) 848-8199

Crosswords

If you're a crossword puzzle fanatic, you spend countless hours working on puzzles. Although you have fun and increase your vocabulary, curling up on your sofa with the *New York Times* doesn't do much for your social life. To meet men while crosswording, join the American Crossword Federation and participate in one of their many tournaments. Each participant races against all the competitors to finish his or her puzzle first. While you're feverishly working on your puzzle, there won't be much of an opportunity to talk with anyone, but during breaks and afterward, you just might find yourself engaged in conversation with an attractive man.

Millions of people enjoy crosswords; 2,500 of them are interested enough to belong to the American Crossword Federation. They range in age from 18 to over 80. Women (who as a group tend to have superior verbal skills) slightly outnumber men. But there *are* men to be met, and you'll find them to be articulate, serious, and moderately introspective.

American Crossword Federation
P.O. Box 69
Massapequa Park, NY 11762

Darts

The British have long enjoyed playing darts at their local pubs, but Americans have only recently begun to get into the sport in a big way. Unlike other activities that challenge eye-hand coordination, darts require a minimum of equipment and space, and can be played in indoor comfort throughout the year. Essentially all you need is a dartboard, some wall space, and darts. Practice refines your visual-motor abilities and will enable you to start tacking up increased points and even make a few bull's-eyes.

Millions of people all over the world play darts. More than 17 million play in the United States, 100,000 of them seriously enough to be members of the American Darts Organization. About 60 percent are men. The majority are between 25 and 55, with a high school education and low-middle income.

You can learn to throw darts in the privacy of your own home or at a local bar, but to play the game on a competitive level (on a singles, doubles, or team basis), you'll need to join a league in your area. The male darters you'll meet prefer a straightforward and simple approach to life. They don't like a lot of pretension or fuss in anything they're involved in. Most are quick, alert, and intent on doing well in whatever is important to them.

American Darts Organization
13841 Eastbrook Avenue
Bellflower, CA 90706
(213) 806-8319

Dinner Lectures

If you enjoy the combination of good food and company, you may want to get involved in a dinner club affiliated with the Associated Clubs Inc. (also known as Knife and Fork Clubs International or Metropolitan Dinner Clubs). Participants meet in a restaurant or banquet hall once a month and listen to nationally known guest speakers. Topics may include humor, politics, science, and personal growth. These dinners also offer excellent networking opportunities to meet and mingle with the business and professional leaders of your community.

National membership in the dinner clubs is estimated at 30,000. There are at least 100 cities with active chapters. Slightly more women than men participate. The average age tends to be high (60 to 70 years old), but younger people usually attend, too. This is a good way to meet men who are established in their careers and comfortable with their lives. They're not doing a lot of soul searching or experiencing existential angst; they know who they are and where they're going. They're very much interested in the people around them and the world at large.

> **The Associated Clubs Inc.**
> One Townsite Plaza, Suite 315
> Topeka, KS 66603
> (913) 232-0892

Dog Shows

Are you a dog lover? If you're one of the millions of Americans who are, you probably own one or more dogs. If you don't currently own one, why not? As a single woman, you could benefit from the companionship and protection they provide. Another benefit of dog ownership is the leisure and social activities available for dog owners. In addition to the obvious things

---

In today's busy world, it's inevitable that some people try to combine their business and social networking. A 1986 article in *Business Week* magazine reveals that most major cities have young executive clubs and business networks. Singles can meet in business attire at local restaurants, exchange business cards, and attempt to win door prizes such as a $1,000 zero-coupon bond. Check with your local Chamber of Commerce to see if one of these clubs exists in your area.

In their book *Finding Love* (New York: Crown, 1989), Drs. Margaret O'Connor and Jane Silverman advise going to places or activities where you know you'll have fun (rather than going to those that attract men but don't appeal to you). They note that going where you'll have a good time will bring out the best in you. Men will be likely to notice and be intrigued by your enthusiasm and obvious pleasure in being there.

like walking your dog and having him or her chase Frisbees in the park, you can also show your dog (provided she or he is registered with the American Kennel Club). Having your dog participate in shows will involve a substantial commitment to training, grooming, and traveling. But dog show enthusiasts feel it's well worth their time and energy. They actually see showing as a sport and enjoy the opportunity to show off their dogs.

It is estimated that 100,000 to 300,000 people are active in showing. A little more than half are female; one-quarter are single. The median age is 42 years. Most are employed in management or in professional positions, with over half earning more than $50,000 a year. People participate as exhibitors, breeders, trainers, groomers, and handlers. Many attend 12 or more shows a year and travel over 3,000 miles annually to participate in various shows around the country.

People who are active in showing are worlds apart from dog owners who keep dogs only as pets. "Show people" are much more competitive and energetic. They're very goal-oriented and pursue their dreams with determination and vigor. Different breeds attract different types of owners. The vast variety makes it impossible to list here all the breeds and the personality characteristics of their owners. After participating in a few shows, you'll undoubtedly make some observations of your own.

For information on the more than 3,500 AKC-sanctioned and -licensed clubs, contact:

American Kennel Club
51 Madison Avenue
New York, NY 10010
(212) 696-8260

Fantasy Games

Did you like dreaming about fairies and pixies as a child? Do you enjoy science fiction stories where the fate of the universe is precarious and desperate battles must be fought against evil and terrifying odds? Are you a would-be actress who wishes she had an outlet for her dramatic energies? If the answer to any of these questions is yes, then you very well might enjoy role-playing in fantasy games. These games can range from silly and humorous to darkly serious. Some are physically arduous, some are mentally complex, and many are both.

The International Fantasy Gaming Society sponsors live fantasy role-playing games. The games are usually played on weekends and range in length from a few hours to two and a half days. They're typically played outdoors with teams of six to eight players and are led by a Loremaster who serves as the team leader. The object of the games is a specific goal such as finding a "lost" treasure, saving a king's daughter, or restoring peace to a mythical land in conflict. Players assume assigned roles and interpret their characters (such as fighter, monk, knight, druid, cleric, princess, or thief) as they see fit. Padded weapons are used so players can fight each other safely.

In addition to participating in the games as a player character, you can be a nonplayer character who doesn't actually compete, or a support person who produces, writes, judges, or photographs the games, runs errands, sews costumes, or constructs buildings. You can also participate in role-playing games in the comfort of your own home through computer bulletin board systems.

About 2,000 people participate in live role-playing games a year. The active paid membership in the International Fantasy Gaming Society is about 500. Local chapters (either established or in the process of forming) are in Colorado, Texas, Massachusetts, Los Angeles, Ohio, California, Georgia, Mississippi, Idaho, New York, Maryland, and Oklahoma. Membership in the society is about 56 percent male. Because there is a large cohort of college students, the average age is brought down into the mid-twenties, but participants range in age from 5 to 67 years. Most of the leaders of the organization are in their thirties. About half are single.

The men you'll meet here are well-balanced individuals. They have the energy and determination to achieve success in their work, but they want more than that out of life. Enjoying themselves is just as important to them. Highly imaginative and creative, they need an outlet for self-expression and discovery. Fantasy games fill the need and allow them the opportunity to temporarily live in a world of adventure and intrigue.

For more information on your local chapter, forming a new chapter, or participating in a national convention or tournament, contact:

International Fantasy Gaming Society
P.O. Box 3577
Boulder, CO 80307-3577

Another source of information is:

Strategy Gaming Society
24508 38th Avenue, Court E
Spanaway, WA 98387

Fishing

Fishing is more than just a way to spend a few quiet hours while catching some sun. Though some people don't approach the activity very ambitiously, many others pursue it as a true sport. If you've never seriously fished, you have little to lose by giving it a try. You might find yourself getting "hooked"! Even if you don't win any trophies, you'll still have something good to eat for dinner if you catch even a small fish.

It's estimated that 60 million Americans fish. Freshwater fishing is much more popular than saltwater fishing, but there are fans of both types. Sixty-eight percent of the fishing population is male.

Freshwater fishermen are usually patient and dependable. They don't like a lot of flash and often prefer to do things naturally and in an old-fashioned way. Saltwater fishermen are more interested in excitement and adventure, but they don't need a constant high. They can enjoy the quiet times as well as the dramatic events in their lives.

To learn more about fishing, contact a local bait shop or read the outdoor sports section in the local newspaper and see if you can connect with a fishing club. The BASS Anglers Sportsman Society, with over half a million members and 2,000 local chapters, is the world's largest fishing organization. It offers many tournaments as well as opportunities to become involved in environmental issues.

BASS Anglers Sportsman Society
One Bell Road
Montgomery, AL 36117
(205) 272-9530

Flying

The commercial airlines serve their purpose, but being a passenger on a jetliner doesn't provide you with a sense of accomplishment or adventure. If you want more from your aviation experience than a small bag of cocktail peanuts and a "feature" film you saw months earlier, consider learning to fly a plane yourself. Flying can be an exciting hobby. It can also have some practical application as well: Imagine flying at your own convenience to a business appointment instead of waiting hours at an airport. There is also the possibility of turning your hobby into a second career as an airline pilot.

Getting a private pilot's license requires a great deal of training. This training takes a minimum of six weeks, but can be stretched out over months or years if you lack the time or money (over $3,000) to do it all at once. Beginners usually take at least 35 hours of ground school and 50 hours of flight time before they can be tested (via a written and practical exam) for their license. Once you obtain your license, you must have made at least three takeoffs and landings within 90 days of any flight. You must also pass a check ride every two years.

About 100,000 people take flying lessons each year. The overwhelming majority of private pilots are men, usually between the ages of 30 and 50. The older ones tend to be businessmen, while the younger ones are looking into training for careers as commercial pilots. Some do it strictly for recreation.

A unique idea to assist single men and women in meeting one another was developed by New Jersey businessman Paul Hartunian in the early '80s and described by William Novak in *The Great American Man Shortage and Other Roadblocks to Romance* (New York: Rawson, 1983). Hartunian's "Love Notes," printed on business-size cards, informed the recipient that the giver was interested in meeting him or her. It stated "Bars and pickup lines are not my style, so I'm hoping to meet you using this card. I'd really like to find out who you are and tell you what attracted me to you." The giver's name and phone number was on the reverse side.

Although the cards are no longer available, you can duplicate the idea by having any print shop make up cards with your own message.

Through flying you'll meet energetic men who like to be in control of their own destinies. They're usually ambitious go-getters who are very successful in their careers.

You can locate a flight school at most airports, or call (800) ICANFLY for the name of a nearby flight school.

Folk Dancing

You may never visit Greece, Israel, Italy, Germany, or Eastern Europe, but you can experience some of the vitality of their people through folk dancing. By learning dances native to these countries, you'll get good exercise and meet some interesting people.

Statistics on people who folk dance are not available. However, informal studies show that men and women of all ages folk dance.

Male folk dancers tend to be interested in a variety of people and experiences. They're usually fairly intellectual and serious about most aspects of their lives, but they also know how to have fun and enjoy moderate physical activity. Those who are of the same ethnic group as the dances in question have a great deal of pride about their heritage.

Folk dance groups can be found in most large cities. Read the entertainment listings of your local newspaper for the names of clubs or groups. Ethnic groups and lodges (such as those for Americans of Greek, Italian, German, Hispanic, Polish, Israeli, and Russian descent) may also have folk dance opportunities.

Garden Clubs

Gardening is a leisure pastime enjoyed by millions of people. But some gardeners don't want to confine their energies and expertise to their own backyard and prefer to beautify and protect their community's horticulture. Others want to learn more about gardening in general or about specific plants and flowers. Some people also seek a social outlet, since gardening can be such a solitary and isolated activity. For all these people (and maybe for you), garden clubs are the perfect solution. These clubs, which can be found in almost every community, offer lectures, demonstrations, and exhibits. Many of them sponsor major flower shows to educate the public on artistic arrangement and horticultural excellence, in addition to helping with arboretums, botanical gardens, parks, and historic gardens.

Over 15,000 members belong to the 188 clubs affiliated with the Garden Club of America. If your community is large, you may also have specialty groups devoted to orchids, roses, azaleas, and so on. Women do outnumber men in garden clubs, but you will find men in almost every club. Many are middle-aged or older. Some specialty groups (such as those for roses and orchids) also attract a good number of men, since they view growing these species as real challenges.

Men who garden are nurturing individuals. Because they don't want to just admire beauty from afar but prefer a hands-on approach, they tend to be active and committed to whatever is important to them.

To connect with your local garden club, contact:

Garden Club of America
598 Madison Avenue
New York, NY 10022
(212) 753-8287

Go

Millions of people in Asia (over 10 million just in Japan) play this intriguing game, and Americans are now discovering it as well. The game is both simple and complex. The equipment consists of a 19-by-19 wooden grid board with 180 black stones and 181 white stones. It starts as an open battlefield with nothing on the board. You lay stones down strategically, trying to make a line of stones that the opponent can't penetrate. At the end of the game, the stones on the intersections are counted and scored. Games can last from 30 to 90 minutes.

Because the game originated in China before the time of Confucius, there is some Buddhist philosophy associated with it. Ignorance and aggression are severely punished. The natural flow of the game has to be respected, as do the rights of the opponent. Change is inherent in the game and a flexible perspective must be cultivated.

The American Go Association has 1,500 members in 140 chapters. The ratio of men to women is 10 to 1. The average age of Go players is in the twenties to thirties because many discover it in college, but there are also plenty of older players. Go players are high achievers (professionals, computer people, and artistic types) who want an immense challenge. They tend to be highly intuitive, dedicated, serious individuals who are open to learning and growing.

Go is not a simple game to learn, but it's well worth the effort. Go players are a small but enthusiastic bunch who have a special bond among themselves and an almost missionary zeal for recruiting new players, so you'll find people in your local chapter who are more than happy to teach you the game.

American Go Association
P.O. Box 397, Old Chelsea Station
New York, NY 10113-0397

Ham Radio

Do you love talking with people? If so, amateur radio is the ideal hobby for you. Becoming an amateur radio operator (better known as "ham") enables you to communicate with hundreds of new friends across town and around the world by using short distance and long distance frequency bands. In addition to the entertainment value, ham radio can save lives. Many operators work as volunteer trained communicators during times of disaster.

There are 1.5 million individuals who operate ham radios worldwide and 450,000 in the United States. Only 10 percent are women. To qualify to operate a ham radio, you must pass the entry-level license exam. The test consists of questions on simple electrical principles and Federal Communications Commission rules, in addition to a five-word-per-minute Morse code exam. Study guides are available from the Amateur Radio Relay League.

Male hams are extremely gregarious. They love to talk and they love people. While it's true that they're intrigued by gadgets, they never allow the material aspects of life to dominate the human elements.

In addition to talking with people over the airwaves, you can meet them face to face by joining one of the almost 2,000 clubs around the country. For further details, contact:

American Radio Relay League Inc.
225 Main Street, Dept. E
Newington, CT 06111
(203) 666-1541

Home Brewing

Many people drink beer, but only a select few can say they actually brew their own. You don't have to be a chemist to make your own at home. It's easier than you might think, and the satisfaction is immense. Brewing your own beer will save you money over the commercial brands while enabling you to experiment with different techniques and ingredients to suit your own taste. With a $50 investment in equipment, you can mix and match over 15 varieties of hops and 30 brands of malts to make a five-gallon batch.

The American Homebrewers Association has more than 8,000 members in 146 clubs. In the three states where home brewing is illegal (Georgia, Alabama, and Oklahoma), people have to pursue their craft underground. Ninety percent of home brewers are men. The average age is 31.

By joining a beer-making club, you'll be able to share information and compare beers with fellow home brewers. You'll meet a variety of men through club meetings, conferences, and competitions. The one thing they have in common is that they're independent thinkers. They prefer to do their own thing and not have others impose their values or tastes on them.

Home brewers have a wicked sense of humor, as evidenced by the names of their clubs:

- Brewbirds of Happiness (California)
- SEIZURE (Southeast Idaho Zymurgical Union for Rectitude and Ebullience)
- Royal Canadian Malted Patrol (British Columbia)
- BURP (Brewers United for Real Potables—District of Columbia)
- Brews Brothers (Washington state)
- Brewmeisters Anonymous (Arizona)
- Worts of Wisdom (California)

American Homebrewers Association
Box 287
Boulder, CO 80306

Humor Organizations

f a sense of humor is your most important requirement for a man, you may want to consider joining a humor organization. Many of the organizations

A tongue-in-cheek suggestion from Linda Sunshine's book *Women Who Date Too Much (and Those Who Should Be So Lucky)* (New York: New American Library, 1988) is to get arrested or have a minor fire or an imagined robbery. These are sure ways to meet cops and firemen!

have small memberships, but your chances of finding a man who will make you laugh are very good. Possibilities include:

**American Association of
Aardvark Aficionados**
P.O. Box 120
Mount Tabor, NJ 07878
(Among other activities, it sponsors a National
Aardvark Week and Miss American Aardvark Contest.)

American Zombie Association
RR1, Box 103A
Menlo, IA 50164
(Requirements for membership are the abilities to drink three
zombies in one hour if male or one if female and to tie a cherry
stem into a knot using the tongue in 15 seconds or less.)

Couch Potatoes
P.O. Box 249
Dixon, CA 95620
(Requirements for membership: List five all-time favorite
TV shows.)

**National Society for Prevention of
Cruelty to Mushrooms**
1077 South Airport Road West
Traverse City, MI 49684
(Tries to prevent cruelty to mushrooms and other neglected or
mistreated forms of life.)

For more ideas, refer to the humor section in the *Encyclopedia of Associations* at your library.

Investment Clubs

If you're like many women, you'd like to gain more financial savvy, but you just don't have any idea of where to start. You may earn an impressive salary but doubt your competence in investing it on your own. While the obvious solution is to place your surplus funds in the hands of a broker, this doesn't do much to increase your investment know-how.

A preferable alternative is to join or start a local investment club. These clubs meet on a regular (usually monthly) basis to pool their money and to decide how to invest it. As little as $30 each month can be invested, offering a unique opportunity to gain valuable investing experience without risking a lot of money. If you do know a good deal about investing, you may still find the club's group discussions helpful for generating leads for your personal portfolio. Another benefit is the business and social networking. Members develop friendships and enjoy social events such as wine and cheese parties or even travel together on the profits they've made.

The mechanics of the clubs are simple and their performance is noteworthy. Members contribute a set amount of money each month, even in down markets when stocks are performing poorly. A discount or full-service broker purchases the stocks they've chosen or sells holdings that members no longer want in their portfolio. Because the clubs use the dollar-cost averaging approach if investing regularly without trying to guess where the market is headed, reinvest all dividends and interest, focus on growth companies, and diversify their holdings, more than half of all investment clubs equal or beat the annual return of Standard & Poor's 500-stock index and professional money managers year after year.

It is estimated that there are at least 29,000 investor clubs in the country. The vast majority of members are college-educated and earn over $61,000 a year. Although members' contributions in the clubs may be small, many have other investments in personal portfolios which average more than $100,000. About 25 percent are under age 40 and a similar number are over 60. Nearly two-thirds are men.

You'll meet men here who like to be self-reliant but also enjoy companionship. They're financially solvent and intend to stay that way. Most are future-oriented and are willing to take a patient approach, making small sacrifices to reach long-term goals.

For further information on starting or joining an investment club, contact:

**National Association of
Investors Corporation**
1515 East Eleven Mile Road
Royal Oak, MI 48067
(313) 543-0612

**American Association of
Individual Investors**
625 North Michigan Avenue
Chicago, IL 60611
(312) 280-0170

Juggling

Juggling is a wonderful activity for people who enjoy the chance to combine challenging eye-hand coordination with a little showmanship. If you like the idea of showing off your expertise while entertaining others, juggling may be right up your alley. You can start with three balls, rings, or clubs and gradually work your way toward as many as ten. Juggling routines can be combined with other activities such as magic, mime, dance, acrobatics, and comedy.

Jugglers are big on enthusiasm but short on numbers. Only 3,500 people worldwide belong to the International Jugglers Association. Over 80 percent are men. The majority have completed at least four years of college. They work in such diverse fields as art, computers, engineering, journalism, management, and sales. The largest percentage (37.5 percent) fall in the 31-to-40 age category; 13 percent are over 40; 31 percent are 21 to 30.

Male jugglers usually have a good sense of humor and have retained some of their boyhood sense of wonder and whimsy. Highly creative, they dislike structure and routine. They much prefer to do their own thing with as much freedom as possible. Although they like attention and admiration, they're willing to work hard to earn it.

The International Jugglers Association has local affiliated juggling clubs which hold meetings and stage festivals.

International Jugglers Association
Box 29
Kenmore, NY 14217
(716) 876-5331

Kite Flying

The next time someone tells you to go fly a kite, take this advice literally. You may not have flown a kite since you were a kid, but it's easy to rediscover the magic. It's hard to think of a better activity on a gorgeous, windy day. Find yourself a spot in the park that will give you some room to maneuver (but strategically located so that you can see and be seen by other people) and get that kite up in the air!

Kite flying is not an expensive hobby, since the wind and air space are free. Kites can be purchased or hand made for a wide range of prices, but a good one (which can last 40 years) may cost $50 to $200.

Like jugglers, kite fliers of the male variety are likely to have retained a little of their childhood selves. Not that they're immature; it's just that they can still enjoy life's simple pleasures. They may be goal-oriented but are not workaholics. Continually pushing themselves past their limits is not their style. These men want to savor the world, not set it on fire.

There's even an association of kite fliers that you may want to explore. With 18 affiliated chapters, national membership in the American Kite Fliers Association is around 2,500. About 65 percent of the members are men. The association sponsors kite festivals and competitions in addition to holding seminars and publishing a bimonthly newspaper.

American Kite Fliers Association
1559 Rockville Pike
Rockville, MD 29852

Living History/War Reenactments

Is *Gone with the Wind* one of your favorite movies? If the film appeals to the romantic in you and you've fantasized about living during the Civil War era (or any other historical period), here's a way to experience the past. It doesn't involve science-fiction time machines or New Age hypnotics. All you need are some costumes, a few authentic props, an active imagination, some knowledge of history, and a number of like-minded people who will help create an unforgettable experience.

Thousands of individuals are involved in reenacting. Instead of taking up golf or stamp collecting, they embrace history as a hobby. These "living history" activities re-create events and lifestyles of the past with as much authenticity as possible. Many of the activities are focused on war experiences (with an emphasis on the Revolutionary and Civil Wars), but some deal with other human pursuits (such as cotillions, parades, weddings). Every participant dresses in costume and assumes a role, speaking in the

Should you meet the man of your dreams at a reenactment, just imagine the type of wedding the two of you could put together. You could play Scarlett O'Hara to his Rhett Butler in a marriage ceremony with all the pomp and splendor you could ever want.

In 1988, two living-history hobbyists had just such a wedding. Charles Sullivan (a college history professor from Perkinston, Mississippi) and Jane Kelly were married at an antebellum mansion in Vicksburg. The genuine Confederate ceremony featured uniformed honor guards and bridesmaids in magnificent hooped gowns of the 1860s.

language of the time. Some women dress in military uniforms and accompany the troops, but most authentic regiments won't allow any females in military uniforms. Instead, women can portray nurses and civilians.

Most of the battles are done over and over again, since there is always something new to be learned and experienced. As many as 10,000 reenactors show up for an event (such as the 125th anniversary reenactment of the battle of Gettysburg in July 1988).

Because of the reenacting organizations' loose structure, an exact number of participants and members is difficult to determine. Civil War buffs number about 30,000. Besides Revolutionary and Civil War reenactments, there are many other periods that living-history fans get involved with, such as the War of 1812 and the French and Indian War. The majority of participants range from their early twenties to their forties. Men appear to outnumber women by 70 to 1 or even more.

Obviously, the men you'll meet here have an interest in history. But they're far from bookish recluses. These are men who are actively and passionately involved in the highs and lows of yesteryear. They're imaginative and have a flair for the dramatic. Whether the one you hook up with plays a private or a general, you'll enjoy the magic he creates on and off the battlefield.

If you're interested in getting involved in a reenacting organization or regiment, you may want to obtain a copy of *The Courier,* a Civil War reenactment publication that will enable you to learn more, obtain props, and make contact with a local regiment. Write to:

The Courier
P.O. Box 1863
Williamsville, NY 14231-1863
(716) 634-8324

For information about other historical periods:

Living History Association
P.O. Box 578
Wilmington, VT 05363

Magic

How many times have you watched a magician and wondered "How in the world did he do that?" If you'd like to find out and perform a few tricks yourself, you can join one of the 275 rings (clubs) affiliated with the International Brotherhood of Magicians. Members come together to practice and discuss their art each month. Once you begin to acquire skills, you can use them just to entertain yourself and friends, or you can practice them more publicly as a volunteer in children's hospitals, shelters, and other settings or as a paid professional at parties.

More than 13,000 people belong to the International Brotherhood of Magicians. Fewer than 10 percent are female. Ages range from 18 to 80. You'll find male magicians to have a sense of whimsy and humor. They're capable of intense concentration and hard work, yet they know how to relax and are never so wrapped up in themselves that they lose touch with the people who are important to them.

International Brotherhood of Magicians
P.O. Box 89
Bluffton, OH 45817

According to Emily Marlin in *Taking a Chance on Love* (New York: Schocken, 1984): "People seem to fall in love when they are busily and happily pursuing a full life rather than a love object." In other words, by participating in the experiences and activities suggested in *this* book you stand an increased likelihood of connecting with someone you can love and who can love you.

Even if you don't meet the man of your dreams in class, at a meeting, or on the athletic field, these activities can bring about positive results in your man-meeting quest. Participation in any activity outside your home will expand your social network. You might meet people, both male and female, single or married, with whom you'll form friendships. These people may introduce you to some of their friends, one of whom may turn out to be *the* man!

Mensa

Tired of meeting men you have to play dumb with? If you're a highly intelligent individual (in the top 2 percent of the population), this may well be a problem you'll encounter over and over again. But a membership in Mensa could change all that. This nonprofit organization brings intelligent people together to enjoy each other's company. Most local Mensa groups meet at least once a month and many offer activities several times a week. Meetings may range from dinner and drinks to concerts, games nights, luncheons, film parties, or lectures by noted authorities. Subgroups specialize in such varied subjects as sports, sciences, history, law, poetry, photography, and astrology. Regional and national meetings expand opportunities to interact with a wide range of people.

To qualify for membership, you must score on a standardized IQ test higher than 98 percent of the general population. In addition to the standard Wechsler Adult Intelligence Scale, scores from other tests (such as the Graduate Management Admission Test, Medical College Admission Test, Law School Admission Test, SAT or GRE of 1250) may be accepted if approved by Mensa's supervisory psychologists. Mensa will send you a preliminary test which doesn't actually qualify you but will help you preview what your scores are likely to be and will prepare you for taking a timed, written examination.

Nearly 55,000 individuals belong to American Mensa and its 140 local groups. The ratio of men to women is 1 to 1. The diversity of the membership can be seen in its range of ages (4 to 94), education levels (high school dropouts to multiple Ph.D.s), economic levels (welfare recipients to millionaires), and occupations (teachers, scientists, computer programmers, engineers, farmers, authors, actors, musicians, factory workers, truck drivers, and executives).

Needless to say, you'll meet incredibly bright men through Mensa. They enjoy stimulating conversations and learning about everything and anything. Rather than cloistering themselves in a library in their free time, they seek the companionship of other intellectually gifted individuals.

American Mensa, Ltd.
2626 East 14th Street
Brooklyn, NY 11235-3992
(718) 934-3700

Miniature Collecting

It's a small world . . . especially if you're a miniature collector. Just about anything can be reduced to a miniature in scales of ¼, ½, or 1 inch. Miniature enthusiasts make and collect buildings (anything from Victorian houses and barns to fire houses, railroad stations, and churches), dolls, nature landscapes, furniture, other furnishings, and animals. The challenge is in finding objects that are accurately scaled, look realistic, and are very attractive.

Many people collect "small" items, but not all are true miniaturists who make and collect scaled pieces. More than 12,000 individuals belong to the National Association of Miniature Enthusiasts and its associated 400 clubs across the United States and Canada. Members range in age from 1 to 80. A little less than half are male.

In addition to meeting men through your local club, your possibilities will increase if you attend regional or national "houseparties." These conventions allow participants to display their collections and increase their skills by attending workshops and exchanging hints with one another.

What sort of men are involved with miniatures? As is obvious when you inspect a scaled miniature, they're extremely detail-oriented, perfectionistic, and neat. But this is not to imply that they have rigid or lackluster personalities. They definitely enjoy whimsy and beauty. Most can be quite charming.

National Association of
   Miniature Enthusiasts
P.O. Box 1178
Brea, CA 92622
(714) 529-0900

Don't have time to pursue any leisure interests? Max L. Marshall, author of the *Re-Mating Game* (White Hall, Va.: Betterway Publications, 1988), says priorities rather than lack of time keep you from getting involved in activities that can increase your chances of finding "Mr. Reasonably Right." He notes that people find time to do the things they want to do (such as cleaning their homes or watching TV); it's not more time that's needed but a shifting of priorities (deciding to take a ceramics class instead of just relaxing around the house, for example).

Model Aeronautics

Model planes kindled the Wright brothers' and Charles Lindbergh's passion for flying. Thousands of other people in all walks of life are similarly devoted to building, designing, and flying model airplanes. If you're looking for a challenging hobby, this is a good one to consider. You can specialize in building your own models (which can take countless hours to perfect) or in piloting the planes, performing aerobatic maneuvers using either control-line planes or remote-controlled models. Flying requires superb eye-hand coordination, excellent strategic skills, intense concentration, and some understanding of aerodynamics. Competitive racing events include rat racing (two or three fliers dance around each other's control cables, racing planes at speeds near 200 mph), control-line combat (planes operated by wires chase each other around the sky, trying to lop off paper streamers attached to their opponent's tails), radio-controlled pylon racing (high-powered planes fly around a pylon course for 10 miles at 190 mph), helicopter maneuvering, mock aerial combat, free flight both indoors and outdoors, and precision aerobatics (stunts such as reverse wingovers, hourglasses, four-leaf clovers, horizontal eights, and six-sided loops).

There are more than 8 million model plane enthusiasts. The most dedicated (160,000-plus) belong to the Academy of Model Aeronautics or one of its more than 2,300 chartered clubs throughout the country. Fewer than 2 percent of members are women. And don't think that modelers are typically young boys. The average age is estimated at 38. Engineers, aviation professionals, and other high-tech types predominate, but you'll also find teachers, truck drivers, farmers, lawyers, and almost every other occupation. Personality types vary. Control-line fliers like detail, precision, competition, and simplicity. Radio-control fliers (the majority of modelers) are more gadget-oriented and like fast action, whereas free-flight modelers are introspective, intellectual, patient, and tranquil.

To become involved in model aviation, learn more about your local group from the nearest hobby supply shop or contact:

Academy of Model Aeronautics
1810 Samuel Morse Drive
Reston, VA 22090
(703) 435-0798

Model Railroads

When you were growing up, you may have wished for a model railroad set like your brother's instead of the doll you got at Christmas. You can make up for lost time now by becoming involved in the fascinating hobby of model railroading. It's easy to start. You can begin on a shoestring by making much of the scenery and even the cars yourself, or you can buy everything you need for the entire layout. Either way, you'll enjoy the challenge of putting together an appealing replica of a railroad station and its surrounding town.

It's been estimated that over a quarter of a million individuals are model railroaders. About 22,000 belong to the National Model Railroad Association. (Benefits include monthly publications and national conventions.) Ninety percent are men. The average age is 46, but this is dropping as younger people become interested in the hobby. There are 127 local divisions throughout the country.

Men active in model railroading are usually detail-oriented perfectionists who are capable of hard work and deep concentration. Whatever they choose to do in life, they'll do well. Although they come across as pragmatic realists, deep down they're sentimental dreamers.

National Model Railroad Association
4121 Cromwell Road
Chattanooga, TN 37421

Motorcycling

If you think of cars when you hear the names BMW and Honda, you're not yet a motorcyclist. But to more than 8 million people, these manufacturers (and others such as Yamaha, Kawasaki, Suzuki, and Harley-Davidson) make motorcycles that are used both for transportation and recreation. Motorcycling gives a sense of freedom that automobiles can't provide. Riding a motorcycle on a sunny day allows you to get closer to nature than any enclosed, four-wheel vehicle ever could.

Motorcycling, both street touring and off-road riding, is largely a male activity. Over 90 percent of the riders are men. But forget the stereotype of a vaguely sinister young dropout gunning his chopper. And there's nothing antisocial about most motorcyclists. The average age is 36. About 78 percent have annual incomes over $25,000 and 54 percent earn more than $35,000 a year. Motorcyclists include college professors, sales reps, computer experts, truckers, and house painters. A little less than half are single.

It's difficult to make any generalizations about cyclists, because they're strong individualists who don't conform to any set patterns. You'll probably find that male motorcyclists know exactly who they are and are content with that knowledge. Unpretentious and down-to-earth, they can only be happy by being themselves. They also like a good amount of freedom in a relationship and will balk at too many demands and expectations.

Local motorcycle dealers can put you in touch with clubs in your vicinity. For the Motorcycle Rider Course nearest you, call toll-free: (800) 447-4700. The American Motorcyclist Association can alert you to the thousands of trail and racing events held each year.

American Motorcyclist Association
P.O. Box 6114
Westerville, OH 43081

New Age Activities

The New Age movement is so eclectic and wide-reaching that it's difficult to define. The most simplistic explanation is that it combines metaphysical, psychic, and spiritual elements to enable individuals around the planet to live in health, peace, and harmony. Its proponents adopt it as their philosophy of choice, or combine it with more traditional religions. Much of the philosophy and many of the practices are borrowed from Eastern and Native American traditions. New Age activities can include meditation, Zen Buddhist philosophy, massage, Taoist traditions, nutrition (macrobiotics or vegetarian), tarot cards, Wicca (white witchcraft), crystals, dowsing, past-life regression, Sufi teachings, positive self-talk, healing arts, astrology, magic, the occult, shamanism, and stress reduction. While some cynics ridicule New Age philosophies and practices, the movement has many devotees; actress Shirley MacLaine is one of the most prominent enthusiasts.

Because the New Age movement is loosely and informally organized, no statistics on its practitioners are available. However, it is believed that thousands of individuals of all ages and both sexes are involved in some aspect of it. Many New Agers are introspective, open-minded, and less traditional than other men.

To find out about the New Age groups and clubs that meet in your area to discuss, learn, and practice these new and old techniques, consult your community's alternative newspaper. These publications can often be found in health food stores and restaurants. Another possibility is to check the postings at your local New Age bookshop (check the Yellow Pages for specialty book dealers).

Parenting

If you're single but have a child, parenting is probably one of the most important things you do in your off-work hours. If you'd like to get support from other people who share your concerns and experiences, consider joining Parents Without Partners. For more than 30 years, this group has dedicated itself to the welfare and interests of single parents and their children. Programs are run in three areas:

- Educational activities (group discussions, lectures by psychologists, lawyers, and other professionals).

In case you don't think that men are looking for love, too, consider the case of Paul Hohendorf, a thirty-something bachelor from Detroit. As profiled in the February 20, 1989, *People* magazine, this catering company vice president has made an art out of fax flirting. He faxed his photo and a greeting card message to offices all over the Americas, Japan, and Australia. More than 4,000 women responded to his international love call. This "modem operandi" may not work for everyone, but obviously it enhanced Paul's social life.

- Family activities (picnics, hikes, camping, bowling for children and their parents).
- Adult social activities (where single parents relate to other adults).

Chapters may also conduct community service programs, fund-raising for national or local charities, or run cooperative exchanges (such as baby-sitting, clothing, home repairs, or toy swaps), or legislative affairs programs.

There are 138,000 members in North America. Thirty-five percent are men. Ages range from 18 to 80; most are over 35. About 85 percent are separated or divorced. Some have young children; others have grown children. Members come from all walks of life; the common denominator is that they seek the companionship and assistance of other single parents. You don't have to be afraid of how these men will react to your children; they understand what it is to be a parent and aren't afraid of the responsibility.

For information on one of the 700 local chapters, contact:

Parents Without Partners Inc.
8807 Colesville Road
Silver Spring, MD 20910
(301) 588-9354

Photography

Using an inexpensive camera at your niece's birthday party does not qualify you as a photographer. But if you admire the work of professional photographers and sometimes wish you could capture such images on film, you may enjoy developing your photographic expertise. Amateur photography is a wonderful hobby that gives you an excuse to get out of the house and experience people and things that might not ordinarily be a part of your life.

Thousands of people engage in photography as a hobby, some more seriously than others. They run the gamut from preteens to senior citizens. Both men and women are shutterbugs, but men seem to get more involved.

By joining a local photography club (ask for information at a camera store), and by getting out into the world to pursue photography, you'll meet men who are introspective but also interested in the world around them. They're visual rather than verbal, imaginative yet practical.

Poker

When you think of poker, do images of hard-drinking gamblers in smoke-filled rooms come to mind? If so, you're harboring an unfair and untrue stereotype of the popular card game. Poker has become a respectable leisure activity that is played by all types of people. The game is easy to learn. In less than an hour even players who don't know a straight from a flush can play and enjoy the game. But poker's strategies require a lifetime to master.

There are an estimated 61 million poker players in the United States. Most belong to private clubs or play informally in private homes. About half of all players are women. Ages range from 18 to 80. Dentists, doctors, lawyers, accountants, senators, business owners, policemen, salespeople, college students, and retirees play poker.

You'll find that poker players have quick minds and good perceptions about other people and what makes them tick. They do like order and precision, but they can also be creative thinkers. Their congenial temperaments cause them to want to spend considerable time with other people rather than on their own. In general, they have a fairly relaxed attitude about money and are comfortable with gambling. You can learn to play poker from a book or from other players. One way to find out about local chapters and tournaments is by belonging to the International Home and Private Poker Players' Association (IH3PA). It has 337 members in 25 states, and holds tournaments.

**International Home and
Private Poker Players' Association**
Route 2, Box 2845
Manistique, MI 49854

Pool

In the past, pool halls have had the reputation of being smoky and somewhat seedy. But now that pool and billiard tables have moved into restaurants, nightclubs, and upscale clubs, the game is attracting a new population. There are several versions of the game. Pocket billiards is the most popular, featuring 15 numbered object balls sunk by a white cue ball into six pockets. The game requires eye-hand coordination, concentration, and strategy, so you'll find it to be challenging without being too physically taxing.

The actual number of pool players is difficult to assess, since many play informally and sporadically. It is estimated that thousands pick up a pool cue at least every now and then. The real enthusiasts, equal numbers of men and women, participate in local and national championships. Most are in their twenties and thirties. In the posher establishments, many have six-figure incomes.

While no one can promise that you'll meet the likes of Paul Newman and Tom Cruise (as in *The Color of Money*) by hanging around a pool hall, you *can* meet some desirable men. Many of them appear laid-back on the surface, but they can be shrewd and calculating in racking up points, both on the pool table and in life.

To find a place near you to play, look in your Yellow Pages for pool/billiard halls or drinking/eating establishments that advertise their pool tables. Or contact:

National Pocket Billiard Association
2635 West Burnham Street
P.O. Box 15365
Milwaukee, WI 53215

Public Speaking

Most people are uncomfortable doing any kind of public speaking. Yet a good many of us need to make some sort of oral presentations as part of our jobs. Even if public speaking isn't a requirement of your job, you may find it beneficial to develop these skills: The ability to communicate clearly is helpful in every aspect of your personal and professional life.

Toastmasters International, a nonprofit organization, has been working for more than 60 years to help people enhance their public speaking and communication skills. More than 6,900 local clubs provide a "learn-by-doing" workshop in which members critique one another's prepared oral presentations, give impromptu talks, develop listening skills, conduct meetings, learn parliamentary procedure, and gain leadership experience by serving as club officers. The typical club has 20 to 40 members who meet weekly or biweekly.

Membership in Toastmasters is approximately 145,000. About 55 percent of the members are men. Most of the men you'll meet here are success-driven and are trying hard to get ahead at work. Others are not as concerned with making it in the business world, but need to be able to communicate with the public or the media as part of their jobs (for example, in the medical, scientific, or social service fields). All the men are consciously working on their communication skills, so you'll find them to be easy conversationalists and good listeners.

For information on your local club, contact:

Toastmasters International
2200 North Grand Avenue
Santa Ana, CA 92711
(714) 542-6793

Sailing

Everyone likes the way a sailboat looks. There's something infinitely relaxing and appealing about the image of the sails gently rippling in the breeze as the boat glides across the water. Many people admire sailing from afar, but have never tried it because sailing has erroneously become known as a difficult, expensive, elitist hobby. In fact, the opposite is true. Individuals with ordinary physical abilities and without any experience or wealth can learn to sail in a matter of hours. The cost of learning to sail and renting or buying a small boat can be reasonable. Once you try it, it's almost inevitable that you'll be hooked.

Men outnumber women in this activity 3 to 1. You'll find men of all educational and occupational backgrounds. They're gentle without being wimpy, active without being hyper, and intelligent without being overly intellectual, and they are sensual. They usually have great tans from spending lots of time on the water.

There's no national sailing club per se, but the American Sailing Association will provide you with information, particularly about sailing schools. The association also has special offers for group rendezvous periodically (listed in their newsletter).

American Sailing Association
13922 Marquesas Way
Marina Del Rey, CA 90292-6000
(213) 822-7171

Scrabble

You probably already know that Scrabble is a great board game. It challenges your vocabulary and spelling skills in a fun way. Unlike other games that rely mostly on luck, Scrabble truly does require some top-notch intellectual skills. Whereas crossword puzzles are usually done alone, Scrabble allows for social interaction. If you'd like to play the game more frequently, consider joining a local club or participating in one of the nearly 80 tournaments offered throughout the country each year.

More than 15,000 people belong to Scrabble Players Inc. Men and women are equally represented. People of all ages play Scrabble. You'll find men who play the game to be articulate in a quiet sort of way. They're well-spoken but they tend to be somewhat introspective and don't necessarily use their verbal skills to communicate their innermost feelings.

To locate the Scrabble club nearest you or start a licensed club in your area, contact:

The National Scrabble Association
c/o Williams & Company
Box 700
Front Street Garden
Greenport, NY 11944
(516) 477-0033

Skydiving

Skydivers claim that their hobby is the most exciting in the world. Once you try it, you may well agree. The thrill of leaving an airplane thousands of feet above the earth and sailing through the sky at 120 to 160 mph can't be duplicated by any other means. There is some risk involved, but innovations in equipment and adequate instruction and supervision make parachuting much safer than in earlier years.

To jump, you'll need a maneuverable main parachute, a reserve parachute, and protective clothing (helmet, boots, jumpsuit, goggles, and gloves). For purposes of economy, parachutists ride together on an airplane. Once the aircraft reaches the desired altitude, the parachutist directs the pilot to fly the plane over the target point on the ground. As the parachutist freefalls, the sensation feels like flying. The freefall is ended after the parachutist checks the altimeter (for example, at 2,500 feet) and pulls the ripcord, which causes the parachute to open. It can then be steered by pulling on a steering line in either hand.

More than 110,000 people skydive each year in the United States. (The U.S. Parachute Association has more than 18,500 members.) Only about

13 percent of current parachutists are women, although recently 25 percent of skydiving students have been women. Ages range from the teens to the eighties. The average age is in the early thirties. Representative occupations include doctor, lawyer, pilot, engineer, mechanic, police, plumber, student, and government official. Parachutists tend to have a higher level of education than the average American.

Men who parachute are searching for a sense of freedom. They lead responsible work lives but they want to break loose during their off-hours. If you're the clinging type, look elsewhere, because a skydiver doesn't want to feel restricted or confined in any way. But if you're dynamic, fearless, and actively involved in the world around you, you might enjoy freefalling through life (as well as the sky) together with another special skydiver.

U.S. Parachute Association
1440 Duke Street
Alexandria, VA 22314
(703) 836-3495

Society for Creative Anachronism

If everyday life has become a bit of a bore, climb out of the rut by escaping to the medieval or Renaissance era. The Society for Creative Anachronism (SCA) offers you unique opportunities to become involved with these long-ago times. Some of the activities are far from relaxing (fighting, jousting, and competing with weapons at tournaments), but all will allow you to leave your mundane concerns behind and live a few hours at a time as an entirely different person in an age totally unlike our own fast-paced, high-tech world.

Once you join the SCA, you'll need to decide on a persona. This can range from an aristocratic lady to a guildsperson (scribe, minstrel, bard, leather worker) to a peasant. You'll assume a Middle English name representative of those times, complete with a title such as Lady, Mistress, or Baroness. When you participate in events, you'll wear a medieval costume (perhaps a long, flowing dress in earthy greens and browns, with a cape or cloak).

In addition to local chapter activities such as meetings, banquets, and small-scale tournaments, regional and national events enable you to meet fellow participants from all over the country. Special events during the large tournaments can include workshops in costume history, brewing, calligraphy, cooking, gaming, dance, revelry, storytelling, chess, darts, archery, and other games, culinary feasts, and traditional fighting activities.

Current SCA membership is about 15,550. All ages belong, but the twenties and thirties predominate. The gender mix is about 50-50. Both singles and couples participate. There are over 600 local chapters scattered across the United States.

While your past experiences may have convinced you that chivalry is dead, a few hours with the men of the SCA will prove you wrong. They enjoy being gallant both on and off the tournament battlefields. Escape from the ordinary by getting involved with this unique organization and its special men.

Society for Creative Anachronism
Office of the Registry
P.O. Box 360743
Milpitas, CA 95035-0743

To get yourself in the mood for time tripping back into the Middle Ages and Renaissance, select an authentic name for yourself by choosing a title, first name, and last name. Mix and match from the columns until you find the name that suits you.

Titles	First Names	Last Names
Lady	Alisoun	De Witte
Baroness	Siobhan	Throckmorton
Viscountess	Caroline	of Oxfordshire
The Honorable Lady	Aidan	of Grandloch
Countess	Rhiannon	O'Roarke
Mistress	Victoria	Murrough
Duchess	Rosalinde	de la Mor
	Genevieve	of Canterbury
	Brielle	Smythe
	Cateline	Ismail
	Fionna	McGrain
	Meghan	Dumas
	Brigid	Thistlewood

Sports Car Clubs

The majority of adults view their cars in a utilitarian way: They're simply vehicles that enable access to jobs, shopping, entertainment, and so on. But to some people, cars are a form of recreation in and of themselves. Some enthusiasts are so enamored of one particular make that they belong to a specific club devoted to caring for and showing that type of car. Others like to take a more active role and get involved in racing as drivers, crew, starters, marshals, and timers.

The Sports Car Club of America (SCCA) has more than 46,000 members in 108 regional chapters across the country. More than 8,000 SCCA-licensed race drivers compete in the 250 amateur road racing events conducted at regional and national levels each year. To drive in SCCA amateur road racing competition, you must obtain an SCCA competition license which requires a medical form certifying that you're in good health, and which then qualifies you to participate in SCCA drivers' training school. You'll need to provide your own safety suit, approved driving helmet, and race car.

An alternative to road racing is amateur autocross (also known as slalom or solo). Drivers compete for the lowest time around a pylon-marked course in a parking lot. A driver's helmet is necessary but a competition license is not. You can compete successfully with your street car. Obviously this event is less risky than road racing while still providing lots of racing excitement.

In SCCA road rallies, family cars are run on public roads at less-than-highway speeds. The driver and navigator complete a predescribed course in predetermined time by following a given set of instructions. Participation can be as relaxed or as intense as you want it to be.

Yet another way to get involved in SCCA events is to train and become licensed as a race specialist, official, or administrator. Possibilities include positions of stewards (overall responsibility for running the race and enforcing the rules), registrars (providing passes, accepting and organizing official race entry forms), course marshals (ensuring all emergency equipment is operational and in place), pit marshals (responsibility for safety in the garage and pit areas), timers and scorers (using stopwatches, microprocessors, and electronic sensors to keep track of every car on every lap), and flaggers (warning the drivers of track conditions).

More than 50,000 individuals read *SportsCar* magazine. The readership appears to be indicative of sports car enthusiasts in general. The vast majority (82 percent) are men; 35 percent are single. The median age is 37, with a

Whether salespeople are selling insurance or cars, they're bound to experience some rejection and failure. It may take following up 30 leads to finally close a deal. They can't afford to get discouraged after the fourth or fifth no-sale, because it's always possible that the next one will be the charm. And that holds true for you in love as well. You can't give up after just a few attempts at meeting and dating, because you never know when it will happen for you. . . .

range from 18 to 79. Over half are college graduates. Fifty percent are in the manager/proprietor/self-employed/engineer/doctor/lawyer categories; the others are in sales, technical, mechanical, or skilled crafts, or in school. The average income is about $55,000, with 19 percent earning $100,000 or more.

If you admire the looks of sports cars and enjoy the adrenaline rush of high speeds, you'll fit right in with sports car enthusiasts. The men you'll meet travel in the fast lane in both work and play. They're action-oriented and aren't happy just sitting on the sidelines watching other people do things.

Interested in learning to race but don't have an appropriate car? Your region's chapter can help you find a race car to rent for drivers' school. It can also refer you to your local chapter and SCCA Drivers' School.

Sports Car Club of America
9033 East Easter Place
Englewood, CO 80112
(303) 694-7222

Square Dancing

Your fashion sense or company dress code may dictate crisp, tailored clothes for work, but you might want to consider donning short ruffled skirts and petticoats in your after hours. This costume may not get you on the pages of *Vogue*, but it will enable you to enjoy a very American form of recreation: square dancing.

If you've never square danced or haven't done it for years, you may be pleasantly surprised if you join a square dance club. You don't have to be especially coordinated to learn square dancing; the various swings, prome-nades, and handholds are easy to perform. The challenge is in quickly responding to the 2,500 possible calls, since square dancers never know what the caller will call out next.

An estimated 6 million people enjoy this invigorating and inexpensive hobby. A large number are married couples over 25, but lots of younger people and singles also participate. As you might expect, square dancing is most popular in Western states, but you can find square dancing clubs all over the country.

Square dancers are among the friendliest men you'll ever meet. They're polite and respectful to women. But if you're looking for a trend-setting maverick, you'll be disappointed. Square dancing men are highly conven-tional and are usually followers rather than leaders.

To find a square dancing club in your community, inquire at a square dancing/Western apparel store (see the Yellow Pages) or contact:

Square Dance Convention
2936 Bella Vista
Midwest City, OK 73110

Stamp Collecting (Philatelics)

You probably barely notice the stamps on the letters you receive in the mail, but they're really much more than small, brightly colored pieces of paper. There's a wealth of history, politics, geography, art, and culture in postage stamps. Small wonder, then, that thousands of people are intrigued by them and are avid stamp collectors. Any types of stamps can lend themselves to collecting. You can specialize in United States stamps or those from any other country around the world. Some people collect stamps relating to cats, famous authors, music, science, or sports. Others specialize in a certain time in history, such as the 19th century.

Getting started in stamp collecting is as easy as buying a ready-made album and a bag of stamps. All you have to do is place the stamps in their corresponding spaces in the album. But for more of a challenge, you should arrange your own collection in the way that is most meaningful for you. A lot of stamp collecting is done in your own home. Stamps can be ordered or exchanged through the mail and then organized in your album or "stock book." For increased pleasure and a new social outlet, you should join a local club or society where you can learn from and socialize with other collectors. You can also meet men at local, regional, national, and international shows and exhibits.

The American Philatelic Society (the oldest and largest stamp association in the United States) has almost 57,000 members. Affiliated as chapters are at least 750 local stamp clubs. Of the total membership, 91 percent are men. Ages range from 18 to the late nineties, with the average being 55. Most members are college graduates. The men you'll meet here are intelligent. They have a lot of curiosity about the world and its people and tend to be well traveled.

The American Philatelic Society offers many valuable services for its members, including insurance for collections, stamps sold by mail, an authoritative journal, publications, and a translation service. It also sponsors correspondence courses and a weeklong summer seminar on philately at Pennsylvania State University.

American Philatelic Society
P.O. Box 8000
State College, PA 16803
(814) 237-3803

Star Trek Fan Club

There are many fan clubs for various entertainers and television shows, but the *Star Trek* fan club deserves special mention because its members are so dedicated. If you've been a confirmed follower of this television show (which ran during the late '60s and can now be seen in syndicated reruns) ever since you first laid eyes on Mr. Spock, you may want to join Star Trek: The Official Fan Club. Membership entitles you mainly to the magazine, which will enable you to meet fellow fans through its pen-pal section and its listings of special events. There are over 300 *Star Trek* conventions a year where you can meet people who share your passion for these science fiction television episodes and movies.

The club has about 35,000 members and continues to grow (at some 50 members a day). Close to 40 percent of the membership is male. Ages vary, but the largest group is between 25 and 37. The men you'll meet here are a little offbeat, but fairly serious and intelligent. *Star Trek* is more than just another show to them; it's something they find deeply entertaining and enriching.

Star Trek: The Official Fan Club
P.O. Box 111000
Aurora, CO 80011

Tiddlywinks

Tiddlywinks may not be a high-profile game, but there are a number of people who are deeply involved with it. They enjoy the mental strategy and physical skills the game requires. Tiddlywinks is actually a sort of war game in which players attempt to capture their opponent's pieces and to control the center area. The game is played on a 3-by-6-foot mat by two or four players. Players attempt to snap small plastic disks into a cup by pressing the edges of the disks with larger ones.

The game is currently most popular in England and the northeastern United States, but the Tiddlywinks Association would like to see more growth all over the United States. They would particularly like more women to join their ranks, as over 90 percent of players are men. Most get involved with the game while attending science and math programs. You can expect these men to be logical, left-brained thinkers who like a sense of order in everything they do. They don't have a lot of use for chaos or spontaneity; they much prefer things to proceed at a predictable, orderly pace.

For information on learning the game, joining one of the local clubs, or participating in regional or national tournaments, contact:

North American Tiddlywinks Association
10416 Haywood Drive
Silver Spring, MD 20902

Vegetarian Groups

If you can't imagine ever doing without pepperoni pizzas or chili dogs, you'll want to skip this section. But if you're a confirmed vegetarian or just toying with the idea of giving up meat for ethical, ecological, or health reasons, you may enjoy belonging to a group of like-minded people. In these groups, you'll be able to exchange books and recipes, share potluck meals, work for improving the environment and animal rights, and generally celebrate a meatless lifestyle. Most cities have at least one vegetarian organization. About 98 local groups (with 2,000 members of all ages) are affiliated with

Vegetarians come in all shapes and sizes, so you won't be able to tell at first glance whether or not a man is a carnivore or prefers veggies. However, if he is sporting a bumper sticker or T-shirt with the following slogans, it's a safe bet to assume that this is not a guy with whom you'll be sharing a filet mignon:

GIVE PEAS A CHANCE
VEGETARIANS ARE SPROUTING UP ALL OVER
LIVE AND LET LIVE
BE KIND TO ANIMALS—DON'T EAT THEM

the nonprofit North American Vegetarian Society. In addition to local educational and social events, national and international conferences are sponsored.

Although exact statistics are not available for the gender breakdown of vegetarians, it is believed that about half are men. Vegetarians can be found in all walks of life. The vast majority are compassionate and concerned about all living things. They feel a strong connection to everything on the planet and try to nurture and preserve life in all forms. Many (but not all) are liberal in their political and religious philosophies. Best of all, they're healthy. The risk of cardiovascular and other diseases is much reduced for proponents of this eating style. If you want a man who will enjoy good health throughout his life, you'll find what you're looking for in a vegetarian club.

North American Vegetarian Society
P.O. Box 72
Dolgeville, NY 13329

Ventriloquism

You undoubtedly enjoyed watching ventriloquists as a child. Now that you've grown up, you may enjoy becoming a ventriloquist yourself. Ventriloquism is fun because you'll amuse yourself while entertaining others. Making a puppet come alive by giving it speech is a real challenge. It takes many years to perfect your routine and not move your lips, but you're guaranteed to enjoy learning and refining these skills. In addition to being a hobby, it can also be a lucrative source of extra income if you perform at parties, conventions, and club meetings.

About 5,000 people practice ventriloquism, more as hobbyists than as full-fledged professionals. Ages range from 3 to 95 and reflect the general population in that the male-female ratio is 50-50.

As you might expect, ventriloquists are excellent communicators. They also have a great sense of humor. Almost without exception, they enjoy children. You'll find "vents" to be friendly and down-to-earth.

You can meet men at the annual North American Association of Ventriloquists convention, and also by performing together at an event. You might even meet an admirer in your audience. For information on joining its 1,750 members, contact:

North American Association of Ventriloquists
Box 420
Littleton, CO 80160
(303) 798-6830

Wood Carving and Whittling

Imagine being able to take a piece of wood and make it into a work of art. That's exactly what wood-carvers and whittlers do. (Whittlers use only a knife, whereas carvers use gouges, chisels, and knives.) Subjects can be animals, human figures, geometric shapes and objects, and abstract representations. Even if you've never considered yourself artistic, you might want to see what happens when you chip away at a piece of wood.

There are probably more than 100,000 carvers in the United States. More than 35,000 belong to the National Wood Carvers Association and one of its 250 chapters. About 80 percent are men.

By joining a local or national organization, you'll enjoy the fellowship of both professionals and amateurs, find markets to sell your work, discover tool and wood suppliers, and exhibit your work. The men you'll meet will be honest, thoughtful individuals with a deep appreciation of nature. As far

Not convinced that a singles bar is bad news? If the suggestions in this book seem like too much trouble for you and you're tempted to take a more direct route by frequenting bars, rent the video *Looking for Mr. Goodbar.* You may change your mind!

as they're concerned, the simple, natural things in life are far preferable to anything overly complicated or artificial.

Further details can be obtained by contacting:

National Wood Carvers Association
P.O. Box 43218
7424 Miami Avenue
Cincinnati, OH 45243

Writers' Clubs

Do you enjoy expressing yourself on paper? Do you feel there's a novel in you just waiting to get out? Do yourself *and* your social life a favor by perfecting your writing skills. Writing is generally a solitary occupation, but most medium-size and large cities have clubs for writers to meet and discuss their craft. Members may critique each other's work and sponsor lectures by editors, agents, and published writers.

Although some writers can be reclusive and uncommunicative (except on paper), the self-selecting nature of a writers' club will ensure that these types won't join. Instead, you'll meet men of all ages and backgrounds who want to share their thoughts and feelings with others. Most are aspiring or beginning writers; chances are you won't meet a really famous writer here (unless he is coming in as a guest lecturer).

To find a writing club near you, look for listings under Clubs, Support Groups, Special Interest or Arts Groups in the entertainment section of your local newspaper. Libraries, bookstores, and colleges may also be able to provide you with names and phone numbers of writers' groups.

C H A P T E R   3

Volunteer, Political, and Civic Work

AS A MEMBER OF YOUR community and a citizen of the United States and the planet, you have certain responsibilities and obligations. Instead of just bemoaning the problems and injustices you see around you, get involved in developing some solutions. Give something back to your local community or the world. Money is certainly needed, but so are *you* needed to make a commitment of your time and energy.

Whether you're more comfortable working on a one-to-one basis with a child or raising funds for a large organization, there is a multitude of individuals and organizations that can put your talents to good use. Try a few of the following possibilities and discover the satisfactions of giving of yourself. An added bonus is the opportunities you'll have to meet men who are also helping on a large and small scale to make this a better world.

SERVICE CLUBS

Any of the following service clubs provides a social outlet as well as multiple opportunities to do good works. The men you'll meet here (and you *will* meet men, since women constitute only 2 to 35 percent of these clubs' membership) are usually quite sociable (as evidenced by their opting to join a club), caring, and action-oriented. Just sitting around discussing problems is not their style; they're doers who would rather right the wrongs and improve their communities and the well-being of others.

AMBUCS

Helping the handicapped is a noble endeavor, and that's what AMBUCS (National Association of American Business Clubs) is devoted to. Their national project, "Scholarships for Therapists," assists deserving students in continuing their studies in physical, occupational, or speech and hearing therapy. Each local chapter also adopts a major civic project within the community (such as raising money to build a rehabilitation center) as well as several minor ones (such as transporting handicapped children to treatment centers). The club is run by its members through a committee structure. Every member serves on a committee. AMBUCS notes that the responsibilities given to members help them acquire skills (such as directing others or communicating ideas) that pay lasting dividends in their careers. Social events are also an important part of each chapter's activities and range from bowling parties to picnics to dinner dances.

Seven thousand members belong to 159 clubs in the USA. The male-female ratio is approximately 90-10, since women were not admitted until 1987. Membership is open to persons of good standing in the community. The only requirements are that the applicant be of good repute and be asked to join by an AMBUC member. To ensure a cross-section of the business community, some clubs classify their members as to their business, restricting the number allowed per classification.

> **National Association of**
> **American Business Clubs**
> P.O. Box 5127
> High Point, NC 27262
> (919) 869-2166

Civitan International

Civitan International is a service club that focuses on helping mentally and physically handicapped citizens. Local chapters can choose the projects most needed by their communities; most support training, facilities, sheltered

If you think that men are more interested in sex or money than love, think again. Love was right after health as the top values in life, according to a recent poll conducted by Louis Harris and Associates for *Playboy* magazine. Ninety-nine percent of the men polled considered love to be important for their happiness. Do your bit to make a man happy: Find someone to love.

workshops, fresh air camps, medical screening of infants, and provide funds and volunteers for the Special Olympics.

There are more than 50,000 members in 1,800 clubs. As the first service club to eliminate the sex barrier, it has a 35 percent female membership. Though some of the clubs are all-male or all-female, 60 percent of the clubs are mixed. There are also singles-only clubs. The average age is the late forties.

Clubs meet weekly or semimonthly. Many convene at restaurants for a meal during the meeting. In addition to civic work, there's a strong emphasis on social activities (dances, sports, picnics).

Civitan International
Growth and Retention Department
P.O. Box 130744
Birmingham, AL 35213-0744
(800) CIVITAN
(205) 591-8910 in Alabama

Cosmopolitan International

Cosmopolitan is a service club whose motto is "Unity, Service and Action." Members develop good citizenship and brotherhood through Unity, contribute to the community through Service, and accomplish defined objectives through Action. Fellowship of members is stressed along with serving others.

Internationally, Cosmopolitan's efforts are concentrated on combating diabetes mellitus (research, education, and patient care). They have established two diabetes centers and will continue to dedicate themselves to this cause because they view it as one of the three largest public health problems in the United States today. Projects of local chapters include raising money for vocational scholarships, contributing to the United Fund, helping with senior citizens' recreation centers, establishing hot lunch programs, and tree planting for beautification.

There are currently about 3,100 members in 92 local clubs in the United States. Less than 10 percent of the membership is female. Ages range from 21 to 90, with an average age of 53. Membership is by invitation, but most clubs are actively striving to increase their membership.

Cosmopolitan International
P.O. Box 4588
Overland Park, KS 66204
(913) 648-4330

Jaycees

The Jaycees (Junior Chamber of Commerce) provide leadership training and personal development for men and women ages 21 through 39. They raise millions of dollars for charity each year on the local, state, and national levels, and donate thousands of volunteer hours to important projects in their communities. Their programs include: Individual Development, Management Development, Community Development, Governmental Affairs, scholarships for students through the Show Pride in America program, fund-raising for the Muscular Dystrophy Association and St. Jude Children's Research Hospital, youth programs, and family life programs.

The United States Jaycees have 240,000 members; Junior Chamber International has over 420,000 members in 90 nations. About 66 percent of the Jaycees' membership is male. The largest age group is the 26-to-30-year-old range. There are 5,000 local chapters throughout the country.

Many local Jaycees chapters are listed in the phone book, but you can contact the national headquarters at:

U.S. Jaycees
P.O. Box 7
Tulsa, OK 74121-0007
(918) 584-2481

Kiwanis

Kiwanis is a worldwide service organization of individuals who want to improve their communities. Their objectives are to emphasize the human and spiritual rather than the material values of life; to encourage the daily living of the Golden Rule in all human relationships; to promote the highest social, business, and professional standards; to develop a more informed and involved citizenship; to form enduring friendships; to render altruistic service; and to build better communities. Through weekly meetings, each local club chooses projects that address the needs of the community. Projects and civic activities can include assistance to the aging, the needy, and youth, encouragement of international understanding, and general community improvements.

More than 300,000 men and women belong to the 8,400 clubs throughout the United States and in 72 other countries. Membership is nearly 95 percent male. Ages range from 18 to over 100; 54 is the average. Individuals of good standing in the community may be invited to become members. To contact the club nearest you and let them know of your interest, call or write:

Kiwanis International
3636 Woodview Trace
Indianapolis, IN 46268
(317) 875-8755

Lions Clubs

Lions Clubs International is the largest service-club organization in the world. An estimated 1,365,000 members belong, in their communities, to one of the Clubs' 40,000 branches. One of their foremost concerns is providing service to the blind and visually impaired. To this end, they operate eye banks for surgical transplants, provide vision screenings, furnish white canes for the blind, provide vocational training and sheltered workshops for the blind, support basic research into eye disease at major medical centers throughout the world, and support guide dog schools. They also provide diabetes screening (since this is the primary cause of adult blindness and a leading cause of death) and support diabetes research. Specific programs are organized to address the needs of senior citizens (such as entertainment at a nursing home, health screening at a senior center, or construction of special housing) and youth (sponsoring international camps to bring young people together to share their cultures and friendship, as well as camps for children with mental or physical disabilities or insulin-dependent diabetes). The Lions also have bought the land and equipment for thousands of recreational facilities in community parks and playgrounds.

Since 1987, women have been eligible for full membership in Lions Clubs. Fifteen percent of new members are women. Membership is by invitation only. Anyone of "legal majority and good moral character and good reputation" is eligible for invitation. Most Lions Clubs include in their membership a cross-section of the business people and professionals in their communities. Ages vary from early twenties to over 100; the average age is about 50.

International Association of Lions Clubs
300 22nd Street
Oak Brook, IL 60521-8842
(708) 571-5466

National Exchange Clubs

The largest exclusively American service-club organization in the nation has branches in hundreds of cities and towns all across the continental United States, as well as in Alaska, Hawaii, and Puerto Rico. Each local club determines the size and scope of its community activities, but the common goals are improving, advancing, and uplifting the human condition and preserving and perpetuating patriotic principles integral to the national heritage. The three categories of service are:

1. Youth
   - Youth of the Month/Year Award Program, given to high school students for scholastic and athletic achievements.
   - Young Citizenship Award for elementary and junior high students.
   - Junior Exchange Clubs for high school students to serve their communities.
   - Sunshine Special Program, in which a group of deserving (orphaned, disadvantaged, disabled) youngsters are selected and treated to special outings at an amusement park, sports events, the beach, the zoo, or picnics.

2. Americanism
   - One Nation Under God program for increasing appreciation of our religious heritages through communitywide prayer breakfasts, assembly programs in schools, and encouraging attendance at religious services.

- Freedom Shrine, in which a mounted collection of 28 of the most important historic American documents (such as the Declaration of Independence) is installed in schools, universities, libraries, state capitols, airports, and city halls.
- Milestones of Freedom, which sponsors quizzes and awards (given to elementary and junior high school students) relating to the documents of the Freedom Shrine.
- Proudly We Hail program to encourage the regular display of the flag by individuals, commercial establishments, and industries by awarding them with a plaque.
- Project Giveakidaflagtowave distributes small American flags to youngsters at parades, fairs, picnics, and school assemblies.
- National Defense program, which educates the community on all aspects of a defense-related issue.

3. Community Service
- Crime prevention through projects such as Neighborhood Watch, Child Identification/Fingerprinting, Police Officer of the Year Award, National Crime Prevention Week.
- Fire prevention through projects such as educating the public, installing smoke alarms in homes of needy families, improving and expanding fire-fighting units.
- Child abuse prevention by increasing public awareness and training volunteers to work with abusing parents and their children.
- Family Days Program, where all club members and their families enjoy special gatherings.
- Book of Golden Deeds program, which recognizes unsung heroes within the community.

In *Risking* (New York: Simon & Schuster, 1977), author and psychiatrist David Viscott notes that personal fulfillment will result in an increased comfort in taking risks of love because "you feel you love yourself more and because you know what's important to you."

The 1,200 local Exchange Clubs have 44,000 members, made up of business and professional men and women ranging in age from young adults to retirees. About 90 percent are men. You can expect men in this club to be a little more conservative and traditional than those in other service clubs. They're firm believers in patriotism, organized religion, and family values.

National Exchange Clubs
3050 Central Avenue
Toledo, OH 43606-1757
(419) 535-3232

Optimist International

Optimist International, one of the world's largest service-club organizations, has more than 167,000 members in 4,000 Optimist Clubs all over the United States, Canada, and the Caribbean. Their motto, "Friend of Youth," reflects their commitment to making a positive impact on today's young people and the future. Their projects include Just Say No antidrug clubs for elementary school children, the Respect for Law program to instill a sense of responsibility to the laws of our communities and the enforcers of those laws, the Help Them Hear program, which provides aids and services to the hearing impaired, the Optimist Oratorical Contest and Essay Contest, which provide scholarship awards to young people, the Optimist Junior World Golf Championships and Tri-Star Sports (a competition in baseball, football, soccer, hockey, and basketball for girls and boys), Youth Appreciation Week, Bike Safety Week (educating kids on safe bicycling through clinics, rodeos, and other events), and Optimist Youth clubs.

Local clubs also sponsor scouting activities, operate camps and homes for underprivileged children, distribute Christmas baskets for the needy, raise funds for community needs, and much more.

Optimist Clubs generally meet weekly for breakfast, lunch, or dinner. Local clubs number from 25 to 100 business and professional men and women. Membership in Optimist Clubs is open to any adult who lives in or does business in the local community served by the Optimist Clubs. But it is by invitation, so you need to contact the club and get invited to a meeting.

Adults of all ages belong to Optimist International. Because membership has been open to women only since 1987, only 8 percent are women. So, you can meet a lot of men in this club while undertaking projects to help the next generation. The men in this club are very compassionate. Regardless of whether or not they have children, they care about young people in general and truly want to help them. As the name implies, they're also upbeat. The Optimist Creed emphasizes positive thinking, inner strength, enthusiasm, and working to achieve the best possible future instead of dwelling on negative events that happened in the past.

Optimist International
4494 Lindell Blvd.
St. Louis, MO 63108
(314) 371-6000

Rotary

The Rotary began in Chicago in 1905 with 19 members. Its continued growth over the years has resulted in 24,462 Rotary clubs in 167 countries and geographical regions. There are now more than a million members.

Rotarians dedicate their time, money, and expertise to a wide range of programs and projects to benefit their communities. Examples from all over the world include:

- Combating drug abuse through hot lines, public seminars, educational materials, and rehabilitation centers.
- Serving disabled persons through camps, corrective surgery, and distribution of medicine.
- Assisting the elderly through free medical care.
- Improving the environment through river cleanups and recycling projects.
- Supporting vocational programs such as job training.

Business and professional leaders who live or work in a local club's territory are eligible to be invited into membership. A candidate must fill an occupational classification, such as banker or university teacher, not already held by an active member of the club. Applicants are reviewed in terms of their character, reputation, service-mindedness, and the ability to attend weekly club meetings. If a meeting must be missed, the Rotarian is encouraged to "make up" within six days by attending a weekly meeting of any Rotary club in the world.

Only 2 percent of Rotarians are women. The average age is 53, but many Rotarians are in their thirties and forties. The Rotary club prides itself on its members' "universally applied tolerance and friendliness," so you'll find that men in this group have these characteristics.

Rotary International
One Rotary Center
1560 Sherman Avenue
Evanston, IL 60201
(312) 866-3243

Ruritan

Ruritan is a civic service organization with the slogan "Friendship, Goodwill, and Community Service." Its purpose is to create a better understanding among people and, through community service, make their own areas better places to live and work. Each club surveys its own community to assess needs and then develops projects accordingly. Nearly all clubs work with 4-H and Future Farmers of America and one in three clubs sponsors scouting. Other programs and projects can include sponsorship of Little League, awarding scholarships, sponsoring safe boating campaigns, working to improve public utilities, investigating air and water pollution, organizing blood drives, and making hospital beds, wheelchairs, and baby seats available for community use.

About 37,000 people belong to Ruritan; 88 percent of them are men. The average age is 52, but this appears to have been decreasing in recent years. Business and professional people may be invited to join.

Ruritan National
Ruritan Road, P.O. Box 487
Dublin, VA 24084
(703) 674-5431

Sertoma

Sertoma is an acronym for "Service to Mankind." This service club has grown from a small club in Kansas City to an international organization with 30,000 members in 38 states plus Canada and Mexico. Sertoma members raise funds and sponsor research and treatment for people affected by speech, hearing, and communicative disorders. Members also work with youth through drug education and scouting.

Be careful of unrealistic expectations in love, such as waiting for the perfect man to come along. In the first place, the supply of perfect men is extremely limited. The second problem is illustrated by the old joke that follows:

Two young women are eating in a restaurant. The first tells her friend that she has finally found the perfect man.

Second woman: "That's wonderful! So why do you still look so unhappy?"

Replied the first: "He's waiting for the perfect woman."

Members of a Sertoma club need to be of good character and reputation in the agricultural, business, institutional, or professional life of the community. They also must fulfill all other membership requirements established by each local club. The average age is 47 and the ratio of men to women is 14 to 1.

Sertoma
1912 East Meyer Boulevard
Kansas City, MO 64132-9990
(816) 333-8300

ENVIRONMENTAL AND CONSERVATION GROUPS

Protecting the environment and wildlife is a major concern to growing numbers of caring individuals. Most environmental clubs have equal numbers of men and women. You'll meet men who truly care about life beyond their own little chunk of turf. They enjoy the outdoors and treasure nature in all its forms.

Audubon Society

When it was formed at the beginning of the century, the National Audubon Society limited its scope to bird preservation. It has since expanded to encompass all aspects of nature. Audubon members are well aware of the interconnectedness of life and of problems with the earth's life-support systems—air, water, and land. The society tries to minimize pollution, influence public policy, and educate people about nature, while taking steps to conserve plants and animals.

If you're a bird, animal, or plant lover, you might want to join the more than 550,000 members in 510 local chapters. Membership is equally divided between men and women. Almost 40 percent are single. The median income is about $41,000. Almost three quarters have had some college. The median age is 45.

As a member, you can join in natural history field trips, attend films and lectures, and work to save endangered species and to protect natural areas by educating people, researching, campaigning, and lobbying.

National Audubon Society
P.O. Box 2667
Boulder, CO 80321

Ducks Unlimited

Ducks Unlimited was founded more than 50 years ago by a group of sportsmen who wanted to save North America's waterfowl. Drought and other factors had caused the duck and goose populations to plunge to unprecedented lows at the time; in later years, the group has also tried to preserve the habitats of other species of wildlife such as the whooping crane, bald eagle, peregrine falcon, and least tern.

The 500,000-plus members who live in every one of the 50 states primarily perform fund-raising activities such as dinners, auctions, shooting and fishing tournaments, and golf outings. They also work with other conservation groups and state and federal government agencies to create habitat awareness nationwide.

Although statistical breakdowns of the membership are not available, it is believed that men predominate, since they form the bulk of the hunting population. Do be aware that many of these men are fervent sportsmen. They love the outdoors and wildlife, but they enjoy hunting and see it as an essential part of wildlife management. If the killing of animals for sport offends you, look for another conservation group.

Ducks Unlimited
One Waterfowl Way
Long Grove, IL 60047
(708) 438-4300

Sierra Club

If you're a nature lover, you probably already belong to the Sierra Club. But if by chance you're not a member, you may want to think about joining. The Sierra Club works on hundreds of conservation issues—locally, regionally, nationally, and internationally. Its major goals are to protect the global environment against threats of acid rain, water and air pollution, hazardous wastes, ozone depletion, and global warming. Past and current projects include lobbying for the Clean Air Act, Arctic National Wildlife Protection, the California Desert Protection Act, national forests and parks protection, and energy conservation.

As a member, you can participate in grass-roots activism to help clean up and maintain the environment through lobbying and public education. Another benefit of membership is the opportunity to participate in national and local outings and trips.

To join this organization (which has 416,000 members in 71 local chapters), contact:

Sierra Club
730 Polk Street
San Francisco, CA 94109
(415) 776-2211

HEALTH ORGANIZATIONS

If you're in perfect health, count your blessings. If you do have some health concerns, you have firsthand knowledge of the devastating impact they can have on the quality of life. Either way, you may want to get involved with a health organization, because working to promote health and to fight disease is one of the most meaningful things you can do.

Most health organizations do not keep track of the male-female ratio, ages, or other demographics relating to their membership. But it is believed that generally an equal number of men and women of all ages volunteer. Some are active in the organizations because they or a family member have the disease or health problem. Others were moved to join just by hearing about an organization and believing in its cause.

Consider joining an organization such as the American Cancer Society, which has more than 2 million volunteers. These volunteers raise funds through special projects such as Jail and Bail (local celebrities are put in "prison" and are bailed out through donations) or Daffodil Days (daffodils are sold to businesses) as well as parties, galas, and balls. In addition, they educate professionals and the public, and help cancer patients and their families. They come from all walks of life but share the common goal of wanting to save lives and diminish suffering.

To get involved with one of the more than 3,300 local units of the American Cancer Society, look up their number in your phone book or contact their national headquarters at:

>**American Cancer Society**
>1599 Clifton Road
>Atlanta, GA 30329
>(800) ACS-2345

Your community has a number of other health organizations that you may be interested in. Look in your yellow pages for the listings under "Health Organizations and Agencies."

OTHER VOLUNTEER AND CIVIC ACTIVITIES

There is a wide variety of human service and civic volunteer opportunities and an equally wide variety of men you can meet by participating in these activities. Give a few of the following a try.

American Civil Liberties Union

The ACLU is a nationwide nonpartisan organization dedicated to preserving and defending the principles embodied in the Bill of Rights. Through public education, advocacy, lobbying, and litigation, the ACLU tries to maintain and expand rights guaranteed by the Constitution for this and future generations. Some concerns and issues they've tackled in recent years include: the rights of homosexuals, prisoners, immigrants, and the homeless; the right to withdraw medical life support; flag desecration as an expression of free speech; reproductive rights (for example, for pregnant women to be admitted to drug treatment programs or teenagers to obtain birth control or abortions); challenging school prayer and nativity scenes on government property.

If you believe in and want to protect our democratic system, you may want to join the more than 275,000 members of the ACLU. Affiliate chapters are found in every state. Members are of all ages, although most tend to be older than 30. Many are lawyers, but you don't have to be one to belong and help. Members can perform office work, raise funds, and lobby Congress and state and local legislatures. Statistics are not available on the gender breakdown of the membership, but more than half are men.

The men you'll meet here will tend to be very liberal. You could safely assume that they respect women and want an egalitarian relationship where both parties function as equals. Usually they operate more on logic and intellectual principles than on emotions. They'll take a stand when they believe it's right, even if it causes some pain or discomfort.

American Civil Liberties Union
132 West 43rd Street
New York, NY 10036
(212) 944-9800

American Red Cross

You're probably familiar with the Red Cross. As the nation's foremost volunteer human services organization for more than 100 years, they've helped millions of people both in this country and overseas prevent, prepare for, and cope with emergencies. Over a million volunteers each year perform such tasks as:

- Feeding, clothing, or sheltering victims of disasters (ranging from small house fires to large-scale hurricanes).
- Collecting, testing, and distributing blood.
- Teaching Red Cross CPR, first aid, water safety, and lifesaving courses.
- Providing military families and veterans with emergency-related communications and social services.
- Giving food and medical assistance to people around the world.
- Administering immunization clinics, health fairs, and blood pressure screening.
- Collecting, processing, and distributing tissues (such as corneas for sight; temporal bones for hearing; skin for burn patients; heart valves for heart defects; bones, tendons, and ligaments for orthopedic procedures) for transplants.

• Providing leadership skills to direct local chapters.

You can always find your local Red Cross chapter in the phone book, but for further information contact:

American Red Cross
Washington, DC 20006

Amnesty International

Writing a letter can be one of the most meaningful ways to spend your leisure time, according to Amnesty International. This group believes that the lives of individuals around the world can be saved by just a single letter to a government. Amnesty International is a worldwide movement of people who believe that governments must not deny individuals their basic human rights. Concerned about the thousands of people who are held in prison because of their beliefs, often without charge or trial and tortured or put to death, Amnesty International works impartially, without considering the ideology of the government or the beliefs of the victim.

To protect human rights, members:

• Seek the release of prisoners of conscience (people detained for their beliefs, color, sex, ethnic origin, language, or religion who have not used or advocated violence).

• Work for fair and prompt trials for all political prisoners.

• Oppose the death penalty and torture or other cruel, inhuman, or degrading treatment or punishment of all prisoners without reservation.

Of the 700,000 members of Amnesty International in 150 countries, 400,000 live in the United States. They belong to 600 community-based chapters of 10 to 25 people who meet regularly to write letters, organize, and publicize actions on behalf of individual prisoners of conscience; work against torture and the death penalty; and participate in special human rights campaigns. The men you'll meet here are articulate, intelligent, caring people. These are not self-centered yuppies. They're deeply concerned about and committed to making life better for everyone. If they care this much about people they've never even met, imagine how well one of them would treat *you* as the special person in his life.

Amnesty International USA
322 Eighth Avenue
New York, NY 10001
(212) 807-8400

Animal Protection

Are you an animal lover? If so, you may want to devote some of your time
to helping them. One possibility is your local animal shelter, run by the
Humane Society, American Society for the Prevention of Cruelty to Animals, or the local city or county government. You can work directly with
the animals, feeding, grooming, walking, and just plain loving them, or you
can help with their "adoptions." Somewhat more women than men volunteer
at these shelters, but your man-meeting opportunities are increased by the
contact you'll have with men who come in to look for a possible pet.
Conversation can be greatly enhanced when a puppy or kitten is around.

Another possible option is joining an animal rights organization such
as the American Anti-Vivisection Society. Believing it is unethical to inflict
suffering and death on animals, this group works to eliminate the use of
animals in research and testing. About 8,000 people belong to the society.
Slightly more women than men seem to join. The age range is preteen to
nineties, with an average in the thirties. Volunteers can help with mailings,
special projects, office jobs, passing out leaflets, staffing tables at local
events, and participating in protests and demonstrations.

Animal lovers are nurturing souls with plenty of compassion for all
living things. You'll find them to be sensitive, centered individuals.

American Anti-Vivisection Society
Suite 204, Noble Plaza
801 Old York Road
Jenkintown, PA 19046-1685
(215) 887-0816

Arts Volunteering

If you're a lover of the arts, consider giving a few hours a week or month
to help support them. Almost without exception, arts organizations continu-

ally feel a financial pinch and rely on volunteers to help raise funds, usher, guide tours, and in other ways. Volunteer possibilities include:

* *Museums:* tour guide, gift shop volunteer, ticket seller.
* *Theater, ballet and opera companies:* usher, ticket seller, stagehand.
* *Symphony orchestras:* usher, public relations, host/hostess for visiting performers.

Ushering is a prime example of a win-win situation. The theater, ballet, or opera company saves money by not needing to hire paid ushers, and you get to attend a performance for free! Fund-raising is another example. The benefit to the arts organization is obvious (the funds raised can be its real lifeblood), but you'll also benefit by increasing your network of friends and acquaintances, by acquiring skills that will enhance your résumé and your potential for success in the business world, and through your enjoyment of the parties and gala events.

Men and women generally participate equally in ushering and fund-raising efforts (except in museums and ballet companies, where women seem to predominate). Most are in their thirties to fifties. You'll find two types of men: those who genuinely love the arts and those who enjoy the prestige and business connections that their association with an arts organization provides. The men who usher tend to be less financially successful than the men who involve themselves in fund-raising.

To get involved, contact the local arts organization of your choice.

Big Brothers/Big Sisters of America

Many organizations address the needs of children, but Big Brothers/Big Sisters is the only national youth-service organization that focuses on a one-to-one relationship between adult volunteers and children. Most of the children are from single-parent homes, but special-needs children (the handicapped, learning disabled, school dropouts, abused and neglected) are also served. The Big Brother or Big Sister functions not as a substitute parent but rather as an understanding friend who listens to the child, gives advice when asked, and spends four to six hours a week with the Little Brother or Little Sister.

You don't have to be a parent, teacher, or social worker to be a Big Sister. All you need is the desire to share a small part of yourself with a young child. As a prospective volunteer, you will be carefully screened and then matched with a compatible child. Professional caseworkers also super-vise the matches and ensure that things go smoothly.

Big Brothers/Big Sisters has more than 485 agencies across the country. You can become either a direct service volunteer for one of the 100,000 children on the waiting lists (if you can devote at least four hours a week for a minimum of one year) or a leadership volunteer (serving on the board or helping to seek financial support from companies, organizations, and com-munity groups). There are currently 75,000 Bigs volunteering. Slightly fewer than half are women. The average age is in the early thirties.

As with any volunteer organization, you'll find concerned and caring men. Big Brothers/Big Sisters meetings and social functions will enable you to meet especially warm and caring individuals. Intimate relationships don't scare them; they truly enjoy communicating and sharing with others.

Big Brothers/Big Sisters of America
230 North 13th Street
Philadelphia, PA 19107-1510
(215) 567-7000

Blood Donation

There are thousands of people who want and need your blood! They're not vampires; they're people just like you who, because of illness or injury, happen to require a blood transfusion. Donating blood is completely safe. To qualify, you must be in good health, at least 110 pounds, and over 17 years old. You're given a miniphysical to check your temperature, pulse, blood pressure, and hemoglobin to make sure you're not anemic. Once you're found to be eligible, a new, sterile, disposable needle is used to take a pint of blood from your arm. The complete process takes about 45 minutes.

Over 4.5 million people donate blood to the Red Cross each year, with hundreds of thousands more donating to other blood collection agencies. Volunteers are allowed to donate every 56 days. Slightly more than half of all donors are women, but this still leaves 2 million or so donors who are

In an article in the May 1989 *Ms.* magazine, author Molly Irvine praises blood banks as one of the best places in town to meet men: "Not only are the donors rigorously screened for AIDS, but blood donors also get Brownie points in heaven."

men. Giving blood is one of the most personal ways to volunteer, so it follows that men who give blood aren't threatened by intimacy and involvement. Giving is truly as important to them as receiving.

Donate at your Red Cross chapter or community blood bank. You never know who'll be lying next to you or whom you might meet while partaking in the refreshments most centers provide after you donate.

Boy Scouts

When you were growing up, you wouldn't have been able to join the Boy Scouts. But now as an adult female, you can get involved in this esteemed organization and play an active role in developing the minds, bodies, and spirits of boys and young men. (Consider it your gift to the younger generation of women!) There are many ways to get involved with scouting, both directly (becoming one of the 500-plus women who serve as Scout leaders) and behind the scenes in administration, fund-raising, and clerical work.

Around 1.5 million adults volunteer in the Boy Scouts. Ages range from 20 to 65 years. Though the number of female volunteers is not available, the overwhelming majority of volunteers are male. The Boy Scouts are organized through 410 local councils nationwide.

As you would expect, men involved in scouting are capable and caring. They have a variety of interests but share a common motivation to help the youth of America develop into good citizens and human beings.

Contact your local council for volunteer opportunities. All local councils are listed in the phone book.

While Boy Scouts are not specifically groomed to become husbands, lovers, and friends to women, the Boy Scout ideals certainly go a long way in preparing boys to develop some pretty impressive characteristics. Any men you'll meet through scouting also share these qualities. After you read the description of a Scout noted in the Boy Scout law, you'll understand why a man involved in scouting can be such a good catch. Who wouldn't want a man who is:

Trustworthy	Courteous	Thrifty
Loyal	Kind	Brave
Helpful	Obedient	Clean
Friendly	Cheerful	Reverent

Community Cleanups

You pick up after yourself in your own home. But your community (indeed, the entire planet) is also your home, and you probably don't give much thought or effort to its cleanliness. Unfortunately, you're not alone in this neglect; most people don't think or do anything about the larger environment. Carelessness leads to an ever-increasing litter problem that diminishes the beauty of parks, beaches, historic sites, and other community treasures. Often, paid groundskeepers pick up much of the trash, but occasionally the community is called on to pick up litter and do whatever else is required (such as clean and restore buildings) to get things looking good again.

Although volunteers in such efforts are often teenagers, people in their twenties, thirties, forties, and on up also participate. Men and women tend to participate equally. All volunteers are concerned citizens who care about their community and are willing to pitch in to have it look as nice as possible. Watch your newspaper for announcements about the next scheduled cleanup.

Goodwill Industries of America

As North America's leading nonprofit provider of vocational services for people with disabilities and other special needs (such as illiteracy, a history of criminal behavior, or lack of work experience), Goodwill helps people overcome barriers to employment and fully participate in the life of the community. Goodwill serves more than 83,000 people a year (of which about 14,000 find competitive jobs in the community) through its 177 autonomous, community-based Goodwill agencies throughout the United States and Canada.

Volunteers serve as members of the governing board of directors, offer expertise as members of the business advisory councils, raise funds, or participate in special events and client-oriented activities such as recreation, social development, education, and personal hygiene. Over 11,000 men and women from all walks of life and ages contribute their time and energies.

Look in your phone book for the Goodwill nearest you or contact the national headquarters at:

Goodwill Industries of America
9200 Wisconsin Avenue
Bethesda, MD 20814-3896
(301) 530-6500

Holiday Dinners

Most communities provide Thanksgiving and Christmas meals to people who would otherwise go without. Indigent, homeless, transient, and ill individuals receive free meals sponsored by churches, civic groups, shelters for the homeless, and concerned citizens. Volunteers are always needed to obtain, prepare, and serve the food. Helping to spread a little holiday cheer among strangers is guaranteed to make your own holiday season more meaningful.

Men and women of all ages volunteer for holiday dinners. Some do it because of strong religious convictions; others do it simply because they care about people.

To get involved, read your local newspaper to see which groups are sponsoring dinners. You can also contact churches, shelters, and organizations like the Salvation Army.

Jury Duty

Quite a few people try to get out of jury duty when they're called to serve. Don't let this be the case when it's your turn. It's your civic duty, after all, and you might even find it interesting. Many cases are routine and mundane, but it's also possible to serve on cases of murder, drug trafficking, white-collar crime, and so on.

If your service lasts more than a day or two, you'll get to know your fellow jurors very well. This is especially true if you get sequestered overnight. There's always a chance that you'll meet someone special. (The composition of the jury can vary anywhere from mostly female to mostly male, depending on both the details of the case and the wishes of the attorneys.)

Little League Baseball

The Little League baseball and softball programs enable children to learn good sportsmanship and improve their physical fitness. Participation in these games has meant a great deal to millions of boys and girls since 1939. Little League prospers because of the volunteer efforts of adults throughout the year. Some 750,000 volunteers manage and coach their local leagues, as well as maintain the fields and serve on the board of directors. Women are allowed to participate in every capacity.

By volunteering in this program, you will meet eight-year-old boys, but you'll also have an excellent chance of meeting adult men in their twenties to sixties. Some are fathers (and some are single fathers) of the participants, whereas others just want to help their communities by working with youth. You'll find the men here to be concerned about other people, enthusiastic, and openly communicative. They care just as much about life's little pleasures as they do about the bigger, flashier, more expensive means of having fun.

For information about the league nearest you or creating a new one, contact:

Little League Baseball
P.O. Box 3485
Williamsport, PA 17701
(717) 326-1921

Make-A-Wish Foundation
of America

How many opportunities do you have to be a fairy godmother and make dreams come true for deserving people? If you become active in the Make-A-Wish Foundation of America, you can experience the joy of cheering up children with life-threatening illnesses. This nonprofit organization began with the fulfillment of the wish of a seven-year-old boy with leukemia who wanted to be a policeman. Local officers granted his wish with a custom-made uniform, helmet, badge, and helicopter ride. In the following years, the organization has granted thousands of wishes to children all over the country. The types of wishes are limited only by the child's imagination. They include destinations (such as trips to Disney World and the Kentucky Derby), occupations (being a fireman for the day), celebrities (meeting a rock star or film personality), and special gifts (a fishing pond in the child's backyard).

The Make-A-Wish Foundation has 71 chapters within the United States. Seven thousand volunteers work in accounting, law, fund-raising, public relations, wish granting, and special events.

Make-A-Wish Foundation of America
2600 North Central Avenue, Suite 936
Phoenix, AZ 85004
(602) 240-6600
(800) 722-WISH

Mothers Against Drunk Driving

Mothers Against Drunk Driving (MADD) was founded in California in 1980 after a 13-year-old girl was killed by a hit-and-run drunk driver who had been involved in another hit-and-run drunk driving accident just two days earlier and was free on bail. The child's mother began a one-woman campaign to save other children from death and other parents from pain. MADD has evolved into an organization with more than 1.5 million members/supporters and 400 chapters nationwide.

Volunteers provide information and materials to teachers and students to help educate the next generation to become responsible drivers, and they educate adults on safe driving through programs such as Project Red Ribbon (between Thanksgiving and New Year's as a safe driving reminder), Drive for Life on Labor Day weekend, and annual candlelight vigils honoring victims of drunk driving. MADD also works with legislators to toughen drunk driving laws and sponsors victim support programs.

You don't have to be a mother to belong; only half the members are female. You just need to be a concerned citizen. The predominant age group is between 30 and 50.

Mothers Against Drunk Driving
669 Airport Freeway, Suite 310
Hurst, Texas 76053
(817) 268-MADD

Neighborhood Crime Watches

No matter where you live, you're not immune from crime. Even small towns aren't completely safe. The police do their best, but they can't be everywhere at once. Therefore, citizens are starting to form their own patrols, taking turns riding or walking around the neighborhood. If you're not aware of one in your area, check with the police department. If there isn't one currently in operation, they can guide you in forming one. Just a few hours a week of your time is all that's required (and often less than that if you have an active group with numerous members). You don't have to carry a gun or make arrests; you are just lending your eyes and ears and alerting the police if you see anything suspicious.

Participating in the meetings and the patrols is an excellent way to meet your neighbors (some of whom may be attractive single men you wouldn't otherwise know).

Open Government Meetings

Not all local and state government meetings are open to the public, but many are. Follow the local issues and attend some meetings on subjects that interest you. Every community has meetings galore: city councils, special legislative sessions, task forces, hearings, and so on. As a member of your community, it behooves you to know what's going on and to voice your opinion. Whether it's rezoning a formerly residential area or an upcoming bond issue, you can surely find topics that matter to you.

Women are still not assuming as active a political role as men. Therefore, you stand an excellent chance of meeting men at these gatherings. Even if you find yourself on the opposite side of an issue with a man who otherwise seems very promising, you may find other things in common, either afterward over coffee or by getting involved on a committee where you will work together.

Political Organizations

All too many Americans are politically apathetic. Not enough people bother to vote, and only a few really get involved with the political party of their choice. But politics affects every aspect of our lives, whether we recognize it or not. The people in political office make and enforce decisions that have implications for all of us. It is therefore to our benefit to become active in the political system.

To do so, you can join either of the two major parties, depending on your personal preference. Democrats are considered to have the more liberal platform, generally supporting social services, government protection of civil rights, and so on. The Republican policies emphasize economic/business growth and a strong defense. This is, of course, a very simplistic definition, and you'll want to investigate the parties more thoroughly if you're not already affiliated. You can locate the Democratic or Republican parties in your phone book. If you're between 18 and 40, you might consider joining the Young Democrats or Young Republicans. Both organizations have between 100,000 and 200,000 members nationally. Most are college graduates, between 23 and 35. Men and women are equally represented.

**Young Democrats
of America**
430 South Capitol Street SE
Washington, DC 20003
(202) 863-8000

**Young Republican
National Federation**
310 First Street SE
Washington, DC 20003
(202) 662-1340

As a political activist, you can support the campaigns of the candidates you prefer. There are opportunities to participate in fund-raising, media relations, and grass-roots organizing. All these activities can enable you to meet large numbers of men, both locally and nationally. Attending a national convention can further improve your odds.

An alternative to the Democratic and Republican parties is the Libertarian party, the third-largest party in the United States, as well as the fastest growing. More than 100 elected or appointed Libertarians hold public office. As the name implies, freedom is stressed: economic freedom which leads to prosperity, preservation of civil liberties and personal freedom, and foreign policies that emphasize nonintervention, peace, and free trade. Principles embodied in the Declaration of Independence and the Bill of Rights are emphasized. Both free enterprise and freedom of expression are valued. Specific beliefs are that military service should be voluntary and a compulsory draft or registration eliminated, that medical research should be returned to the private sector away from the bureaucracy, that antitrust laws and other regulation of business should promote a free, openly competitive marketplace, that allied nations should take responsibility for their own defense needs, that drug laws should be repealed, that the minimum wage should be repealed, and that the government should get out of education and let private schools teach.

Almost a quarter of a million people are registered Libertarian voters in the United States. There are about 150 local or regional affiliates in all 50 states. Libertarian party membership is roughly 60 percent male; meetings are attended mostly by men. The majority of members are in white-collar occupations and college-educated.

In *Making Love Happen* (Latham, N.Y.: British American Publishing, 1989), author and romance consultant Rebecca Sydnor notes that women who leave romance totally to chance are placing themselves in a position of weakness. Eventually, she believes, they'll act out of desperation and settle for men who aren't right for them. She doesn't feel that it's unnatural or artificial to set the stage for the type of love you want; meaningless casual affairs or remaining in an unsatisfying relationship are far more unnatural.

Activities with the Libertarian party could include participating in fairs, assisting at mailing parties, and introducing candidates to neighbors and the community.

The men here will tend to be well-read (Ayn Rand's *The Fountainhead* and *Atlas Shrugged* are favorites), thoughtful, and independent. They're tolerant of lifestyles and beliefs that differ from theirs. If you're tired of men who try to get you to change to their ways and impose on your freedom, a Libertarian could be a welcome change.

Libertarian Party
1528 Pennsylvania Avenue SE
Washington, DC 20003
(202) 543-1988

Public Broadcasting

The hundreds of public (also called educational) television and radio stations throughout the country do an excellent job of providing top-notch news, music, and cultural programs on a shoestring budget. Because money is always tight, volunteers are welcomed with open arms. If you care about quality broadcasting and are an enthusiastic fan of PBS (Public Broadcasting Service) or NPR (National Public Radio), it's in your best interest to give them some of your time as well as money. You can help out with some of the office work or assist in taking care of the record or film libraries. Several times a year, most stations hold major fund-raising campaigns during which volunteers answer phones, catalog donations, and assist with other tasks.

Demographics on public broadcasting volunteers are difficult to provide, since they vary so much according to the locale (a station near a retirement community will tend to have more older volunteers, for example). Men seem to volunteer more frequently. The vast majority are college-educated professionals.

The men you'll meet here are cultured and intellectual. They enjoy the finer things in life and won't settle for inferiority in anything that touches their lives.

Contact your local station to volunteer.

Relief Efforts

It's an unfortunate fact of life that natural and manmade disasters occur and cause human suffering. Fortunately, there are always people who offer a helping hand to those affected by hurricanes, tornadoes, earthquakes, famine, war, crime, and accidents. Volunteer efforts include fund-raising; conducting drives for food, medical supplies, and clothes; rebuilding homes and other structures; and administering first aid and solace to victims. The rewards of helping are obvious. Volunteers feel an intense personal satisfaction knowing that they are taking action to help others who are desperately in need.

Both men and women get involved in relief efforts. Certain aspects seem to attract each of the sexes. For example, usually more women than men prepare meals in shelters, whereas men predominate in many of the collecting and distributing activities. You'll find the men here to be spontaneous, responsive, and active individuals. Instead of just thinking about problems, they do what's necessary to solve them. They know how to make life better for themselves and others.

You can get involved in the next relief effort by reading your local newspaper or watching the news on television and learning what needs to be done. Ad hoc groups usually form, and established groups (such as churches and charitable organizations) are always glad to have another volunteer. The Red Cross is involved in many relief efforts, so you can also contact your local chapter.

Rescue and Emergency Care

Performing rescue and emergency care can be highly stressful, but also very rewarding. While you might not want to be a firefighter, ambulance driver, or paramedic as a full-time career, you may enjoy doing it as a part-time volunteer. The qualifications vary by city or agency, so check within your community to see whether you have what it takes (or can acquire the skills) to perform this essential volunteer work. The fire department will be able to tell you about its volunteer force and can also direct you to the ambulance/paramedic service.

Only about 6 percent of volunteer ambulance drivers and fire department workers are women. Ages range from 21 to 60. There's a wide variety of education backgrounds and occupations as well. The men you'll meet doing this type of work like the excitement of emergency situations, but they generally have low-key, easygoing personalities. They care deeply about people and feel good about providing these services to assist the community.

SANE/FREEZE

Everyone wants a just, environmentally safe, and peaceful world. Unfortunately, only a fraction of the population takes any action to promote this goal. If you care about ending the arms race and abolishing nuclear weapons, you'll want to think about joining SANE/FREEZE. The nation's largest disarmament organization, SANE/FREEZE believes that most of the billions of dollars spent by the military could be better utilized to preserve the environment, end drug abuse and drug-related violence, and overcome poverty and homelessness. They see the world as a family of nations with a shared destiny and a common imperative for just and peaceful living.

As a SANE/FREEZE member, you can work on campaigns to educate the public and Congress about global peace (for example, working to close nuclear weapons plants or lobbying to reduce arms). Nationally there are about 170,000 members in 250 local chapters. Ages range from high school students to senior citizens. Slightly more than half are women.

The men you'll meet in this organization are concerned, thoughtful individuals who care deeply about the fate of the planet for this and future generations. Many tend to be on the liberal side. They care about the United States, but they also care about the rest of the world.

SANE/FREEZE
1819 H Street NW, Suite 1000
Washington, DC 20006
(202) 862-9740

Very Special Arts

The arts are among the most satisfying of all human endeavors. Dance, drama, music, literature, and the visual arts enable feelings, thoughts, and creativity to be expressed. This is especially important for people who are physically or mentally challenged. Very Special Arts, founded by Jean Kennedy Smith in 1974, is an organization dedicated to coordinating arts programs for those with disabilities. Sponsored projects include playwriting for teenagers and senior citizens, dance for the blind and visually impaired, opera for the disabled, creative writing for hospital patients and institution residents, art programs (including bringing artwork created by Very Special Arts participants to hospital patients), and special projects for infants and preschool children with special needs, as well as hospitalized veterans.

Very Special Arts is unable to provide statistics about their volunteers, but they do depend on volunteers to help with their festivals, school programs, special projects, performances, and exhibitions. In the United States, more than a million individuals with physical and mental challenges participate in Very Special Arts activities.

As a volunteer, you'll be integrated into the network of local, state, and national organizations, including educational and cultural institutions, arts agencies, associations for the disabled, and health and rehabilitation organizations. This means that you can meet a variety of parents, teachers, trainers, artists, and health specialists. All the men you'll meet will be caring, compassionate individuals who enjoy the arts. They know how to celebrate life and the human spirit. A relationship with one of them should be truly special.

Very Special Arts
John F. Kennedy Center for the Performing Arts
Washington, DC 20566
(800) VSA-3336 or (202) 662-8895

CHAPTER 4

Education

NO MATTER WHAT YOUR AGE, socioeconomic status, or level of formal schooling, the need to continue learning persists throughout your life. Don't just do it for job advancement; do it for the joy of learning. Education can truly enrich your life by enabling you to acquire new skills, develop new ways of thinking, and meet new people.

Challenge yourself intellectually by enrolling in classes and seminars regularly. Whether you never attended college or have a doctoral degree, you can sign up for college courses ranging from accounting to zoology and everything in between. You don't even need to work toward a degree; simply take interesting classes on a noncredit basis. Also look into other educational opportunities, such as those offered by your community schools, hospitals, financial services firms, and business/professional seminar companies. You'll learn a lot . . . and are likely to meet a lot of men in the process!

COLLEGE

College offers a wide range of opportunities to meet men while improving your mind. Although women slightly outnumber men in the number of bachelor's and master's degrees earned, there are still thousands of men of all types enrolled in institutions of higher education.

Meeting men at school is safe and easy. Unlike many other situations in which you have to size someone up in a few minutes, a semester-length course gives you several months to get acquainted. Conversation occurs naturally before, after, and sometimes even during class.

Another nice aspect is the diversity of college students. Every race, religion, ethnic group, and nationality is represented at many schools. Different socioeconomic classes, interests, and personalities can be found as well. And don't feel that all college students are young enough to be your kid brother. More and more adults are returning to college for career growth or for personal enrichment.

Keep the following information in mind when selecting college courses.

20 Best Majors for Meeting Men *(ratio of men to women)*

Engineering   5.6 to 1
Dentistry   4.1 to 1
Osteopathic medicine   3.5 to 1
Chiropractic medicine   3.3 to 1
Optometry   3.1 to 1
Theology   3.1 to 1
Architecture   3 to 1
Medicine   2.57 to 1
Physical sciences   2.57 to 1
Geography   2.3 to 1
Agriculture and natural resources   2.2 to 1
Philosophy   2.1 to 1
Economics   1.94 to 1
Computer and information sciences   1.85 to 1
Banking and finance   1.8 to 1
Law   1.7 to 1
Protective services   1.63 to 1
Religion   1.5 to 1
Political science   1.5 to 1
Veterinary medicine   1.3 to 1

Lisa Birnbach, author of *Lisa Birnbach's College Book,* noted in an interview (*People,* September 17, 1984) that women who want to meet men should consider attending Cal Tech, an engineering and science school in California where only a fraction of the 900 students are women. But don't get your hopes up if your SAT scores or grades weren't anything to brag about. In recent years, the average student who was offered admission had scores of 650 verbal, 750 math, and was in the top 10 percent of his or her high school class.

20 Worst Majors for Meeting Men   (*ratio of women to men*)

> Home economics   15.6 to 1
> Elementary education   13.2 to 1
> Interior design   8.1 to 1
> Dance   7.3 to 1
> Library science   6.1 to 1
> Social work   6.1 to 1
> Allied health   4.2 to 1
> Art history   4 to 1
> Crafts   3.1 to 1
> Foreign languages   3.1 to 1
> Public relations   2.4 to 1
> Psychology   2.2 to 1
> Sociology   2.2 to 1
> English   2 to 1
> Anthropology   1.8 to 1
> Painting   1.8 to 1
> Advertising   1.7 to 1
> Journalism   1.7 to 1
> Area and ethnic studies   1.6 to 1
> Drama   1.4 to 1

OTHER EDUCATIONAL EXPERIENCES

College isn't the only place where you can learn new skills and acquire new knowledge. Your community is full of other educational opportunities. Be sure to take advantage of some of the following.

Business Seminars

No matter what your niche in the business world, you can benefit from a motivational or informational seminar every so often. These one-day seminars can rejuvenate your enthusiasm for your job (as well as other areas of your life) and help you achieve more success.

You probably receive mailings for such seminars each month. Two of the biggest and best-known companies offering these seminars are:

CareerTrack
3085 Center Green Drive
Boulder, CO 80301-5408
(800) 334-6780

Recent offerings include In Search of Excellence seminar, How to Give Exceptional Customer Service, How to Deal with Difficult People, The One-Minute Manager, Taking Control of Your Work Day, Self-Esteem and Peak Performance, Business Writing Skills for Professionals, and How to Make Presentations That Win Approval.

Fred Pryor Seminars
2000 Johnson Drive
P.O. Box 2951
Shawnee Mission, KS 66201
(800) 255-6139

Representative seminars include Successful Communication Skills, Business Writing for Results, How to Manage Priorities and Demands, How to Turn Your Work Group into a Winning Team, Assertiveness Skills for Managers and Supervisors, How to Supervise People, How to Get Things Done, and How to Work with People.

Seminars are regularly offered in most major cities, usually in hotels. Generally at least half the attendees are men and often the ratio is higher. Most are college graduates, in middle to upper management positions, with a median age between 35 and 44. The average salary is above $50,000. As you might suspect, the men you'll meet at these seminars (by sitting near them or going out for lunch together) are take-charge individuals, but they're not so egotistical that they think they know it all. They're generally open to new ideas and people.

Community School Adult Education/ Noncredit Courses

How about learning something just for the fun of it? Not to earn credits, not to acquire new skills or knowledge that could significantly change your life (although you might enroll in a course that winds up doing just that), but simply because a course sounds like it might be intriguing or pleasurable! Every community offers adult education as part of its public school system. Generally held at night for a couple of hours a session over the course of two to three months, these courses touch upon a vast variety of subjects. Colleges usually offer similar courses at night or on the weekend. These noncredit courses are worlds apart from the standard courses listed in their catalogs. Examples of community school and noncredit courses include:

Renovate Your Home Yourself	Effective Public Speaking
Drawing on the Right Side of the Brain	Writing Your First Novel
	Introduction to
Beginning Chinese	Wine Appreciation
Photography	Starting Your Own Business
Beginning Birdwatching	Stress Management
Assertiveness Training	Magic
Financial Planning	Auto Repairs
How to Buy Antiques	Vegetarian Cooking
Desktop Publishing	

Many school systems and colleges will mail brochures about these courses to nearby residents or advertise them in the newspaper. If yours doesn't, contact the adult education department of your city or county school system or the community education/noncredit courses department at the college of your choice.

Because the scope of offerings is virtually unlimited, it's impossible to detail what types of men you'll find in each course. Use your own intuition and experience as well as the rest of this book to pinpoint the personality characteristics of men who might be attracted to certain courses.

Continuing Education

If you're in a profession or occupation that requires a certain amount of continuing education credits each year, it's imperative that you regularly attend professional seminars. Even if you're not required by your licensing board or employer to attend these educational workshops, it's still a good idea to do so to keep up with new trends in your field and revive your enthusiasm for your work.

The man-meeting opportunities provided by continuing education vary according to the specific field. If you're in a male-dominated profession, you'll obviously find more men in the courses you attend. To enhance your

According to Eric Weber, author of *The Divorced Woman's Guide to Meeting Men* (New York: Morrow, 1984), the body language that has an "astonishingly magnetic effect on getting men to approach you" is the smile. He notes that it's a simple, low-risk, nonthreatening overture that requires minimal courage and doesn't have to be rehearsed beforehand. Give it a try.

opportunities for meeting men at professional seminars if you're in a female field such as health care or early childhood education, look for more generic courses which may attract men in related fields. For example, nurses or occupational therapists could attend a course in "Humor and Healing," which could appeal to physicians as well. Preschool teachers might think about a workshop in "Developmental Cognition," which might also be chosen by psychologists.

Finding out about seminars, workshops, and conventions shouldn't present any difficulty for you if you belong to a professional association. You'll receive many advertisements for seminars in the mail, and you can read about them in your professional journals and newsletters.

Dale Carnegie Training

The Dale Carnegie organization is dedicated to helping men and women develop their potential and achieve success in business, family, and social life. They offer training in communication, human relations, public speaking, management, sales, and customer relations. Instead of being in a passive lecture format, these classes are highly interactive. Students present reports and talks and practice problem-solving and decision-making techniques. Everyone listens to all presentations and offers positive and constructive feedback.

If you'd like to improve your business and personal relationships, develop more leadership skills, enhance your communication and public speaking skills, and formulate a more positive and enthusiastic outlook on life, these courses can be most helpful. Each course consists of fourteen 3½-hour sessions. They are generally held in the evening.

More than 3.5 million people have graduated from Dale Carnegie courses. Over 170,000 enroll each year. About two-thirds are men. Although there is a wide range of ages among participants, the majority are in the 25-to-49 group. Over 34 percent have a bachelor's degree.

The men you'll meet here are ambitious and motivated. Even if they don't start out as good communicators, the course will help them improve their conversation skills.

Dale Carnegie training is available in 1,077 cities across the United States. Local licensed representatives are listed in the white pages of the phone book. For more information, write:

**Dale Carnegie and
    Associates Inc.**
1475 Franklin Avenue
Garden City, NY 11530
(800) 213-5800

Dance Instruction

Dancing is one of the most enjoyable activities around, but all too many people never get a chance to participate because they lack a dancing partner or feel too self-conscious about their lack of skills. Dance instruction can alleviate both these concerns. You don't need a partner for group dance lessons. It's even okay if you have two left feet. Professional dance instructors can teach virtually anyone to dance and make it fun to learn. Lessons are available in ballroom, swing, Latin, disco, and country-western. You can find listings under Dance Instruction in your Yellow Pages. In addition to the large national chains like Fred Astaire and Arthur Murray, your community will have some smaller local schools. Investigate a few schools before you give any time or money to dance instruction. Only you, of course, can determine which instructors, students, and facilities you like best.

Dance schools have an undeserved reputation for being a haven for elderly widows or socially awkward people with limited social outlets. True, there are a lot of senior citizens in the daytime classes, but younger people enroll in the classes held at night. Most are not desperately searching for a lover (although they're open to the possibility)—they simply want to learn to dance or improve their dancing skills.

Financial Seminars

If you really want to be in control of your life, it's imperative for you to take charge of your finances. Every day you allow to go by without learning how to manage your money is another day your money isn't working for you. So start acquiring some knowledge about investing. Stock brokerage firms, banks, insurance companies, and financial advisers all offer seminars on stocks, bonds, limited partnerships, and tax-saving tips. Read the Sunday and Monday business sections of your newspaper for listings and advertisements of these seminars.

More men than women enroll in financial seminars. Most are in their forties to sixties, although some are as young as the late twenties or early thirties. They are realistic and pragmatic, but are also comfortable with taking some chances in life and with dreaming big dreams.

Gardening Seminars

Gardening is a very satisfying activity for many people. Working the earth, planting seeds, trimming hedges, and growing flowers and vegetables can be extremely rewarding. If you have a passion for gardening, you'll enjoy learning more about your hobby by participating in seminars offered by your local garden club, botanical garden, commercial nursery, or greenhouse. Topics can range from growing roses to landscape design to pest control.

The nature of the seminar will determine the ratio of men to women in the class. A course on flower arranging will be predominantly female, but a landscaping class may have more male participants. Most of the men will be home owners in their thirties and forties. They are interested in making

---

Between ages 25 and 34, there are 119 single men per 100 single women. After age 34, single women outnumber men. By age 65, there are only 26 single men per 100 single women. This should serve as inspiration for you to start your man hunt right now. There's no time to delay. (Based on U.S. Census Bureau study, "Marital Status and Living Arrangements," March 1985.)

---

the grounds of their home as attractive as possible and enjoy nurturing growing things.

Health Seminars

There's nothing more precious than your health. Take advantage of the educational seminars offered by hospitals, medical clinics, and health professionals in your area. If you're healthy, you can attend wellness workshops to learn how to stay that way. If you do have some health concerns and problems, you can find seminars that focus on your specific ailment(s).

Women tend to enroll in such courses more than men, but men are beginning to see their value and are participating in more of them. Most are in their mid-thirties or older. Some have serious health problems, whereas others are into preventive maintenance. Don't write them off as hypochondriacs; they just have a genuine interest in promoting their health.

Read your local newspaper to find out what seminars are being offered. You can also contact hospital education departments and health organizations (such as the American Heart Association). Be on the lookout for advertisements on bulletin boards in your physician's office (for example, an allergist may hold seminars on coping with allergies) or even in your grocery store; dietitians sometimes sponsor seminars in which participants walk through food stores and learn which products are healthful and which aren't. Psychiatric hospitals and clinics also hold seminars on mental health topics such as stress management and interpersonal relations.

Home Repair and Improvement Courses

If you're a home owner, you probably care a great deal about the appearance and function of your house or condo. It's the biggest investment you'll ever make in your lifetime, so any improvements to your home will benefit you in the long run by increasing its resale value. The psychological benefit is, of course, the enjoyment that having your home exactly the way you want it brings. Your financial gains and personal satisfaction will be even greater if you do a lot of the work yourself. You can learn how to do home repair and improvement projects by attending a course given by your local home improvement/hardware store. Typical courses may include basic plumbing, tile laying, wallpaper hanging, and deck building.

You'll find very few women in these classes. They're attended mainly by men in their late twenties through fifties. Many are successful in their jobs, but they're not such workaholics that they can't devote some of their weekend hours to fixing up their homes.

Language Classes

It's an unfortunate fact of the American educational system that its students are usually unable to speak any foreign languages. If a foreign language would be helpful for you on your next vacation or in your job, consider enrolling in a language class. In addition to classes at your local college and community school adult education program, you can find classes at schools like Berlitz under Language Instruction in the Yellow Pages.

Classes often attract more men than women, especially in languages such as Spanish, Arabic, Chinese, Japanese, German, and Russian. Men in these classes are often studying these languages for business purposes. They tend to be very serious about their work and are interested in doing anything that will help them get ahead.

Music Lessons

Whether you'd like to brush up on your childhood musical skills or want to learn an instrument you've never played, music lessons enable you to experience the joy of making music. Group lessons are less expensive than individual sessions and can also put you in contact with men who share your interest in music. Find out about music lessons through your community school's adult education program or read the listings under Music Instruction in the Yellow Pages. A music store could also advise you on lessons in your area. Lessons in piano, organ, guitar, banjo, flute, recorder, saxophone, and more are probably available in your community.

There's usually an equal number of men and women in music classes. A large percentage of the men are in their twenties or younger or in their sixties or older, but you'll find a few sensitive souls in their thirties and forties who yearn for something more in their lives and believe that making music would provide fulfillment.

Obedience Training

If you have a lovable but unruly dog, do both of you a favor and sign him or her up for obedience training. A good instructor can teach you to handle your pet more effectively. You'll enjoy your dog a whole lot more if she or he is more responsive to you and your commands.

Obedience classes are attended equally by men and women. A majority are in their twenties to forties. All types of men attend these classes. Most are educated and informed. They believe that owning a pet is a responsibility that shouldn't be taken lightly. Loving but firm discipline is something they're striving to learn. (Keep in mind that these are also qualities needed for parenthood, so many of these men are prime father material.)

You can locate obedience training classes under the headings of Obedience Training, Dog Training, or Pet Training in your Yellow Pages. Your veterinarian can also make some recommendations. (Or ask a dog-walker you pass every day—he just may be your special partner!)

Real Estate Seminars

Many real estate firms offer seminars in buying and/or financing residential or commercial real estate. If you've thought about buying a home or investing in some other properties but didn't think you knew enough to take the plunge, why not attend one of these seminars and learn more?

The seminars on the basics of home buying and mortgaging are attended equally by men and women. Most are young (in their twenties and early thirties) professionals looking into buying their first home. The seminars on commercial or rental properties are more likely to attract men, since women tend to lack the finances and the confidence to become real estate tycoons. These men are apt to be financially stable businessmen in their thirties to fifties.

To find out about these seminars, read the real estate section of the Sunday edition of your local newspaper. You can also ask real estate companies whether they offer any seminars.

It's possible that you'll meet a terrific guy while attending a seminar or workshop. One woman attended a real estate seminar in 1978 and later married the instructor, Tom Hopkins, who earns $10,000 per course and does 172 seminars a year. His company grosses $10 million annually. He and his wife Debbie live in a Phoenix suburb in a six-bedroom, five-bath, $1 million house with a pool, a gazebo, and, in the driveway, a Rolls. Obviously Debbie doesn't regret attending the seminar!

Red Cross Courses

There aren't too many courses more practical than those offered by the Red Cross. You never know when you'll need first aid or CPR skills. Courses are low-cost, and many employers will pay your way so that you'll be certified to perform these services in the workplace.

In addition to swimming and lifesaving courses, many Red Cross chapters offer boating courses which are heavily attended by men. To qualify, you must have a Red Cross swimming certificate or pass a brief test in the water. Courses include Introduction to Paddling, Fundamentals of Canoeing, Basic River Canoeing, Fundamentals of Kayaking, Basic River Kayaking, Basic Outboard Boating, Basic Rowing, and Basic Sailing.

If you want to train to be part of a disaster relief team, the Red Cross offers a two-hour mini-course in Providing Red Cross Disaster Health Services. You can meet a lot of caring and capable men in these courses. Contact your local Red Cross for information.

Religious Education

Even if you balked at attending Sunday school as a child, you may feel different about religious education now. When you attend by choice rather than by parental coercion, you may find that you actually enjoy learning more about the religion you were raised in or about other religions and philosophies that are new to you. Most churches, synagogues, and fellowships offer adult religious education. These can range from the standard Bible studies of fundamental Christian churches to workshops such as "Ethics in Urban Living" at Unitarian churches.

Men and women of all ages attend religious education classes. The type of men you'll meet varies according to the specific church, but almost without exception they are sincerely interested in promoting their spirituality.

Sports Lessons

Lessons in many sports are available in your community. To find out about these activities:

- Read your local newspaper's sports and entertainment sections.
- Ask salespeople in sporting goods stores and look for posted advertisements.

A quote in Julia Grice's *How to Find Romance After 40* (New York: Evans, 1985) from an older woman about available men: "There's not a handful out there, but a landfull."

Her optimistic attitude could help you view the man-searching process in a more positive light.

- Check your Yellow Pages. Most communities will have listings under Golf Instruction, Skiing Instruction, Diving (Scuba and Snorkeling), Karate and Other Martial Arts, Yoga, Gun Safety and Marksmanship, Rifle and Pistol Ranges, Tennis Instruction, Swimming Instruction, Sailing Instruction, Skydiving and Parachute Jumping, and Riding Academies/Stables.
- Inquire at the college that's closest to you. Most physical education departments offer a range of courses (tennis, swimming, basketball, fencing, bowling).
- Look into courses offered by your community school's adult education department.
- Contact the sports associations listed in Chapter 1.

Tutoring

You're wrong if you think that only kids use tutors. One of the most common types of adult tutoring is preparation for graduate school entrance exams like the GRE (Graduate Record Examination), GMAT (Graduate Management Admission Test), LSAT (Law School Admission Test), and MCAT (Medical College Admission Test). If you've been toying with the idea of graduate school but are afraid you wouldn't pass the entrance exams, these programs will increase your confidence as well as your score. Look for programs (such as Stanley Kaplan) under Tutoring or Educational Consultants in your Yellow Pages. Many of them also offer business writing and speed reading classes that can enable you to perform your job more effectively.

There's usually an equal number of men and women in these classes. The median age is about 25, which means that half the students are older and already established in their careers but still interested in improving themselves and their situations through education.

CHAPTER 5

Great Escapes

EVEN IF YOU'RE HAPPY WITH your job, your home, and your friends, you still need to get away from it all every so often. Escaping from your normal routine can be a refreshing experience, fully rejuvenating you so that you'll be better able to deal with the demands of your everyday life when you return. To use your vacation time wisely, put some thought and energy into selecting the kind of trips and adventures that are best for you. Why opt for just another uninspired stay at the usual cottage at the beach when there are so many other options that will broaden your horizons, educate you, soothe your frazzled nerves, invigorate you, and increase the possibilities of meeting an interesting man?

The following listings are not all-inclusive, but are a good starting point. Although there are a variety of tours, schools, expeditions, and adventures, they have in common the opportunity for you to learn a new skill, do something useful, restore your body and mind, be challenged physically or mentally, see new sights, and meet new people. Each listed option merits further exploration. They are not necessarily recommendations. It is up to you to investigate the specific details of any trip, school, or experience that appeals to you. You're the only one who can determine which ones meet your own needs.

ACTIVE VACATIONS

For many people, vacations are synonymous with doing nothing more energetic than drinking, eating, sunning, and splashing in a pool. But for others, only a lot of action will do. They want to test their physical limits and to enjoy pushing their bodies to the max. Read the following listings to see whether any of them sound enticing. Also see the next section on Learning Vacations as well as the last section on Luxury Vacations, since both of these also offer activities of a physical nature.

Adventure Trips

Instead of traveling to cities in the United States and abroad that really aren't that much different from your own, why not expand your horizons and see something totally exotic? Wilderness magazines usually carry ads for many companies that lead adventure trips. (*Great Expeditions* magazine is a great source for information and ideas. Call (604) 852-6170 to find a copy in your area.) One of the most prominent packagers of adventure treks, tours, safaris, and expeditions is:

Himalayan Travel
P.O. Box 481
Greenwich, CT 06836
(203) 622-6777

They offer such trips as:

- African safaris and expeditions. Participants camp and experience the real Africa in four-wheel-drive vehicles. Included are a Kilimanjaro climb, a chimpanzee safari, and touring Morocco, Botswana, and Egypt.
- Asian treks. Participants climb the mountains in Nepal, India, Burma, Bhutan, Thailand, and Indonesia.
- Expeditions in Ecuador, Argentina, and Peru.
- European treks in Greece, Spain, and Switzerland.

About 750 people sign up with Himalayan Travel each year. The sexes are equally represented on most trips, although the African camping safaris and more physically demanding treks attract more men. The majority are between 30 and 65 years old. About half are single. Participants come from all walks of life. For some, it's that once-in-a-lifetime big trip, whereas others come back every year. You'll find all participants to have a genuine love of travel, adventure, and the outdoors.

Bicycle Tours

If you enjoy bicycling and seeing new sights, combine the two in a bicycling vacation. There's a wide variety of bicycle tours to choose from. Some involve stays at luxury inns, whereas others focus on camping out at night. Some last only a couple of days, others as long as three weeks. Some are gentle and easy; others are rugged and adventurous. They can specialize in wildlife and wilderness, culture/art, history/wine tasting, and so on. You can tour the United States or go abroad, explore tropical environments or subalpine terrains.

On most bicycle trips, even beginners can participate. Even if you haven't pedaled for years, you shouldn't have any difficulty if your tour provides a van shuttle you can ride in if you become too tired. (The support van also enables you to avoid cycling with a heavy pack on your back, can perform repairs as needed, and serves refreshments). The majority of participants find that they can comfortably ride 50 miles a day, or about three to five hours.

Read any bicycling magazine for more choices, but one of the most impressive bicycle touring companies is:

Backroads Bicycle Touring Inc.
P.O. Box 1626
San Leandro, CA 94577
(800) 533-2573
(415) 895-1783 in California

Among their many tours are singles-only trips to the California wine country and five- to six-day trips in the Idaho Sawhills, on the northwest Oregon coast, in Arizona's red rock country, Montana's Glacier National Park, southeast Vermont, and the Shenandoah Valley. They also feature trips abroad to France, Ireland, New Zealand, Bali, Australia, and China.

More than 8,000 people travel with Backroads each year. Most are Americans. There is usually an equal number of men and women. Forty percent of the participants are single (and, of course, 100 percent are single on specially designed trips for this group). The average age is between 30 and 50. About a third of the participants are beginners, a third are at the intermediate level, and a third are advanced cyclists. Tours that seem to appeal most to single men are the wine country, New Mexico, Canadian Rockies, and Colorado Rockies.

Getting to know people on a bicycle tour is very easy. When you're cycling together, friendships readily develop. There's a sense of camaraderie as the group forms a cohesive whole who looks out for each other and enjoys one another's company. You'll find men on such tours to be sociable, energetic, and adventurous without being foolhardy.

Canoe Trips

Canoe USA tours are often referred to as "soft adventure" trips. You spend your days actively paddling through the wilderness, but at night you're treated to the amenities at a country inn. Rather than cooking your own meal and camping out at the end of a tiring day as in most adventure trips, you enjoy a gourmet meal and a comfortable bed.

Two- to five-day trips are available in Vermont and Maine in the spring, summer, and fall, and central Florida in the winter. Participants are offered a variety of canoes to use, including tandem and solo ones. After a mini-clinic on safety procedures and basic paddling techniques, they paddle scenic rivers and stop by midafternoon, staying overnight at quaint country inns along the way.

Each tour is composed of 10 to 20 participants. The male-female ratio is 50-50. Ages range from the mid-twenties on up. About a third are single. You can meet well-balanced men here. They're not as adventurous as the ones you'll find on more rugged expeditions, but they don't want to sit at home, either. They enjoy being active and independent, but they also like to be pampered. They're true nature lovers who find much pleasure in the outdoors.

Canoe USA
Box 610-BR
Waitsfield, VT 05673
(802) 469-2409

Cattle Drives and Ranches

You may be a city slicker, but there could still be a little cowgirl in you. Experiencing the Old West through a cattle drive or ranch stay is not for everyone. The days are long and you're guaranteed to be saddle sore for the first few days. The accommodations (bunkhouses or tents) are far from fancy. But if you love horses and the outdoors, you'll enjoy participating in a cattle drive or working on a ranch helping to brand, vaccinate, rope, and trail cattle. Riding a horse while herding cattle from one place to another is demanding work, but it offers a challenge and satisfaction that no other vacation can provide.

Most cattle drives are limited to about 20 participants. Some ranches can hold larger numbers of people. Men and women are equally represented. They range in age from children to senior citizens and come from all over the United States and Europe. Occupations include students, lawyers, police officers, doctors, accountants, teachers, and construction workers.

The men you'll meet may be as urban as you are, but they're eager to get in touch with their more rugged and natural selves. They enjoy testing their fortitude and don't like opting for the easy way out.

Contact:

Joe and Iris Bassett
Schively Ranch
1062 Road 15
Lovell, WY 82431

or

MW Ranch
19451 195th Avenue
Hudson, CO 80642
(303) 536-4206

Covered Wagon Trips

To see the West the way the gold miners and pioneers did in 1843, try a two-, three-, or four-day covered wagon trip along the Oregon, Mormon, and Pony Express trails in Wyoming. Participants ride horses, ride or drive wagons, or walk. They sleep in teepees and cook meals over an open fire. These wagon train trips really make history come alive as you gain the perspective of our forefathers and foremothers in their struggles to settle a new land.

Each group is composed of about 25 people. They're equally divided between men and women, married and singles. The average age is about 40. Most are upper-middle-class professionals and business owners. You'll meet men here who have a sense of adventure and a willing imagination. They're good-natured and good-humored. On these trips you can get to know a man very well, without any illusions, as you camp out, cook, and ride together.

Trails West
65 Main Street
South Pass City, WY 82520
(800) 327-4052

Equestrian Holidays

If you're an accomplished horsewoman (or would like to be), vacationing at a Caribbean equestrian center would be a terrific experience for you. Chukka Cove, in Jamaica, offers lessons in riding, jumping, and polo. Mountain treks for a few hours or a few days are also available. Other activities include snorkeling, golf, tennis, deep-sea fishing, sightseeing, shopping, and nightlife in Ocho Rios. Guests stay in attractive villas.

Several hundred guests visit each year. There appears to be about a 2 to 1 ratio of women to men, but there are more men involved in polo. About half are single or travel solo. Both beginners as well as advanced polo players and riders are accommodated. The average range of ages is 30 to 45. Most are college graduates in professional or management jobs.

The men you'll meet here are typical of polo enthusiasts. They tend to be highly successful in the business world, somewhat aggressive, and aware of proper social protocol. In addition to other guests, you can also meet guest instructors such as Captain Mark Phillips (husband of Great Britain's Princess Anne) and Jack LeGoff (former trainer for the U.S. Olympic polo team).

In their book *Woulda, Coulda, Shoulda* (New York: Morrow, 1985), Dr. Arthur Freeman and Rose DeWolf note that successful brainstorming focuses on "increasing the probabilities" rather than trying to guarantee a specific end result. Think of my book as a brainstorming tool. It can't guarantee that you'll meet your ideal man, especially on the first try, but it can increase the probabilities of connecting with him or, at the very least, meeting new friends who will introduce you to other people. Expanding your social network improves your chances of finding Mr. Right.

Ask your travel agent for details or contact:

Chukka Cove Farm Ltd.
Richmond Llandovery, P.O. Box 160
Ocho Rios, Jamaica, WI
(809) 974-2239

Farm Vacations

You may be an urban sophisticate, but there are probably times when you'd love to escape from the city. Life on a farm could be just what you need to recoup from the stress and pace of city living. There are numerous farms throughout the country that welcome guests. Your hosts will provide you with room and board. You can help feed the animals, milk the cows, or operate farm machinery. In addition to farming, you can usually hike, participate in winter sports, fish, boat, or tour the countryside.

If you're a single parent, this can be an ideal vacation for you and your child to enjoy together. Many singles also travel solo for this unique experience.

Your travel agent can help you arrange a farm vacation. Michel Farm vacations is one resource for host farms in southeastern Minnesota and northwestern Iowa. Contact them at:

Michel Farm
Route #1, P.O. Box 914
Harmony, MN 55939
(507) 886-5392

Heli-Skiing

If you've become bored with the typical ski areas and want more of a challenge, consider heli-skiing. This is truly the most exciting type of skiing around. Skiers are flown in a helicopter to remote areas such as open snowfields, glaciers, and forests. SportStalker is a company that books heli-skiing tours in the mountain ranges of British Columbia from December to May. The terrain makes the skiing far more challenging than that encountered at the usual resorts and offers exquisite scenery as well. It also makes for riskier conditions (for example, avalanches), but the guides and helicopter pilots are well-trained professionals. Participants stay at lodges with Jacuzzis, massage therapy, indoor swimming pools, and so on. Specially designed skis and poles are provided at no extra cost.

More than 4,800 international guests participate in Canadian heli-skiing each season. The vast majority (as high as 90 percent) are men. Most are in their mid-thirties or slightly older and in the medical, dental, or legal professions. Participants are advanced intermediate to expert skiers. These trips are not the place for beginners to learn how to ski, but Intro-Week programs are offered for good intermediate skiers to master heli-skiing technique. Prior to the trip, it's recommended that you have skiied regularly for at least three seasons on different types of terrain and snow conditions. An exercise and stretching program should be started eight weeks in advance.

The men you'll meet heli-skiing are unique and sophisticated individuals. They don't just want to be part of the crowd but continually seek bigger challenges and new experiences. Since they push themselves to succeed at work, it is only natural that they also push themselves to achieve new skills and expertise on their vacations.

SportStalker
P.O. Box 772968
Steamboat Springs, CO 80477
(800) 525-5520

Horseback Riding

Do you love horseback riding? Does roughing it appeal to you? If so, you'll enjoy a horseback riding vacation. One of the top horseback touring companies is:

Warner and MacKenzie Guiding and Outfitting Ltd.
Box 2280
Banff, Alberta, Canada TOL OCO
(403) 762-4551

All their trips are done within the boundaries of Banff National Park in Canada. They supply everything needed for the rides, including guides, cooks, meals, accommodations, horses, and saddles. Participants usually camp out at night, although some lodge trips are available. Trips range from overnight on weekends to nine-day trips for experienced riders. Besides riding and seeing the sights, excellent opportunities are available for photography and fishing.

During the summer season (May to October), about 1,200 guests participate. The ratio of men to women is approximately 1 to 3. This is due to the tendency for most women to travel with one or two companions. But the ratio of single women traveling alone vs. single men traveling alone is 1 to 1. The average age is around the early thirties. The majority come from Canada (55 percent) and the United States (40 percent); the balance are from overseas. The most popular trip for single men appears to be the six-day full circle ride.

Men on these trips may not live like cowboys in real life, but a riding vacation appeals to a deep need within them. It enables them to explore the wilderness, challenge themselves, test their limits, and be self-reliant. This isn't a macho yearning in the negative sense of the word; it's simply a longing to be one's own man and experience the satisfaction that childhood heroes seemed to enjoy in those old Westerns.

Hostels

Don't make the mistake of confusing hostels with hotels. They both provide accommodations for travelers to eat, sleep, bathe, and relax, but there's a world of difference in terms of price and atmosphere. Hostels generally cost $4 to $14 a night and resemble dormitories in their no-frills approach. A few have cafeterias, but most provide only a fully equipped kitchen for the guests to cook their own meals. There is no maid service; you provide for your own needs. Beds come with mattresses, pillows, and blankets; each traveler brings a sleeping bag (or rents one) to use in place of sheets. All hostels have common rooms for socializing. Rules include no alcoholic beverages or illegal drugs, no pets, and no smoking. Hostels are closed during the day from 9 to 5. Lights are out and quiet is expected from 11 p.m. to 7 a.m.

The appeal of hostels goes far beyond their low cost. They offer a unique type of intimacy and hospitality. Unlike the typical hotel lobby, which guests rarely use and even more rarely use to mingle, the small common areas and shared kitchen facilities make it easy for guests to start up conversations and really get to know each other. Other features are the location and unique environment of hostels. They're found in big cities like Boston, Baltimore, Los Angeles, New York, Portland, San Francisco, Seattle, San Diego, and Washington D.C., as well as in more remote areas near national parks and attractions.

Of the 5,000 hostels worldwide in 69 nations and the more than 200 in 41 states in the United States, one is located in a lighthouse on the California coast, another is in a dude ranch in the Rockies, and others are in a mansion in Philadelphia, a converted lifeguard station on Cape Cod, a castle in West Germany, a sailing ship in Sweden, a tree house and geodesic dome in the forest in Brunswick, Georgia, and a World War II battleship (a floating hostel) in Fall River, Massachusetts.

You can arrange your own vacation in which you stay at one hostel for three days (generally the maximum allowed length of stay, unless permission is obtained from the hostel manager) and then move on to another. Depending on where you stay, your activities can include hiking in California's Redwood National Park, attending the New Orleans Mardi Gras and Jazz Festival, biking in Maine, sightseeing in Boston, or snowshoeing and cross-country skiing in Montana. Or you can take one of the World Adventure trips offered by American Youth Hostels. Most of these trips involve bicycling (skill levels ranging from moderate to tough terrain, 35 to 60-plus miles a day) or hiking (from moderately hilly elevations under 4,000 feet, 4 to 7 miles a day, to mountainous terrain elevations over 10,000 feet, 10-plus miles a day). Trips are available in New England, Canada, New York's Finger Lakes, Pennsylvania Dutch country, the Wisconsin Bikeway, the Midwest, Northwest, Alaska, California coast, San Francisco Bay area, Southwest (Utah and Arizona), Yucatán in Mexico, Europe (Belgium, Holland, France, Switzerland, England, Italy, Germany, Austria, Iceland), New Zealand, and Jamaica.

For even more adventurous types, there's a canoeing/camping trip along the United States–Canadian border (the Boundary Waters region of northern Minnesota); horsepacking/rafting in the Colorado Rockies; sailing on an 80-foot schooner and whale watching off the coast of Massachusetts; mountain cycling on all-terrain bicycles in Colorado canyons; llama trekking in New Mexico; snorkeling and beachcombing in Mexico; and windsurfing in Venezuela. If you'd rather sit back and relax, there are motor trips by jeep, van, bus, train, or ferry to New England, New Mexico, the West (Arizona, Wyoming, Colorado, Utah), Pacific Northwest (Puget Sound, British Columbia, Portland), Alaska, Guatemala, Mexico, Peru, Bolivia, Italy, France, Spain, and Great Britain.

More than 4 million hostelers belong to the International Youth Hostel Federation. Nearly 110,000 belong to the United States affiliate, American Youth Hostels. The ratio of men to women is about 1 to 1. The majority are in their twenties and thirties, although 13 percent are between 36 to 55 and 8 percent over 55. The World Adventure trips, bicycling, and the more exotic, rugged adventure trips attract more men than do the hiking or motor trips. (But this is not to say you couldn't meet a man on one of these trips, since a sizable number of men participate in these as well.) It's very possible that you'll meet some non-American men in addition to the domestic variety. At some of the major urban hostels, the percentage of foreign visitors can be as high as 70.

There is such a diversity of people who stay at hostels that it is impossible to pinpoint exactly what type of men you'll meet. Any age, background, and occupation is a possibility. The one common denominator is their openness to new people and experiences. They're friendly, spontaneous, and easygoing in their general approach to life.

To apply for membership in American Youth Hostels, contact them at:

American Youth Hostels
P.O. Box 37613, Dept. 867
Washington, DC 20013-7613
(202) 783-6161

Outward Bound

There are many adventure vacations currently available, but Outward Bound deserves special mention as the world leader in adventure-based experiential education. Founded in Britain in 1941 as a program for adolescent boys, the program has since expanded to 32 schools throughout the world, including 5 in the United States.

As a nonprofit educational organization, Outward Bound offers a non-competitive outdoor experience that enables every participant to achieve success. Activities include rock climbing, rappelling, snorkeling, backpacking, whitewater canoeing, kayaking, rowing, sailing, running, snowshoeing, backcountry skiing, ice climbing, bicycling, and camping skills such as outdoor cooking, emergency first aid, and navigation. Courses range from 3 to 28 days. Special programs are available for the visually impaired, hearing impaired, people with diabetes, college students, families, people over 40, and professionals who want to prevent or reverse career burnout.

Students learn by doing. During the first few days, training focuses on developing the stamina and basic skills needed for the rest of the adventure. Participants then work as a group to achieve common goals (such as navigating through a series of streams or climbing over a 14-foot wall) under the guidance of instructors. Depending on the length of the course, one to three days are spent alone. Courses end with a student-led expedition and a short marathon (bike ride, long swim, or run).

By the end of the course, students have gained both competence and confidence. They know themselves better, having examined their personal values and goals. They've become more self-reliant while also developing leadership and teamwork skills. Participants return to their lives reenergized and ready to tackle new challenges.

Thousands of people participate in Outward Bound each year. Most are not experienced outdoors people; many are beginners. Sixty percent are men and 40 percent are over 25. Participants come from all walks of life.

The men you'll meet here may have already achieved success in their lives, but they're not content to rest on their laurels. They want to continue to grow and take new risks. If they're not self-assured and capable when they embark on their adventure, they will be by the time it's over.

Contact the national office or any of the five Outward Bound schools.

Outward Bound USA
384 Field Point Road
Greenwich, CT 06830
(800) 243-8520
(203) 661-0797
in Connecticut

Voyageur Outward Bound School
10900 Cedar Lake Road
Minnetonka, MN 55343
(800) 328-2943
(612) 542-9255 in Minnesota

Colorado Outward Bound School
945 Pennsylvania Street
Denver, CO 80203
(303) 837-0880

Hurricane Island Outward Bound School
P.O. Box 906
Rockland, ME 04841
(800) 341-1744
(207) 594-5548 in Maine

North Carolina Outward Bound School
121 North Sterling Street
Morganton, NC 28655
(704) 437-6112

Pacific Crest Outward Bound School
0110 S.W. Bancroft Street
Portland, OR 97201
(503) 243-1993

Scuba Diving

Diving and snorkeling enthusiasts believe that no scenery can compare with that found underwater. They flock to places like the Bahamas, Jamaica,

Curaçao, Fiji, Australia, and Cozumel for water sport adventure. If you've never explored these locations or have never tried diving, you'd probably find a scuba diving vacation to be the experience of a lifetime.

There are numerous options for this type of vacation. Most feature stays at island resorts. Ask your travel agent for recommendations. A unique diving vacation involves sailing on a ship that specializes in water sports. The *Ocean Quest* is a 340-passenger floating resort that offers snorkeling, scuba diving, and underwater photography lessons. You can enjoy terrific dining, entertainment, and casinos as well as ready access to water sports.

The male-female ratio is usually about equal. All ages participate. Both beginners and advanced divers can enjoy this.

The men you'll meet here are independent and inquisitive. They enjoy experiencing new things and undertaking new challenges.

Ocean Quest International
512 South Peters Street, Suite 202
New Orleans, LA 70130
(800) 338-3483

Sport Fishing

You may have done a little fishing during one of your past vacations. If you enjoyed yourself, you may want to consider doing it more intensely, devoting most of your time to getting a prize catch. Alaska offers some of the most

If you're willing to travel to Alaska, you'll meet more men than you can handle! Consider the case of Talkeetna, a town where single men outnumber available women 20 to 1. Once a year, they invite all the women in the world to a weekend bash. About 50 women show up each year. A bachelor's auction is held where the men offer themselves to the highest bidder. You don't have to stay the winter just because you bid (starting at $2.95) on a bachelor; all you're entitled to is a drink and a dance. The bachelors seek women like themselves—strong, unmaterialistic, and adventurous. Two of them have actually found wives at one of these bachelor balls. If you're warm-blooded, you might want to check it out for yourself.

exciting sport fishing amid spectacular scenery. Your travel agent can help you select a sport fishing vacation such as that offered by Alaska Wildland Adventures. Their two- to six-day sport fishing camp will enable you to catch king salmon, silver salmon, rainbow trout, and halibut. Participants are entitled to eight hours of guided drift boat fishing a day, with nonguided fishing available in the evenings. Lodging is in rustic heated cabins. Your stay can be extended to include trips to the Columbia Glacier, Arctic air tours, and yacht cruises through the Inside Passage.

Men tend to predominate on these trips. You'll find your fellow participants to be patient and introspective individuals who have a sense of adventure.

> **Alaska Wildland**
> **Adventures**
> P.O. Box 259
> Trout Lake, WA 98650
> (800) 334-8730

Surfing

Catch a wave and a great vacation at the same time by surfing in an exotic location such as Peru or Costa Rica. Worldwide Surfing Adventures is a company specializing in foreign surfing vacations. You pack your surfboard and they do the rest, arranging for accommodations and transportation. Nonsurfing activities include windsurfing, whitewater rafting, sightseeing, and parties at night.

More than a thousand people go on these vacations each year. Over 90 percent are men. They range in age from 15 to 65. Students as well as blue-collar and white-collar workers are represented. Twenty percent are beginners.

You'll meet men who are action-oriented individualists. They like to take risks and aren't easily discouraged.

> **Worldwide Surfing**
> **Adventures**
> Morris Overseas Tours
> 418 Fourth Avenue
> Melbourne Beach, FL 32951
> (407) 725-4809

Even though she's a Hollywood script analyst, Cecille Avallone couldn't have rewritten the way she met her husband to be any more unusual. Cecille took her first rafting trip on the Colorado River in 1986. Although it wasn't love at first sight (she thought he was a roughneck who worked on oil rigs, and he thought she'd never successfully complete the trip because she was dressed inappropriately in nice clothes), Cecille got to know instructor Jim Hall very well during the seven-day trip. Shortly after the trip was over, Jim proposed and Cecille accepted. Their relationship was profiled in the November 7, 1988, issue of *People*.

Whitewater Rafting

For an exhilarating challenge, whitewater rafting is hard to beat. Riding the rapids gives you the opportunity to test your courage, develop your paddling skills, and view scenic waterways. Most people who try whitewater rafting find it an experience like no other they've ever had and usually book another trip soon after.

USA Whitewater Inc. is a company that manages reservations for four professional rafting outfitters. They offer trips ranging from half a day to nine days. (On the overnight trips, participants camp out on the river or stay in a bunkhouse lodge or cabin.) Twelve different rivers in seven (mostly Eastern) states are available, or custom trips can be planned. The number of people in the boats can range from one to ten.

Forty thousand people participate in the raft trips each year. Usually only about one-quarter are women; there's an even higher percentage of men on the roughest and most challenging trips. Both beginners and advanced rafters participate. The mix of married and single participants is about equal. The average age is somewhere in the mid-twenties to mid-thirties. Most are college graduates employed in professional fields such as medicine, law, and architecture. They lead ordinary enough lives which are generally fulfilling but they find themselves yearning for adventure and excitement. For a few days, whitewater rafting provides that adrenaline rush.

USA Whitewater Inc.
P.O. Box 277   (800) 624-8060
Rowlesburg, WV 26425   (304) 454-2475 in West Virginia

Wilderness Trips

If you enjoy wilderness experiences, look into the opportunities offered by the Sierra Club. This conservation organization sponsors more than 275 outings annually. Local chapters and groups offer more than 8,000 outings a year. Some possibilities are ski touring, backpacking, cycling, or canoeing in Alaska's Arctic Wildlife Refuge, Virgin Islands National Park, Montana's wilderness, and Madagascar.

Sierra Club
730 Polk Street
San Francisco, CA 94109
(415) 776-2211

For another wild adventure, try a vacation at an Audubon Camp affiliated with the National Audubon Society. Possibilities include:

- 7 or 12 days in western Wyoming, photographing mountain scenery and wildlife, floating down the Snake River in Grand Teton Park, hiking, rock climbing, square dancing, canoeing, and playing volleyball.

- 6 or 12 days in Maine, studying birds and the environment.

- 8 days in the Pacific Northwest, investigating the ecology of ancient forests (from 200 to 1,000 years old).

- 8 days in Texas, exploring the landscape of Big Bend National Park, relaxing in a mineral hot spring, floating the waters of the Rio Grande, or horseback riding.

- 6 days in Greenwich, Connecticut, identifying and learning about birds, photographing nature, and stargazing.

- 6 days at Sanibel Island, Florida, photographing nature.

- 8 days at Yellowstone, photographing nature during winter, exploring on cross-country skis.

- 7 days in southeast Arizona, learning about plant and animal life in the Chiricahua Mountains.

Participants must be 18 or older. They reflect the general Audubon demographics: mostly college-educated, almost half single, and men and women are equally represented.

Audubon Ecology Camps and Workshops
National Audubon Society
613 Riversville Road
Greenwich, CT 06831
(203) 869-2017

Hawaii is more than the glitter of Waikiki. To really see Hawaii at its best, go on an Eye of the Whale tour. They offer five-day whale-watching and trade-wind sailing trips, in addition to a seven-day sailing/hiking adventure (across the crater floor of the world's largest active volcano, Kilauea) and a ten-day hiking odyssey. Islands explored are Kauai, Molokai, and Hawaii. Nature study, adventure, and relaxation are combined for an unforgettable experience. The marine/wilderness adventures emphasize hands-on experience and group participation, including taking photographs and recording vocalizations of whales and porpoises, hoisting sails and taking the helm. Accommodations are in scenic inns, cabins, and sailing yachts.

About 200 people participate in these adventures each year. Each group tour is composed of four to ten people and two naturalist guides. The proportion of men to women is 40–60, possibly because women more frequently travel in pairs. But 65 percent of the participants do travel solo. The range of ages is 30 to 70, with 45 being the average. Most come from the east and west coasts and are well-educated (doctors, lawyers, teachers, computer analysts). You don't need to be an experienced sailor, snorkeler, or hiker to participate; the only requirement is good general health.

Eye of the Whale
P.O. Box 1269
Kapaa, Hawaii 96755
(808) 889-0227

Yet another wilderness outfit is American Wilderness Experience, whose comprehensive and innovative listing of adventure/wilderness vacations includes:

- Snowmobile trips during the winter at Yellowstone National Park.
- Horseback trips in the western United States and Canadian Rockies.
- Llama trekking through the wilderness of Colorado or Wyoming.
- Fishing trips in Alaska, Wyoming, or Canada.
- Backpacking in the western United States.
- Whitewater rafting in the western United States.

- Canoe trips in Vermont, New York, and Minnesota.
- Hiking and sea kayaking in the Alaska wilderness.

Of the many participants each year, 40 percent are single; 45 percent are men. The largest age group is 30 to 45. Most popular among the men are the horseback, rafting, and snowmobiling trips.

American Wilderness Experience
P.O. Box 1486
Boulder, CO 80306
(800) 444-0099
(303) 494-2992 in Colorado

LEARNING VACATIONS

Vacations aren't necessarily a time to deactivate your brain. It can be very fulfilling to use your time off from work to learn something new. Possibilities range from active sports to archaeology. Maybe one of the following will be right for you.

Academic Study Trips

To challenge your intellect, meet some men, and earn college credits, nothing beats study sessions offered by major colleges and universities. Usually held in the summer for three-week sessions, these programs are sponsored by American educational institutions but are held abroad. Imagine studying Shakespeare or Chaucer at Oxford! The University of California at

In their best-selling book, *Smart Women, Foolish Choices* (New York: Clarkson N. Potter, 1985), Drs. Connell Cowan and Melvyn Kinder note that 80 percent of all single women seem to be interested in a select 20 percent of the available men. You don't have to be a skilled statistician to realize that these numbers can't work very well for the majority of women. If you learn to keep an open mind about the type of man who can make you happy, you might find that you're interested in 30, 40, 50, or even a higher percent of the men you'll meet . . . and this will significantly increase your options.

When you're traveling abroad, keep the following signals in mind for how men around the world react to seeing an attractive woman. This will help you recognize when a man is interested.

A Frenchman kisses his fingertips.

The Greek strokes his cheek.

The Italian presses his forefinger into his cheek and rotates it.

An American lifts his eyebrows.

(Based on *Do's and Taboos Around the World,* edited by Roger E. Aytell, New York: Wiley, 1985.)

Berkeley can enable you to do just that. They also offer travel/study opportunities in Paris, Scotland, Venice, and Kyoto.

Thousands of people have participated in these courses. Usually about 20 to 50 enroll in each travel/study experience. Slightly more women than men participate. Although younger people do attend and enjoy themselves thoroughly, the age range is typically between 40 and 60.

By participating in a study session abroad, you'll meet brainy men from the United States and Europe. They have a great deal of intellectual curiosity and prefer companions with similar qualities.

Your local college may sponsor such courses, or you can contact:

University of California Berkeley Extension
Marketing Department 14
2223 Fulton Street
Berkeley, CA 94720
(415) 642-3112

Archaeology

For more than a thousand years, a primitive people, the Anasazi, farmed the land around the Mesa Verde Plateau in southwestern Colorado. At the beginning of the 12th century A.D. there were at least 10,000 Anasazi; by the end of the 13th century they had all disappeared. No written records were left behind, but the artifacts of their daily life were well-preserved.

Archaeologists are still conducting research into these people, their lifestyle, why they abandoned the area, and where they went.

The Crow Canyon Archaeological Center, situated in the middle of this area (4 miles from Cortez, Colorado, and 400 miles from Denver), carries out research attempting to solve the mystery of the Anasazi. The center allows participants without any formal training to work with its archaeologists at the excavation sites and laboratories. The low-cost tuition paid by participants covers dormitory-style housing and meals.

Most field seminars last a week. The Winter Lab program, which includes artifact analysis, cataloging, and processing, runs for two weeks. Hundreds of novices, ranging from young adults to retirees, participate in the research. Men and women are equally represented. The men you'll meet have a great deal of intellectual curiosity and interest in other people.

Crow Canyon Archaeological Center
23390 County Road K   (800) 422-8975
Cortez, CO 81321   (303) 565-8975 in Colorado

Crafts

Anderson Ranch Arts Center is a nonprofit educational organization that offers workshop programs in ceramics, painting, photography, woodworking, furniture design, and printmaking. Each summer, some 70 one-, two-, and three-week workshops are led by nationally recognized artists and craftspeople, for novice through professional levels.

The ranch is located in the mountain resort community of Snowmass Village, Colorado (ten miles west of Aspen). It features a mixture of historic log cabins, barns, and modern studio facilities. On-campus housing and a dining hall are available; faculty and students dine together. Off-campus condominiums are also available. Smoking is not permitted in any ranch buildings. The Aspen/Snowmass area offers many cultural activities such as classical music, ballet, art, and theater, in addition to outdoor activities such as hiking, whitewater rafting, and gold-medal fishing.

Each summer, more than 900 workshop participants come from all 50 states and several foreign countries. About 43 percent are men. The average age is 42. Twenty percent are novices, 43 percent are serious amateurs, and 37 percent are professional artists.

The men you'll meet here are both creative and practical. They're not into mind games like other artists can be (such as some painters or sculptors). These men just want to honestly communicate in a meaningful way.

Anderson Ranch Arts Center
P.O. Box 5598
5263 Owl Creek Road
Snowmass Village, CO 81615
(303) 923-3181

Fly Fishing

Whether you want to learn how to fish or to improve your skills and technique, a weekend at a school for saltwater fly fishing will be fun and informative. And what better place to do this than "The Sportsfishing Capital of the World"? Less than two hours from Miami International Airport, the Florida Keys are the perfect tropical setting for instruction and recreation.

The Florida Keys Fly Fishing School holds weekend classes that incorporate films, slides, discussions, and field exercises. The school specializes in teaching how to use fly rods to catch the tropical flats species such as tarpon, bonefish, snook, redfish, and mutton snapper. Topics include casting, sighting fish, fly selection, tying, and presentation; tackle selection; knots; wind problems; fighting fish; and flats etiquette. The school does not offer any actual fishing in the program, but most students opt to extend their stay to fish in the Everglades National Park or on the flats around Islamorada. Students usually stay at the Plantation Yacht Harbor Resort. Equipment is available from most of the top manufacturers, so it is not necessary to bring your own fly fishing gear.

The school hosts about 20 students per session. About three-quarters are men and 25 percent are single. The average age is between 30 and 45. Most are college graduates, upper-income professionals with a large percentage in the medical field.

The song "Some Enchanted Evening" describes seeing a stranger in a room full of people and the chance encounter leading to love. Note that the lyrics specify a *crowded* room.

Staying home alone does not lead to meeting the man of your dreams, even in a romantic musical. Find your own crowded room where you can meet some interesting strangers. . . .

As you might expect, you'll meet active outdoorsmen who love a challenge. They know how to relax, but they don't just vegetate. Having fun while doing something useful is more their style.

Florida Keys Fly Fishing School
P.O. Box 603
Islamorada, FL 33036
(305) 664-5423

Golf Schools

If you've toyed with the idea of taking up golf but don't know which end of the club to hold, a week or weekend at a golf school can set you on the right course. If you already know the game but want to improve your skills, golf school can be an enjoyable vacation. Most schools are held at luxurious resorts and allow some time for nongolf activities such as other sports and cocktail parties. Individualized group instruction is offered, usually in the morning on practice tees, with the afternoons allotted to actual play on the golf course. Students are often videotaped and also receive a computer analysis of their biomechanics.

Some schools have as many as a thousand participants a year. Men usually outnumber women by more than 2 to 1. The weekend participants tend to be younger (twenties and thirties) than those who attend for the full week. Most are upper middle class.

The men here are usually calm and even-tempered. They like to put a lot of thought into everything they do, and this approach has made them successful in life.

For a listing of more than 80 golf schools, contact:

National Golf Foundation
1150 South U.S. Highway One
Jupiter, FL 33477
(407) 744-6006

Hang Gliding

Hang gliding is an exciting sport, but it can seem intimidating if you've never tried it. The best (and safest) way to experience and learn hang gliding is to take a course at a United States Hang Gliding Association Certified Flight School.

Kitty Hawk Kites is the largest USHGA Certified Flight School. Located at Nags Head (a beach resort town in North Carolina's Outer Banks), the school has taught at least 140,000 students to fly during the last two decades. Beginner lessons include classroom time on the basics of flight and five flights at the training site. Tandem towing is offered, whereby an instructor is paired with a student on a ten-minute, 1,500-foot training flight. Advanced lessons are also available. Flying over the soft sand helps reduce the injury rate, since the sand is very forgiving. (The injury rate is roughly one in every thousand participants and usually involves wrists or arms.) More adventurous (or foolhardy!) students can fly over mountains.

In addition to hang gliding camps and vacation packages, climbing classes, Jacuzzis, roller skating, windsurfing, and stunt kite (kites that perform aerobatic maneuvers controlled with two or four lines) flying lessons are available.

An estimated 15,000 students participate in Kitty Hawk's programs each year. Two-thirds of the students are men. About 57 percent fall between the ages of 21 and 35. The majority are beginners. The most common occupations/professions are college student, engineer, military, medical, and computer programmer. Most come from Washington, D.C., New York, Virginia, North Carolina, and Ohio. Requirements are a weight of 90 to 225 pounds. Students participate year-round. The spring and fall are particularly recommended because the Outer Banks aren't so crowded.

You'll meet risk-taking men here who are dynamic and unafraid. They want more from life than guarantees and safety.

Kitty Hawk Kites
P.O. Box 1839
3941 S. Croatan Highway at Jockey's Ridge
Nags Head, NC 27959
(919) 441-4124

Homebuilding

Anyone who has ever designed or built his or her own house will tell you it's one of the most meaningful and satisfying experiences you can have. If you're tired of cookie-cutter or unaffordable homes, take matters into your own hands. For a real learning and working vacation, consider attending a two-week course where you'll learn to map out a floor plan, build a model, and draft a set of preliminary blueprints based on materials specifications, cost estimating, energy calculations, and mechanical and electrical design. In addition to theory, you'll learn problem-solving and actual construction techniques on building sites. Classes are personalized so you can get what you want out of them, but you should leave with the knowledge and skills that will enable you to participate in the construction of your dream house at whatever level suits your time, budget, and interests.

At the Yestermorrow Design/Build school (which also includes a one-week cabinetry and four-week renovation course), up to 100 students enroll each summer. They're housed at a nearby lodge and provided with meals. About 65 percent are men. Students are accepted from age 17 up; some participants have been in their sixties. Students come from all over to this unique school: London, Hawaii, the Dominican Republic, Sweden, and throughout the United States.

The two-week Design/Build course is for laypeople; design or construction experience is not necessary. You can participate even if you've never picked up a hammer before. Although there are many types of men who go to this school, the common element is their interest in their living environments. They truly care about where and how they live, and want to have some control over it rather than be at the mercy of someone else's idea and work.

Yestermorrow Inc.
P.O. Box 76A
Warren, VT 05674
(802) 496-5545

Oceanography

Project Ocean Search (POS) is a series of intensive field-study programs conducted each year by the Cousteau Society. A limited number of participants are allowed to join a Cousteau Society team on expeditions to remote island areas. Sessions typically last 12 to 14 days with about 35 participants per session. Although not required, scuba diving is strongly recommended for full participation. Participants and staff are housed in tents. Sleeping gear and eating utensils must be provided by each participant.

Past POS sessions have ranged from Wuvulu in Papua New Guinea to Mosquito Island in the British Virgin Islands. Less remote locations include

Thomas W. McKnight and Robert H. Phillips suggest in their book *Love Tactics* (Garden City, N.Y.: Avery, 1988) that the love you've always dreamed of is most likely to materialize as you pursue your own destiny and attempt to find your ultimate personal satisfaction and happiness in your own way. Use this book to do just that.

Santa Cruz Island off the southern California coast. Daily activities include diving and snorkeling, exploring the environment above the water, and lectures on island ecosystems, marine biology, history of the area, and literature about the sea.

Both men and women participate, ranging in age from 16 to 45. You'll find men here to be adventurous, less materialistic than most, and open to self-discovery and promoting healthy change within themselves.

For more information, contact:

Project Ocean Search
Cousteau Society
930 West 21st Street
Norfolk, VA 23517
(804) 627-1144

Photography Tours

As opposed to a photographic workshop, which concentrates on photographic technique in a structured format, photography tours emphasize travel experiences with professional photographers. Most photo tours focus on nature. This can include iguanas in the Galapagos, polar bears in Manitoba, antelope in Botswana, wildflower meadows in the Canadian Rockies, bison in Yellowstone, pueblos and canyons in the American southwest.

Photo tour participants are generally enthusiastic amateurs, but some are professional photographers. Beginners can sign up; all that's needed is 35mm equipment. The number of men and women is about equal. Most are 35 to 55 years old.

The men you'll meet here are highly visual yet analytical. They're sensual *and* intellectual. They can be somewhat into themselves, but they're able to relate to other people with whom they have something in common.

Some options include:

Close-Up Expeditions
1031 Ardmore Avenue
Oakland, CA 94610
(415) 465-8955

Joseph Van Os Photo Safaris
P.O. Box 655
Vashon Island, WA 98070
(206) 463-5383

Rowing

Three to seven days at a rowing school can teach you the basics or help you perfect your stroke. Sculling in a single shell gives you a complete aerobic workout and tones the shoulders, back, abdomen, arms, and legs. It also provides you with a sense of exhilaration as you move yourself across the water and an inner peace at being one with the craft on the placid waters of a lake.

The Florida Rowing Center provides instruction for beginning to advanced rowers. (The only prerequisite for participation is reasonable swimming skills.) Each student is videotaped and critiqued daily. Participants usually stay at the Palm Beach Polo and Country Club, a luxurious resort facility adjacent to the center. Nonrowing activities can include bicycling, hiking, golfing, polo, shopping, and dining in Palm Beach. Sculling is in season at the Florida Rowing Center from mid-November to mid-May.

More than 300 students participate each season; 60 percent are men. Ages range from early teens to mid-seventies. The average age is the late thirties. Students come from all over the United States and Canada. They are mostly college graduates and their principal occupations are medicine and law (although there is a wide range of participants with diverse backgrounds).

Florida Rowing Centers Inc.
1140 Fifth Avenue
New York, NY 10128
(212) 996-1196

Sailing/Boating

Sailing is invigorating and soothing at the same time. Acquiring sailing skills gives a real sense of accomplishment and opens the door to a variety of travel experiences all over the world. A vast number of sailing schools exist in prime locations all over the country. Each has its own personality and characteristics, but all of them can enable beginners to learn how to sail and experienced sailors to sail better.

Just a few schools are listed below.

Annapolis Sailing School. The school bills itself as the first and largest sailing school in the country, with more than 80,000 people served to date, more than 120 boats, and its own marina personnel to maintain the boats. It offers courses for two, three, or four days, including:

- Become a Sailor in One Florida Weekend (lecture, classroom instruction, and instruction aboard the sailboat).
- Three-Day New Sailors Mini-Holiday (students command their boats while instructors on an escort boat supervise).
- Florida Sun Coast New Sailors Vacation Course (five-day course includes classroom instruction, on-board sailing instruction, cruising, and navigation).
- Weekend Introduction to Cruising (on a large sailboat, students learn the rudiments of chart reading and navigation, plus the operation of the engine, galley, and electrical systems).

The school has six locations: in St. Petersburg, Florida; Marathon, Florida; Charleston, South Carolina; Greenport, Long Island, New York; St. Croix, Virgin Islands and Annapolis, Maryland.

> **Annapolis Sailing School**
> P.O. Box 3334
> Annapolis, MD 21403
> (800) 638-9192
> (301) 267-7205 in Maryland

Chapman School of Seamanship. The school offers a two-week recreational boating course and a one-week course in handling small boats, in addition to career programs in Professional Mariner Training, Yacht and Small Craft Surveying, and Yacht Buying.

Contact them at:

> 4343 S.E. St. Lucie Blvd.
> Stuart, FL 34997
> (407) 283-8130

Florida Sailing and Cruising School. This school offers programs to develop and improve cruising skills while on a vacation. Both "ashore" and "afloat" classes are offered. They include:

- Basic Sailing (three days of sailing in a boat of 20 to 30 feet in moderate winds and sea conditions).
- Basic Coastal Cruising (two days of cruising in local and regional waters as both skipper and crew of an auxiliary sailing or cruising vessel up to 35 feet).
- Advanced Coastal Cruising (acting as skipper and part of the crew of a 30-to-50-foot vessel, day or night, in coastal or inland waters).

Florida Sailing and Cruising School
3444 Marinatown Lane NW
North Fort Myers, FL 33903
(800) 262-SWFY
(813) 656-1339 in Florida

Steve and Doris Colgate's Offshore Sailing School. Concentrated learning opportunities include Learn to Sail, Introductory Racing, Advanced Sailing, and Advanced Racing. Courses range from six to eight days and are given at South Seas Plantation, Captiva Island, Florida; Tortola, British Virgin Islands; St. Lucia; and Cape Cod, Massachusetts. Contact them at:

Steve and Doris Colgate's Offshore Sailing School
16731 McGregor Blvd.
Fort Myers, FL 33908
(800) 221-4326
(813) 454-1700 in Florida

Smithsonian Study Tours and Seminars

The Smithsonian Institution of Washington, D.C., offers a vast variety of well-planned study tours, seminars, and research expeditions. All are learning experiences guaranteed to broaden your intellectual horizons.

Study Tours. Travelers experience in-depth exploration of an area of the United States or a multitude of foreign countries. A study tour typically lasts from three days to three weeks. Past tours have included:

- Baja whale watch. Exploring islands from San Diego to San Ignacio Lagoon.
- Okefenokee. Canoeing in a wildlife refuge.
- Civil War sites. Studying battlegrounds in Virginia.
- New York City. Exploring art deco architecture.
- British theater. Attending theatrical productions and meeting performers.
- Mexico. Observing village celebrations and customs.
- India wildlife safari. Viewing rare species of birds and animals.

Seminars. Topics are explored in depth during seminars that combine classroom study with related tours led by top scholars. Seminars last no more than five days and generally take place in Washington, although a few are held in other cities. Examples of offerings include:

- Washington: Examine air power and the Battle of Britain.
  Learn about animal communication at the National Zoo.
  Study contemporary furniture design and visit working studios.
  Study African art.
- Fort Pierce, Florida: Study marine life at the Smithsonian Research Station on Florida's east coast.
- Tucson, Arizona: Study astronomy at Smithsonian's Whipple Observatory.

The Smithsonian attracts about 6,000 travelers a year, ranging in age from 30 to 75 (with a median age of 55). Two-thirds are singles; about half are men. The more active, outdoor trips attract more single men. The Smithsonian notes that its travelers reflect the demographics of the general membership, which has the highest income and educational levels of any magazine readership.

The men you'll meet on Smithsonian study tours and seminars are well-educated professionals. The ones who participate in the seminars tend to be a little more traditional and intellectual. Those on the study tours want to combine mental and sensory stimulation. They're extremely bright, but they don't just want to ponder information in books; they want to see, hear, smell, taste, and touch the wonders of the world.

The trips require Smithsonian membership ($20 a year; it includes their monthly magazine). A free biannual travel newsletter is available. Contact:

Smithsonian Associates Travel Program
1100 Jefferson Drive SW
Washington, DC 20560
(202) 357-4700

Waterskiing

If you're an avid water-skier or have always wanted to learn, a waterskiing school could be the perfect vacation for you. Most schools, in addition to providing ski instruction in their lakes, also offer other outdoor activities such as swimming, badminton, volleyball, and basketball. Some schools videotape students so they can later review their performance; others provide mental training sessions and a skiing psychology library.

Several hundred students enroll each year in the average waterskiing school. The male-female ratio is about 3 to 1. Ages range from 8 to 68. The average age is usually in the early twenties. Almost two-thirds of students are competitive skiers; the rest are strictly recreational. The men you'll meet tend to be active, energetic individuals who enjoy a moderate amount of risk. They're outgoing but not overly gregarious. Although they can work well and cooperatively with others, they're independent types who prefer to rely on themselves and their abilities rather than letting someone else assume responsibility.

Consider the following schools.

Benzel Skiing Center
P.O. Box 216
Groveland, FL 32736
(904) 429-3574

Bill Peterson Ski School
P.O. Box 835
Windermere, FL 32786
(407) 876-5966

**Mike Seipel's Barefoot
    International Ski Schools
    and Traveling Clinics**
140 South Main Street
Thiensville, WI 53092
(800) 932-0685

**Mike Suyderhoud
    Water Ski Center**
P.O. Box 2052
Redding, CA 96099
(916) 222-8826

Writers' Retreats and Workshops

Is the Great American Novel somewhere deep inside you, but you just haven't had the opportunity to let it out? If you yearn to be a published author and wish that your life permitted you to sit down and write, a writer's retreat may be just what you need to get started. A retreat will let you escape from the demands of your everyday life and devote yourself to your writing. Classes and seminars will provide instruction, while your fellow aspiring writers will support you in your quest.

Consult writing magazines such as *The Writer* and *Writer's Digest* (available at libraries and bookstores) for advertisements about these retreats. One possibility is the Writer's Retreat Workshop, offered for ten days every summer and fall in a Victorian house in Bristol, Connecticut. This experience draws participants with ideas for a novel or novels in progress. Classes are offered in the morning, while afternoons are reserved for working on assignments. Evenings may feature more instruction or entertainment. A professional writer directs the courses and provides New York literary agents and editors as guest speakers. About 12 people from all over the country participate in each session. The male-female composition averages about 50-50, with some sessions having more men and others more women. The average age is 40. Most participants are unpublished writers, but the goal of the workshop is to complete the novel for submission to a publisher or agent.

Obviously, you'll meet men here who have been bitten by the writing bug. Getting published is their dream and hope. If you share their aspirations, you'll find camaraderie that doesn't exist in many other places. Contact:

Write It/Sell It Seminars
74 Bolton Road
P.O. Box 139
South Lancaster, MA 01561
(508) 368-0287

A woman is quoted in *Smart Women, Foolish Choices* by Drs. Connell Cowan and Melvyn Kinder (New York: Clarkson N. Potter, 1985) as defining the qualities of the perfect man: Richard Gere's body, Dustin Hoffman's grin, Lee Iacocca's business savvy, Robert Redford's charm, and Pat Boone's commitment to family.

Don't limit your love life by harboring such unreasonable expectations. Keep an open mind for a real man who has his own special qualities.

HELPING VACATIONS

Vacations are typically a time to be good to ourselves. Most people relax, take it easy, and indulge themselves. But a small minority of vacationers choose to look beyond their own needs and do something constructive to help someone or something else. And in the long run, they themselves gain a great deal in the process. People who have participated in the following helping vacations are enthusiastic about what they've accomplished and feel they took away something valuable from the experience. The knowledge, skills, and sense of satisfaction cannot be duplicated by other types of vacations.

Center for Coastal Studies

The private, nonprofit Center for Coastal Studies conducts research that protects great whales, threatened marine ecosystems, and Cape Cod's unique environments. The center accepts volunteers to collect data on whales April 15 to October 30. Volunteers are expected to work eight hours a week. Housing is not provided; volunteers need to find their own in the Cape Cod area. The men you'll meet on this project are nature lovers who are interested in all aspects of life.

Center for Coastal Studies
59 Commercial Street
Box 1036
Provincetown, MA 02657
(508) 487-3022

Earthwatch

Earthwatch is a nonprofit institution that supports scientific research worldwide through its Earth Corps of citizens and scholars working together to improve our understanding of the planet. Each year 3,000 volunteers work in 27 states and 46 countries. They pay a share of the costs of the research project as well as covering their own lodging, board, and travel expenses. Tax deductions are available for some of the expenses as a contribution to scientific research.

Participants perform such functions as tagging fish, measuring acid rain, and interviewing rural residents. Expeditions have included:

- Art and archaeology: archaeoastronomy, architecture, textiles, folklore, and art history.
- Geosciences: paleontology, volcanology, climatology, geology, oceanography, glaciology, and limnology.
- Life sciences: conservation biology, ornithology, botany, applied ecology, mammalogy, herpetology, wildlife management, primatology, entomology, and zoology.
- Marine sciences: ecology, mammalogy, herpetology, ichthyology, and invertebrate biology.
- Social sciences: public health, nutrition, and medical and economic anthropology.

Women slightly outnumber men in Earthwatch projects. Volunteers range in age from 16 to over 80. The largest percentage (25 percent) is between 36 and 45. Most are professionals, students, educators, managers, scientists, and engineers. Most stay two to three weeks. The men here are active and open-minded individuals.

Earthwatch
680 Mount Auburn Street
Box 403
Watertown, MA 02172
(617) 926-8200

Foundation for Field Research

The Foundation for Field Research is a nonprofit organization that coordinates field research projects relating to anthropology, archaeology, art history, astronomy, botany, ecology, entomology, ethnobotany, ethnology, folklore, folk medicine, geology, herpetology, historic architecture, marine biology, ornithology, paleontology, primatology, and zoology. Interested members of the public contribute both their physical and financial assistance. These volunteers participate under the guidance of professional scientists and researchers. They cover their own travel expenses (airfare is usually tax-deductible) and share the cost of the expedition as well as giving their time and skills. Lengths of stay can vary from two days to one month. The majority of projects are from one to two weeks.

Past research projects have included:

• Observing chimpanzees' use of tools in Liberia, West Africa.
• Digging at archaeological sites in Europe, the United States, and the Caribbean.
• Taking a census of whales in the St. Lawrence River, Canada.
• Collecting plants in Grenada, West Indies.
• Making architectural drawings of historic adobe buildings in Mexico.
• Tracing and mapping a volcano that erupted in Texas 32 million years ago.
• Patrolling a beach in Mexico collecting eggs and raising hatchlings to protect giant leatherback turtles from extinction.
• Canoeing down the Missouri River in Montana to study prairie dog colonies.

More than 400 volunteers participate each year. Men and women are equally represented. The age range is 13 to 86, with an average of 45 years. The only requirement is a willingness to work for the scientists toward project goals. Volunteers have included doctors, housewives, students, teachers, managers, secretaries, factory workers, librarians, lawyers, and retirees.

Many of the men you'll meet here are playing out fantasies of being archaeologists, oceanologists, or primatologists. They may always have dreamed of doing this type of work, but practicality won out and placed them in more pedestrian careers. Rather than just bemoan their fate, however, they've chosen to make their dreams come true . . . if only for a week or two. It's not every man who takes action and tries to bring romance and drama into his life, so consider these men to be special indeed.

Foundation for Field Research
P.O. Box 2010
Alpine, CA 92001-0020
(619) 445-9264

Habitat for Humanity Work Camps

If you were a former United States president, what would you do with your vacation time? Travel to Tahiti? Ski in the Alps? Not if you're Jimmy Carter!

This former president picks up a hammer instead and helps build homes for needy families. Thousands of other people from all stations of life have joined him in this worthwhile endeavor. Maybe you should consider spending your next vacation doing the same. When the week is over, you'll be physically tired but emotionally energized.

Habitat for Humanity is an ecumenical Christian housing ministry that seeks to provide decent shelter for the poor. Through donations of money, materials, and volunteer labor, Habitat builds and rehabilitates houses. These buildings are not simply given to needy families; instead, home owners are required to participate in the construction project. The finished houses are sold to partner families for no profit (most Habitat houses in the United States average $30,000) with no-interest mortgages. Recipient families are chosen without regard to race or religion. No government funds are accepted for these endeavors.

Habitat has 400-plus affiliate projects in the United States and Canada. There are also projects in 26 developing countries. More than 3,000 homes are built each year. To become involved with this organization, you can join an affiliate in or near your community. But there are also work camps where individuals spend a week or more at a project outside their area. Participants perform construction tasks as well as office work. Volunteers pay for transportation to and from the work camp. In some areas, housing is available for volunteers; in others, individuals find their own housing.

About 400 people join work camps each year. The ratio of men to women is about even. You don't have to know anything about construction to participate, nor do you have to be a member of a Christian church, although Habitat *is* a Christian organization. Women participants tend to be in their twenties to early thirties and fifties to sixties, whereas the male participants' ages encompass the whole range equally from 18 to 70.

You may not meet a former president, but you *will* meet a variety of men by volunteering in one of these projects. Without exception, you can expect to find warm, caring men whose faith is important to them. These men choose to express their spirituality and love for humanity by taking direct action to help solve one of the most pressing social problems of our time: the lack of affordable, decent housing.

Habitat for Humanity
Habitat and Church Streets
Americus, GA 31709-3498
(912) 924-6935

Smithsonian Research Expeditions

As one of our nation's treasures, the Smithsonian Institution has a wide variety of museums and archives. Volunteers are needed to contribute their time, talent, and financial resources to Smithsonian research. They work with curators at the Smithsonian or at field sites around the country and the world.
Past projects have included:

- Documenting the annual rodeo in Cheyenne, Wyoming.
- Photographing the Festival of American Folklife in Washington, D.C.
- Excavating slave quarters and a cemetery at a Caribbean sugar plantation in Montserrat.
- Monitoring the Arenal volcano and studying local vegetation in Costa Rica.
- Preparing museum collections of animal bones for transfer to a new facility in Washington, D.C.

The men in the research expeditions have a thirst for experience. They want to work hard and make a contribution. They're intelligent, dynamic, and committed, but they don't have such an overinflated opinion of themselves that they mind getting dirty, doing hard, physical labor or menial duties, and working as part of a team.

Associates Research Expeditions
1100 Jefferson Drive SW
Washington, DC 20560
(202) 357-1350

Volunteer Vacations Program

Anybody who enjoys hiking needs to be concerned about the nation's trails. There are fewer miles of trails in America today than there were 40 years ago. Trails have been lost to urban development, logging roads and logging operations, and many other side effects of "progress." To help build new trails and rebuild substandard ones, the American Hiking Society's Volunteer Vacations Program recruits trails enthusiasts from around the country

In her book *How to Find Romance After 40* (New York: Evans, 1985), Julia Grice gives a gentle reminder that there's more to life than the boob tube. She notes that TV watching is nonproductive in that it doesn't offer much opportunity to meet men. The only eligible men are on the screen and you can't get to them! Use this book to find a way out of your house and into the life of a real, living man!

and then sends teams to public lands where trail work is needed. The program operates in the winter, spring, and summer. About 300 volunteers take up picks and shovels each year. Food and shelter are provided by public agencies or by grants from corporations. Volunteers travel to the work site, usually at their own expense, and spend two weeks working on the projects. The work is so rewarding that half the volunteers return.

Complete information about volunteers is not available, but you can expect to find a lot of men in their twenties through forties. These are men who really care about the environment and are willing to pitch in to make a difference. Many are folksy types who are most comfortable with living simply and in accordance with nature.

For more information, contact:

American Hiking Society
1015 31st Street NW, 4th floor
Washington, DC 20007
(202) 385-3252

PERSONAL GROWTH VACATIONS

A vacation is a perfect time for personal growth, learning more about yourself and others, developing a personal philosophy, and establishing healthier ways of living. The following listings, many of which have a decidedly New Age flavor, will enable you to do just that. Also see the following section on Luxury Vacations, since many of the listings in that section (especially the health-oriented spas) will also enable you to accomplish these goals, but in plusher settings.

Communes

To experience a lifestyle different from what you're probably used to, try a few days at a commune. Life in an alternative community can be both relaxing and stimulating. You may not want to live on one permanently, but a short stay at a commune can help you learn more about yourself and other people. If you've experienced the loneliness of the urban single life, a short stay in a group situation in the country will be an eye-opening experience. Consider the following two options.

East Wind. This community of 40 is a democratic, nonviolent, egalitarian cooperative. Adults and children work, learn, and play together. Each member at East Wind is required to work 48 hours a week in areas such as child care, agriculture (vegetable growing, dairy, and cheesemaking), maintenance, and making rope hammocks and nut butters. Food (with an emphasis on vegetarian, although nonvegetarian meals are available), clothing, shelter, medical coverage, transportation, and child care are provided for members. Leisure activities after work include reading, listening to music, watching television, canoeing, caving, backpacking, and swimming.

Eventually East Wind would like to become village-size, with several hundred people. They'd like a heterogeneous population—people of all ages, backgrounds, and interests. Current members range in age from 1 to 64, with 30 being the average age. There are often twice as many men as women. Although of varied beliefs and personalities, the men are generally open-minded, tolerant, and unconventional.

If you'd like to join the 60 to 100 individuals who visit this community in the hills of the southern Missouri Ozarks, contact:

East Wind Community
Box EWB4
Tecumseh, MO 65760
(417) 679-4682

Sirius Community. Sirius differs from East Wind in its size (21 adults), gender ratio (50-50), and orientation (Sirius has more of a spiritual emphasis). Most of its members are employed in nearby Amherst, Massachusetts, in social and health services, solar construction, domestic service, media, and education, but they are required to contribute eight hours of work each week to community projects. Members spend evenings and weekends together.

Visitors can stay in a private or shared room for a weekend or sometimes longer. Vegetarian meals are served. Visitors participate in meditation and work such as cooking, building a new community center, cleaning, doing office work, and gardening. Recreation includes walking in the woods, swimming, skating, slide shows, bonfires, storytelling, and singing.

Members range in age from 1 to 63, with an average between 35 to 40. They honor a common spiritual essence but follow such diverse spiritual practices as Native American traditions and yoga. You'll find men here who are peaceful, spiritual, and committed to making the world a better place. Contact them at:

Sirius Community
Baker Road
Shutesbury, MA 01072
(413) 259-1251

Himalayan Institute

The Himalayan Institute is a nonprofit organization that teaches holistic health, Eastern and Western philosophy, psychology, and meditation. The ultimate goal is the personal growth of the individual and the betterment of society. Programs offered by the institute include:

- Weekend seminars on topics such as Transition in Vegetarianism, Overcoming Habits and Addictions, From Hatha to Kundalini (Yoga), Meditation and Self-Therapy, Freedom from Stress, Fasting and Cleansing, Biofeedback and the Art of Self-Regulation, Turning Barriers into Bridges, Exploring the Light Within, Myths and the Development of Consciousness.
- Self-Transformation Programs from one to three months in which students participate in meditation, yoga, and duties around the institute.
- Graduate-level academic study in Eastern philosophy, contemporary psychology, holistic health, and research methodologies.

- Stress management and holistic health programs: ten-day to four-week sessions concentrating on weight loss, nutrition, exercise, relaxation, and biofeedback.
- Annual International Congress: Held every June, these four days of study and introspection have included topics such as "Science and Spirituality" and "Creativity."

The Himalayan Institute is located in the Pocono Mountains of northeastern Pennsylvania, a 2½-hour drive from New York City. There are branch and affiliated centers in New York City, Buffalo, Pittsburgh, Chicago, Milwaukee, Indianapolis, Dallas/Fort Worth, Washington, D.C., and Minneapolis, as well as Germany, India, Italy, the West Indies, and Canada. But to get the most out of a weekend or longer getaway, the main campus in Honesdale, Pennsylvania, is recommended.

Double-occupancy rooms are provided for all seminar participants. Vegetarian meals are served in the dining hall. Coffee and other beverages with caffeine are not available. Smoking is not allowed. In accordance with the rest of the health-promoting policies, lights are required to be out by 10 p.m.

A few thousand people participate in the institute's programs each year. During the spring and summer, about 30 people take part in weekend programs; about 40 percent are men. All ages participate, but the majority are in their thirties and up.

Because of the retreatlike nature of the institute, planned social activities are not included in the program. But it is possible to meet the opposite sex through classes and seminars, in the dining room, or by skiing, playing tennis, swimming in the pond, and engaging in other sports activities. The men you'll meet are trying hard to live joyfully and creatively. They're intelligent, aware of themselves and others, and are open to different ideas.

For weekend or longer stays promoting relaxation and personal growth, contact:

Himalayan Institute
RR1, Box 400
Honesdale, PA 18431
(800) 444-5772

Kushi Institute

If you're into healthy eating (or would like to be), you might enjoy a vacation stay at the Kushi Institute. Located in the Berkshire Hills of western

Massachusetts on 600 acres of woodlands, meadows, and streams, the institute attracts people of diverse ages, backgrounds, and interests from all over the world. Macrobiotic education is the focus here. Participants learn to eat and cook in the macrobiotic style. Other classes include Oriental philosophy, shiatsu massage, and alternative medicine. Special seminars are available in spiritual topics, dealing with the development of consciousness toward an understanding of ancient and future worlds by meditation, chanting, and study of the teachings of Jesus, Buddha, and Lao-tzu.

Several hundred to a thousand people participate in the institute's programs each year, equally divided between men and women. The men you'll meet here may not have achieved total peace within themselves and the world at large, but they're well on their way. They enjoy quiet contemplation, intellectual discussions, and simple living.

Kushi Institute
Box 7
Becket, MA 01223
(413) 623-5742

Yoga Ashrams

For a vacation experience where you live with a quiet exhilaration and a profound sense of mental and physical well-being, try a yoga ashram. You don't have to be an expert in yoga to benefit from these programs. All you need is a willingness to follow their principles and routines. At most ashrams, guests awake early to meditate. After yogic and breathing exercises, a vegetarian brunch follows. Later in the day, guests can walk around the grounds, swim in lakes and ponds, help cook in the kitchen, or garden, read, or meditate. A second yoga class in the afternoon is followed by dinner and then evening meditation and inspirational readings.

Most ashrams attract more women than men, but you'll find men of all ages (from their twenties to sixties) and from all parts of the country. Most are quiet, introspective individuals who try to live their lives in as healthy and simple a manner as possible.

Consider these:

Sivanda Asrama Vrindavan Yoga Farm
14651 Ballantree Lane
Grass Valley, CA 95949
(916) 272-9322

Sivananda Ashram Yoga Ranch Colony
P.O. Box 195
Woodbourne, NY 12788
(914) 434-9242

Yoga Retreat
P.O. Box N7550
Paradise Island
Nassau, Bahamas
(809) 326-2902

LUXURY VACATIONS

The previous sections of this chapter notwithstanding, there are times when nothing but a luxury vacation will do. Pampering yourself in plush surroundings can be therapeutic. Your whole outlook on life can be improved by a stay at a resort or spa or on a cruise.

Club Med

Club Med is the world's largest vacation village organization, with 110 clubs in 33 countries, all in exotic, scenic, and stress-reducing settings. Locations in the Western Hemisphere include Colorado, Florida, Mexico, the Bahamas, Haiti, Martinique, the Dominican Republic, and Guadeloupe. More distant clubs can be found in Japan, China, Thailand, Malaysia, Indonesia, Israel, Egypt, Turkey, Morocco, Spain, Portugal, France, Switzerland,

---

In the movie *The Big Chill,* the young lawyer played by Mary Kay Place notes her troubles with the men she's met:

1. They're married.
2. They're gay.
3. They're recently divorced and not ready to make a commitment.
4. They're recently divorced and too ready to make a commitment.
5. They're crazy.

It doesn't have to be this way in real life. With the help of this book, you can do better than this unfortunate film character. Get started now.

Austria, and Italy. There's also a new cruise ship (*Club Med I*) that offers seven-day Caribbean and Mediterranean cruises.

Other resorts can be found in these locations, but Club Med is more than just an ordinary resort. The Club Med concept emphasizes freedom. Guests leave behind the concerns and habits of their normal daily lives, even to the point of not carrying a wallet. The vacation package covers transportation, lodging, three meals a day, wine and beer with lunch and dinner, most sports and leisure activities, and evening entertainment. For the few things not included in the package, "pop-it" beads you can wear are exchanged for drinks and other purchases, and settled at departure time.

Sports are an integral part of Club Med vacations (although it's also possible to do nothing but relax). Both the serious athlete and novice can enjoy scuba diving, water and snow skiing, deep-sea fishing, kayaking, swimming, tennis, squash, horseback riding, golf, volleyball, basketball, soccer, softball, archery, and boccie ball. A new activity is the circus schools, where adults as well as children can learn to flip, tumble, swing, twirl, fly, jump, and balance. Tightropes, trampolines, flying trapezes, and unicycles are all available.

More than a million people vacation at Club Med each year. About 60 percent are single. The median age is 35, with a median household income of $60,000. Although Club Med originally had a "swinging singles" image, it now offers many provisions for families and children.

The congenial atmosphere found at all Club Meds will make it easy for you to connect with men from all over the world. It's difficult to generalize about the men you'll find here. Some come for the sports, while others come to relax. Some are gregarious, others are more introverted. But the one thing they all have in common is their desire for a terrific vacation. Together you and the man of your choice can make sure that you both enjoy yourselves.

Your travel agent can tell you more, or call toll-free: (800)-CLUB MED.

If the person you're looking for is one in a hundred, screen a hundred till you find him. If you're seeking a man who's one in a million, you'd better start looking, because you're going to be very busy meeting and weeding out a lot of men!

Concord Resort Hotel

Northeasterners know that the Concord is truly in a class by itself. It has it all: downhill and cross-country skiing (lessons available), indoor and outdoor pools, miniature golf, health club, horseback riding (guided trails and instructor available), ice skating and horsedrawn sleigh rides during winter months, 45 holes of golf (including the top-ranking "Monster"), 24 outdoor tennis courts, 16 indoor tennis courts, indoor and outdoor basketball and volleyball, and nightly entertainment, shows, and dancing. Special events include sports forums with heroes of the major leagues, tennis tournaments and exhibitions with star players, and skating and skiing shows.

But most exciting for singles is the hotel's commitment to them. The Concord has a singles section in the outdoor pool. Round robin seating at meals allows guests to sit wherever they want. Parties, video disco, and Meeters Digest (offering written summaries about guests so anyone who's interested can contact that person) also increase man-meeting opportunities. Singles weekends are offered that include champagne parties, dancing, backgammon, and bridge tournaments. Even single parents weekends are available.

The Concord is a large resort (almost 1,300 rooms), ensuring a sizable number of guests at all times. According to the owners, thousands of singles have met at the Concord. They believe that all the activities offer excellent opportunities for singles to meet. They also estimate that men outnumber women, probably because of the superior athletic facilities which attract so many men. Most are professionals. A large number come from the New York area, but there are also many from New England, Washington, Pennsylvania, the Midwest, and Canada.

For information about this resort, which is 1¾ hours from New York City and 3 hours from Philadelphia, with access to an airport, contact:

Concord Resort Hotel
Kiamesha Lake, NY 12751
(800) 431-3850 (reservations)
(914) 794-4000 (hotel)

Cruises

Ever since the television show *The Love Boat* portrayed cruising as the ultimate romantic vacation, thousands of Americans have rushed to experience it for themselves. They've discovered the many appealing features of cruising: lots of food, fascinating sights, and great entertainment in an all-inclusive package which is often less expensive than other types of vacations. There's no guarantee that you'll meet your ideal man on a cruise, but it doesn't hurt to try. At the very least, you'll enjoy a relaxing vacation for mind and body.

Different people want different things from cruising. Some enjoy sedate cruises, while others want a rowdier time. Some are into gambling, while sports and fitness activities are the most important consideration for others. Gourmets want the best possible cuisine; weight watchers want to eat lightly and maybe even shed a pound or two. You'll have to explore your own interests and desires before you sign up for a cruise.

In terms of meeting men, there are a few hints that can help you choose a ship. The longer the cruise, the older the passengers. If you're looking for a man 50-plus, a cruise that lasts a month or more is where you'd be most likely to find him. Busy people in their twenties and thirties generally cruise for three to seven days. These shorter trips, generally in the Caribbean, attract a fun-loving crowd who like to drink and gamble. Carnival Cruise Lines is especially known for being singles-oriented, as is the Commodore Cruise Line. For the most sophisticated crowd, the Cunard's *Queen Elizabeth II* draws very upscale passengers. Lines that offer sports-oriented cruises (such as Norwegian Caribbean's Dive In program with diving instruction or Royal Viking's sports decks with jogging and par courses, deck tennis, and driving tees) attract more men. You may find more men on cruises with a specific theme (jazz, movies, wine, music, photography, computer science, murder mysteries, Trivial Pursuit). Obviously, ships with the largest number of passengers will also have the greatest number of singles (for example, the Norwegian Caribbean's *Norway* with over a thousand passengers).

Entire books have been written on cruising. You'd be well advised to consult one of them. (You can find them in the travel section of your bookstore or library; space considerations in this book do not permit detailed descriptions of the numerous ships available. A travel agent can also offer helpful advice.)

Mystery Vacations

On a vacation, the last thing you'd want to be faced with is crime. Unless, of course, it's a special mystery vacation where a "murder" is the focal point.

Trains, ships, and country inns all sponsor these exciting adventures, which usually last about three days. A professional acting troupe stages a murder, with guests participating as suspects and characters. Guests quiz each other for clues that will lead to solving the mystery. If you're a mystery buff, you'll really enjoy this amateur sleuthing. In addition to the luxurious accommodations and meals, the advantage of such vacations is that you'll meet a lot of people. Barriers between strangers are quickly broken as guests play fantasy roles and try to collaborate to acquire more clues.

Mystery vacations attract a great many solo travelers. Men and women are equally represented. The majority of participants is between the ages of 25 and 50. The number of participants can range from 20 to 80.

The men you'll meet here have both creative and logical abilities. They like to relax, but not to "veg out," and they enjoy a mental challenge.

Ask your travel agent for recommendations. One possibility is:

Pickwick Productions Mystery Train
Station-Box 162
Laguna Beach, CA 92652
(800) 822-CLUE in California
(714) 494-6800 outside California

Ocean Voyages

Do you dream of setting sail for a distant, exotic port such as Tahiti? Do you fantasize about winning the lottery and gliding along the Mediterranean aboard a luxury yacht? If so, you may need to look beyond the usual Caribbean cruise liners for your next vacation. There's a company that will

---

John Schultz and Kathleen Van Diggelen met in a way that few other couples have . . . on a television show. A *Love Connection* date brought them together. Though that first date was less than wonderful, they later fell in love and were married. The wedding (pictured in the February 15, 1988, issue of *People*) took place on TV, naturally. A judge married them on *Hollywood Squares.* Television usually doesn't do much for anyone's love life, but it certainly made all the difference to John and Kathleen!

help put you on a boat to carry you off to the most adventurous and unusual journey you can imagine . . . and at a surprisingly affordable cost (enabling you to take your dream trip even if you don't win the lottery!).

Ocean Voyages Inc. has over 150 vessels that sail to the Galapagos Islands, Grenadines, Greek islands, the Turkish coast, Hong Kong, Samoa, Fiji, Hawaii, Alaska, and Mexico. Some are luxury sailing and motor yachts, while others offer more rustic accommodations. All will provide you with the kind of experiences you would find sailing the world on your own yacht. You can learn to sail, snorkel, navigate, or just relax. All of the vessels come with a skipper (often the owner of the boat), and most also have a chef on board. Both veteran sailors and novices can be accommodated.

The number of passengers on each boat ranges from 4 to 15. Men outnumber women 55 to 45. Somewhere between 35 and 60 percent of travelers are single and travel solo. Ages range from the twenties to sixties. You'll find interesting and well-educated men who are adventuresome enough to break away from "touristy" travel and experience something completely new.

Ocean Voyages Inc.
1709 Bridgeway
Sausalito, CA 94965
(415) 332-4681

Spas

If you've never tried a spa vacation, you don't know what you're missing. Whether you want to be pampered or want to work hard at becoming healthier, there's a spa for you. Choosing the one that best suits your needs can be tricky because there are so many (in the United States and abroad). Fortunately, there's a service that will help pinpoint the right spa for you. Spa-Finders (784 Broadway, New York, NY 10003-4856) is the world's leading "spa-only" travel service. Their experts will suggest the ideal spa to match your interests and budget (and contrary to popular opinion, spas don't have to be expensive; many cost no more than other vacations) and get you the best rates on accommodations and transportation. All this is free of charge. Call them at (800) ALL-SPAS or send $4.95 for their catalog of spas.

Spas vary widely in terms of their clientele. The beauty and fitness ones generally attract more women than men. Those that have a special appeal to men tend to be ones that offer special activities such as rugged sports or golf/tennis/skiing. You can also find men at New Age spa/retreats or, to a lesser extent, weight-loss spas.

Windjammer Barefoot Cruises

Instead of being merely another passenger on an ordinary ocean liner, try a more adventurous way of cruising. Windjammer Barefoot Cruises specializes in small, informal cruises aboard their special large sailing schooner. The traveling is easy and relaxed. You dress very casually, enjoy the sights, and do whatever moves you at the moment. These ships don't have social directors; it's up to the passengers to make their own fun. Sunning, swimming, snorkeling, scuba diving, beach or masquerade parties, shopping at island boutiques, or taking your turn at the wheel are all possibilities. Although cabins are comfortable, some passengers choose to sleep on deck under the stars. Perhaps best of all, seasickness seldom occurs aboard large sailing schooners because the wind prevents the rolling motion that is usually the cause of mal de mer.

Trips include 6 days in the British Virgin Islands, West Indies, Trinidad and Tobago; 13 days in the West Indies, Grenadines, Leeward, and Windward Islands; and 19 days visiting all the islands. A special reduced airfare program is available. For singles traveling alone, the company will find a cabinmate for you or make arrangements for you to have a private cabin until you find a special cabinmate on the cruise.

About 25,000 people sail with Windjammer each year. The company proudly notes a 70 percent return rate, attesting to the satisfaction of the passengers. Age ranges vary according to the length of the ship's voyage and its itinerary. Older, retired travelers tend to partake in the two-week sails, while younger people choose the six-day cruises. About half are single travelers, with a 60-40 male-female ratio. The *Flying Cloud* (which sails from the British Virgin Islands) is the predominant "diving" ship, so it attracts a great many young travelers interested in water sports.

If your idea of romance is elegant dining and dancing in formal evening clothes, you'd be happier on a luxury liner. But if you like things natural and simple, and tropical islands complete with waterfalls, hidden caves, and dense foliage matter more to you than crystal chandeliers and fancy plate settings, a Windjammer is your type of boat. The company offers special singles cruises, but your chances of meeting a man are good even on a regular sailing. The men you'll meet will be unpretentious and will like to party.

Dr. Joyce Brothers in *What Every Woman Ought to Know About Love and Marriage* (New York: Simon & Schuster, 1984) explains why singles bars are seldom a place to meet Mr. Right. In a two-month research project, psychologists armed with stopwatches observed how long men spent getting to know women in singles bars. Men judged the women in seven seconds or less—obviously an insufficient amount of time for any meaningful contact. If you don't make an impression in those first few seconds, you'll never get another chance. That's why it's preferable to go places and engage in activities where you can really get to know men under less stressful and superficial circumstances.

They're not out to impress anyone with their sophistication; they just want to relax and have fun. With the casual ambiance and intimate atmosphere on board, they (and you!) will leave the restrictions and confines of the workaday world behind.

Ask your travel agent for more details or contact:

Windjammer Barefoot Cruises
P.O. Box 120
Miami Beach, FL 33119-9983
(800) 327-2601 outside Florida
(800) 432-3364 in Florida
(800) 233-2603 in Canada

CHAPTER 6

Community Resources

SOME OF THE BEST OPPORTUNITIES for meeting men aren't especially glamorous or exotic, but they definitely merit attention. Many of them are already a part of your life. Most of them are so obvious that you may have inadvertently been overlooking them as a means of connecting with the opposite sex. This is unfortunate, because all the activities you perform on a regular basis (such as shopping, eating out, banking, maintaining your car) are equally a part of men's lives. Men go to stores, restaurants, banks, and service stations just as you do.

Because such places are patronized fairly equally by men and women, they can function as an excellent romantic meeting ground. Best of all, they're located in or near your immediate neighborhood, thus decreasing the likelihood of your meeting a geographically undesirable man. Chances are that any man you meet in your local laundromat or grocery store will live in the vicinity. This convenience can be an added bonus to potential relationships.

Make a concerted effort to take full advantage of all occasions that you use these community resources. Keep an open mind and positive attitude when you find yourself in any of the following places. You should also experiment with some of the ones you're not currently utilizing, incorporating them as you see fit. It really is possible to find love at the salad bar or the hardware store, so don't underestimate any of the suggestions.

STORES

We all find ourselves in a variety of stores on a regular basis. To varying degrees, we spend significant time and money buying food, clothes, drugs and toiletries, sporting goods, books, hobby supplies, and home furnishings. Regardless of whether you live in a small town or a big city, your community offers a multitude of things to buy.

Most women enjoy the experience of shopping, but they tend to pursue it with tunnel vision. The only purpose of a shopping expedition, as far as they're concerned, is the acquisition of particular items. Shoppers become so engrossed in the hunt for the perfect magenta sweater or so determined to get in and out of the grocery store quickly that they overlook the potential man-meeting opportunities that shopping offers.

Whether they like it or not, men also have to shop. This is particularly true for unattached males who have no one else to do it for them. It's theoretically possible, then, that for every shopping trip you go on, there's a single man also engaged in a similar mission.

Begin to view shopping as a way to come into contact with a vast number of available men. By looking at where they shop and what they buy, you can discern certain characteristics of individual men and make a more informed decision about which of them you'd like to get to know better. The following listing of stores, shops, and services, while not exhaustive, will give you some starting points for evaluating and making the most of the shopping/man-meeting opportunities in your community.

Antique Stores

Antiquing is a leisure activity enjoyed by both men and women. Any person who admires the craftsmanship and style of furniture and ornamental items from long ago has trouble resisting the urge to browse in an antique shop, whether it's a local store or one that requires an hour's drive. Antique collectors make a point of regular visitations, because they never know where or when the perfect treasure will turn up.

Starting up a conversation here is effortless, since antiques lend themselves so readily to discussion. With any piece of furniture, you can debate its age or recommend techniques for restoring it. Your fellow antiquers are likely to be well-educated and moderately affluent. Although they favor tradition in home furnishings, they are not necessarily conservative in their political or social beliefs. Men who shop for antiques are interested in making their homes comfortable and attractive, but are generally not so rigid in their tastes that they would be unwilling to combine their possessions with those of the right woman (if things developed to the point of moving in together). So if you own an Early American dresser that you couldn't bear to part with and he's looking at art deco, don't panic! You can still make a compatible couple.

Auto Supplies

Save yourself time, money, and grief by learning to perform as many automotive repairs and maintenance routines as possible. At the very least, you can change your own oil. Browse around auto supply stores to learn about what parts and supplies are available to fix your car or enhance its performance or appearance.

As you might expect, a majority of the customers will be men. But you may be surprised at the varied types of men you'll find here. Not all drive a pickup truck or dropped out of school in the eighth grade. There are college graduates who drive Volvos, Saabs, and BMWs and prefer not to place their prized possessions in someone else's hands. Most of these men are competent and informed. They like to be in control rather than just allowing things to happen to them. Make eye contact with someone here who looks interesting and see if he initiates conversation (or be brave and ask him a question about oil filters!).

Bookstores

Even in our electronic age, there's still something very satisfying about books and magazines. Turning pages may not be as technologically advanced as running a computer program, but it provides as much stimulation, education, and entertainment as you could ever want. Unfortunately, all too many people nowadays are neglecting the art of reading and instead opt to fill their time with nonstop work, television, and other diversions that may not be half as rewarding. Don't lose the reading habit! Patronize your local bookstore regularly.

You'll often find more women than men in the general fiction section, but the ratio will be reversed in favor of the men in the mysteries and science fiction. Other good bets are art, architecture, and photography, biographies, business, gardening, health, poetry, and psychology/self-help. You can also find a few men browsing through cookbooks.

As for the different types of men you'll find in each area of the bookstore:

- *Art, architecture, and photography:* This is a sophisticated individualist who has high standards for everything (including the women) in his life.
- *Biography:* He's interested in other people and finds something of value in almost everyone.
- *Business:* There may be some workaholic tendencies, leading him to be so absorbed in his work that he neglects everything else.
- *Gardening:* He's a nurturer who loves to care for things (plants, children, pets . . . and maybe you!).
- *Health and fitness:* Two possibilities here: he's either in excellent physical shape and wants to stay that way or he's a hypochondriac who devotes all his energies to worrying about his health.
- *Poetry:* Expect romance from this man; you won't be disappointed.
- *Psychology/self-help:* He's more than willing to analyze his feelings and is always open to self-improvement.

Meeting men in bookstores is usually easier than in libraries. Bookstores lend themselves to browsing and close proximity, and talking isn't frowned on. A number of them have coffee shops or cafés where patrons are allowed to sit and thumb through books over a cup of cappuccino. This also offers an excellent opportunity to make contact with the man of your choice. Bookstores often hold readings and book signing parties. Obviously, the right opener in any bookstore situation is any comment about books: the one he's looking at or the one you're considering or looking for.

According to Michael Leimer, owner of Gingolet Books in Minneapolis, a bookstore is "a better place to meet people than a herpes clinic or Young Republican rally." Dan Odegard, owner of Odegard Books, also in Minneapolis, notes the open attitude of most people who browse in bookstores: "Maybe that makes them more able to be approached" (in the *Minneapolis Star Tribune*, November 8, 1985, "Bookstores a new kind of 'singles hangout' for some," by Colin Covert).

Clothing Stores (Men's)

If you like to give gifts of clothing to the men in your life, take advantage of the opportunity to watch and meet male shoppers. While there are, of course, other women shopping for men's clothing (especially before Christmas), you'll still find that the majority of shoppers here are men buying clothes for themselves.

Break the ice by asking a promising-looking man for his opinion about the yellow paisley tie or the size of the sweater you would need for your six-foot-two, 200-pound brother. Do be sure to mention whom the gift is for so that he knows you're not buying it for a boyfriend.

Because all men (whether they like it or not) have to shop for clothes from time to time, you can find men of every type and description here. It stands to reason that you'll find more white-collar types in the suit/business shirt/tie sections. More rugged types will gravitate to the outdoor wear, jeans, and flannel shirts. The sweater section is a fairly neutral ground, drawing a variety of men.

Collectibles

A multitude of people of all ages and both sexes collect stamps, coins, comic books, baseball cards, celebrity autographs, movie memorabilia, and more. These hobbies can be profitable as well as fun, since many of the items can go up in value and be shrewd investments. Visit some of these specialty stores and see if you want to pursue collecting. Stamps and coins are usually combined into one store, although there are some stores that deal exclusively with one or the other. Comic books and baseball cards are often found in the same store. Autographs and movie memorabilia can be in stores devoted to them (usually in big cities) or in flea markets, comic book stores, and so on.

Collectors tend to be fanatical about their hobby and are usually delighted to discuss their latest acquisitions. In addition to learning a lot from talking to them, you may strike up a friendship.

Most people who collect have both practical and fanciful aspects to their personalities. They are materialistic but they go beyond mere acquisitiveness. They collect not just for the sake of buying and owning the actual objects but also for the history and drama that is behind every collectible. Although it may not be immediately apparent, male collectors do have a sense of romance which can transport them—and you—far beyond the cares and burdens of everyday life.

If you're willing to give up sex until you marry, you might meet a man through the National Chastity Association. This is a nonreligious group of more than 350 who want to reserve sexual relations for marriage. They believe that premarital sex can get in the way of romance and that attraction between men and women should emphasize the intellectual rather than the physical.

Do you want to just say no? If so, contact:

National Chastity Association
P.O. Box 402
Oak Forest, IL 60452

Different personality traits tend to choose each collecting specialty. A brief guide is offered below.

- *Stamps:* This adventurous and imaginative man enjoys traveling to exotic places. Because he easily becomes bored with people and things, he needs constant change and stimulation in his life.
- *Coins:* He's happiest with things that are familiar and predictable. Because he's not comfortable with things he can't control, he likes to have hands-on involvement in everything that affects him.
- *Comic books/baseball cards:* This man will always retain a youthful outlook on life no matter what his age. He tends to form very close friendships and often idolizes people he cares about.
- *Autographs:* People fascinate him. An astute observer of human behavior and characteristics, he's extremely interested in even the smallest details about a person.
- *Movie memorabilia:* He's imaginative and creative. But he often doesn't use these abilities to their fullest potential because of his tendency to cling to the past rather than dealing with the present and planning for the future.

Computer Stores

Computers are here to stay—and most men are delighted about it. Because computers require the logical, left-brained thinking favored by a majority of males, they've taken to these electronic marvels like a duck to water. You'll always find a large number of men at stores that sell computers and software. Usually the men significantly outnumber the women.

But women can't avoid being part of the computer age. For both business and personal reasons, it's essential for anyone of either sex to be computer-literate. If you don't already own a computer, consider acquiring one to make your life easier. If you do have one, keep up with all the current software so that your machine can be used to its maximum potential.

Speak up when you see a man who's looking at software you're familiar with. If you know from personal experience or you've heard either good things or bad about the program in question, let him know. Software can be expensive, so most shoppers are grateful for any guidance that will help them make the right decision.

Because men of all personality types and in almost all walks of life use computers, it is close to impossible to make any generalizations about those that you'll find in computer stores. It should be mentioned, however, that the men who buy computer games can be a different breed from those who buy serious programs such as word processing, data bases, spreadsheets, utilities, and so on. The gamesmen tend to be escapists who focus more on play than on work. They may be charming and fun, but the little boy in them can make them irresponsible at times.

Cooking/Kitchen Supplies

If your experience has been limited to men who live on carry-out pizza, you may be pleasantly surprised that there actually are men who can make a meal from scratch. More and more men are getting interested in gourmet cooking. If you're a culinary genius yourself, spend some time in cooking stores and buy some new gadgets that will make cooking easier and more pleasurable. If you're not into cooking, visit one of these stores anyway and see if you don't get enticed into trying to upgrade your skills. Browsing around these stores will also put you in contact with men who enjoy food and its preparation.

Cooking hints are the order of the day here. If you know of a knife that works like a dream for peeling off the zest of lemons or a pan that's perfect for making blackened fish, share your knowledge. You may end up exchanging phone numbers as well as recipes.

The men you'll find here are typically well-educated professionals who aren't locked into old-fashioned sexual stereotypes. They tend to be innovative and sophisticated. But be aware that there can be a significant ego in these men. They're proud of their accomplishments and want to be constantly stroked and admired. If you become involved with one of them, make sure you're appreciative of all his efforts.

Craft Supply Stores

Creating something attractive and/or functional is extremely rewarding. If you haven't done any handicrafts since the orange and purple ashtray you made in fourth grade, think about learning something like stained glass or ceramics. Most communities have stores that sell craft supplies and equipment.

Craft stores can be a wonderful setting in which to meet a man . . . if you choose them (both the store and the man!) wisely. A general-purpose craft store contains a wide range of supplies, but most are for minor or cutesy crafts, which tend to attract more women than men. Stained glass, on the other hand, is every bit as much for men as it is for women. Glassmaking, ceramics, basketry, and woodworking are also good bets. You can meet a professional craftsman here as well as talented amateurs. Most men who pursue craft activities find it deeply satisfying. They tend to be well-balanced individuals with a positive attitude about life.

Department Stores

The individual departments of a large store offer opportunities similar to those in specialty stores. For example, the electronics department in a department store isn't much different from a store that carries only electronics. The book department is much like a bookstore. The clothing, furniture,

Crossroads, a shopping mall in Boulder, Colorado, has held singles nights which offer pre-Christmas sales as well as the chance to spice up love lives. Singles of all ages can enjoy shopping and dancing to live music. The admission price to the dance is a new toy, donated to the Toys for Tots program.

If your community doesn't have an event like this, it could be worth your while to organize one.

In the '70s, many women wore T-shirts that read: "You have to kiss a lot of frogs before you meet your prince." Two decades later, this continues to be a fact of life. So—start puckering!

sporting supplies, and cookware departments all have atmospheres similar to those of single-purpose stores that specialize in these respective items.

As far as meeting men, the only difference between a department store and a specialty store is that the specialty store attracts men who are extremely interested in that area. If you want to meet a true book lover, go to a bookstore. The man browsing in the book department may be interested in reading, but he probably isn't as passionate about books as someone in a bookstore. Similarly, a man who's walking around the cookware department may, in the process of killing some time, have just wandered in without much of a purpose or real interest, whereas the man who patronizes a cooking store is apt to be a gourmet who really knows his way around a kitchen.

Drugstores

Granted, it's easier to pick up a bottle of shampoo at the supermarket when you're doing your food shopping, but a full-scale drugstore offers a much greater selection of toiletries, cosmetics, and sundry items. Don't cheat yourself out of the opportunity to choose from 30 types of mousse (as opposed to the 4 or 5 that your food store offers).

Most men aren't quite as interested in shopping for toiletries as women, but they do patronize drugstores to pick up prescriptions and over-the-counter products. While waiting in line at the cash register or while perusing the cold remedies section, you can strike up a conversation with a fellow shopper. Because every conceivable type of man shops at drugstores, it's impossible to make any generalizations. But it's possible for you to learn something about any man by simply looking at what he's buying. Having ten prescriptions filled is not a good sign (he's either a hypochondriac or is genuinely not a very well man). Similarly, if he's buying more hair and skin care products than you, you may want to think twice about initiating any contact with him (unless you like vain men). Remember that your own shopping basket is also on display to men who are checking *you* out!

Laxatives, feminine hygiene products, and depilatories aren't ideal props for making a wonderful first impression. If you must purchase something that can be a little embarrassing, do so discreetly.

Electronics Stores

Consumer electronics can be costly, but they can also be a lot of fun. Technology continues to grow at a frantic pace, developing, modifying, and enhancing adult toys in the audio and video fields. If your sound system, TV, or VCR is showing signs of wear and tear or doesn't have all the features you want, think about treating yourself to something new. (You deserve it!)

Because of the variations in price, quality, and features of these items, it truly pays to shop around. Visit as many stores as possible and find out what deals they offer. While you're becoming an informed consumer, you just might connect with someone who's also shopping for a video recorder. Ask for his input in helping you make your decision. You can meet just about any type of man in one of these stores. Men of all ages and occupations use audio and video equipment, so you'll find a wide variety of electronics shoppers.

Grocery Stores

There's no getting around the need for food shopping. If a single person is going to eat, he or she has to make regular trips to the supermarket. But rather than sleepwalking down the aisles, capitalize on the experience.

It would follow that a couple who met in a supermarket would opt to be married in one. Vic Radeka, a divorced auto mechanic, and Debbie Francis, a pharmaceutical sales representative, met at the first singles night at a Publix supermarket in Davie, Florida. A year later, they exchanged wedding vows at Publix. The couple dressed formally, the store was decorated with flowers, and the cash registers were closed during the ceremony. The wedding was featured in the October 25, 1987, issue of *People* magazine.

People-watching in grocery stores can be fascinating. Looking at the items in fellow shoppers' carts, trying to figure out why they're buying those things and guessing their life circumstances, is an intriguing activity for the amateur psychologist. Why, for example, is the woman in the red coat purchasing 20 cans of garbanzo beans? Is the man in the cookie aisle buying graham crackers for his children or does he eat them himself for comfort?

In addition to people-watching, grocery stores also provide an unparalleled opportunity for man-meeting. It's easy enough to start a conversation with someone when you're both waiting in line or to comment on the condition of the asparagus as you each pick some out. And to streamline the process even more, many food stores are offering singles nights with activities such as raffles, dancing in the aisles, music, and bowling (using paper towels for pins and cans of pork and beans as the ball). The atmosphere of these events is very conducive to mingling. You know that everyone is there for the same purpose: to meet someone. The disadvantage is that the singles nights can eventually become very similar to the bar scene. Instead of meeting people under more natural circumstances, you're put in a contrived situation that can lead to artifice and game playing.

Pay attention to the clues you'll find in a man's shopping cart. (Remember that this works both ways. *Your* shopping cart is also on display. Canned spaghetti or white bread is not going to score points with men of any sophistication.) If he has lots of frozen dinners and cold cuts, he probably lives alone and doesn't cook much for himself. If there's a good deal of fresh produce, chances are he's into health and fitness. Two sirloin steaks, wild rice, artichokes, a bottle of wine, and flowers is not a good sign; he is probably already with someone and is planning a romantic dinner for two.

Hardware/Home Improvement Stores

If hardware and home improvement stores are bewildering to you, it's high time you changed that to your advantage. Hardware stores were once strictly the province of men, but women have since discovered the benefits of being handy with a hammer, screwdriver, wrench, and saw. Instead of being at the mercy of carpenters, plumbers, and other tradesmen, you can save money and make sure that home repairs and improvements are done right by doing them yourself. Spend some time in your local home improvement store and learn about its wares. Tackle a few beginner projects on your own and gradually develop your expertise.

Partner shopping is similar to job hunting, according to Susan Page in *If I'm So Wonderful, Why Am I Still Single?* (New York: Viking, 1988). In both pursuits, you must be organized, systematic, keep your self-esteem up, dress well, and put on a good face.

As far as man-meeting goes, these stores are winners. The majority of customers are still men. Most are very willing to share their knowledge and give you some practical hints about successfully completing your project. You can meet many types of men here. While the very wealthiest usually don't bother doing their own repairs and instead hire someone, you won't find just blue-collar workers either. Many professional men are interested in maximizing the beauty and comfort of their homes and prefer to do it themselves. Restoring older homes is an increasingly popular leisure activity and business, so you'll find many creative and dynamic types browsing around home improvement stores.

Health Food Stores

Supermarkets and health food stores are worlds apart. The traditional grocery store entices us to buy on impulse, usually things that aren't all that good for us, whereas the health food store compels us to make intelligent choices and take care of our bodies. If you don't already shop in a health food store from time to time, consider going to one and learning more about their products. Start with some herbal teas or try some grains to make gradual changes in your eating habits. (Beware of any store that smells like vitamin pills. Look for stores that have a fresh produce section.)

Most men who shop at health food stores are friendly and open. They enjoy comparing opinions about different products and sharing nutritional information. But be forewarned. If you're looking for a happy-go-lucky, party-type of guy, you'll be sorely disappointed with a health food enthusiast. These men are thoughtful and serious. They're willing to make sacrifices for the sake of their health and the well-being of the planet. If this describes you as well, hurry to your nearest natural food store and see whether you can find romance among the bulgur and tofu.

Hobby Stores

Piloting a plane is a challenge that takes years to master. If you don't have the time or money to invest in lengthy training, consider piloting a miniature plane—one that's radio-controlled. While you stand with your feet safely planted on the ground, you can have your plane take off and land and even do some stunts. Radio-controlled boats and cars are also available. Your local hobby store sells model boats, cars, planes, and electric trains.

Don't automatically assume that all the hobbyists at these stores are junior-high age. Grown-up boys like these toys just as much as their younger counterparts do. Expect these men to be responsible and mature; they may play with miniature cars in their off-hours, but they're just as comfortable in the adult world of business. Best of all, they're not so stressed out that they experience physical or emotional health problems. Because they know how to relax and let off steam, they can be a lot of fun.

In terms of conversational tidbits, you'll want to ask for advice if you're making a purchase. Inquire as to whether he races his car/plane/boat with a group of people and whether you might join them. By utilizing skill and strategy, you can end up winning the race . . . and maybe even his heart.

Music Stores

More males than females buy records, tapes, and compact disks. Some of this statistical disparity can be traced to teenage boys, who prefer to spend their allowances on rock or heavy metal music, whereas girls tend to buy makeup and clothes instead. But this doesn't mean there are no males over the age of 20 at your local music store. To the contrary, men of all ages browse and buy here. Add to your own collection and to your musical enjoyment by paying a visit to one of these stores.

Musical tastes can be very revealing. A man's choices can instantly tell you something about him (provided he's shopping for himself and not for his 16-year-old nephew).

- *Hard rock/heavy metal:* He likes a great deal of physical excitement. If you want an active life, here's your man. He'll keep you on the go. Just don't expect any stimulating intellectual discussions with him.

- *Soft/pop rock and folk:* He may lack the passion and intensity of other men, but there are many other advantages to this man. If you want a stable, traditional, and comfortable relationship, he'll be perfect for you.
- *Oldies:* Because he's convinced that the best years of his life are behind him, he's in a perpetual time warp where his thoughts and feelings haven't matured. He can be a lot of fun, but he refuses to grow and change.
- *Jazz/New Age:* He'll keep you guessing. You'll never quite know what to expect from him, since his spontaneous and imaginative nature leads him to continually experiment and try new things.
- *Classical:* This is a man who's intellectually and emotionally complex. His multidimensional personality results in his having a variety of characteristics, some of which are paradoxical (such as being both tough and tender).
- *Country-Western:* A man who likes this kind of music is open and honest. You'll always know where you stand with him.

Office Supply Stores

Whether you're one of the growing number of individuals with an office at home or simply need some pens, paper, or envelopes for your personal use, office supply stores can be a fascinating place to shop. The variety of writing instruments, notebooks, and desk organizers at the larger stores is truly amazing. Rather than settling for whatever the local supermarket may carry in the way of stationery, go shopping at a store whose specialty is office supplies. Perk up your notetaking with a pink legal pad; get your desk into

An article in the June 2, 1986, *Newsweek* claimed that single women over 40 stand a better chance of being struck by a terrorist bomb than of getting married! Don't let these statistics get you down. Plenty of women of all ages find partners and are married each year, especially those who *want* to. You don't have to become a statistic. Prove the odds wrong by connecting with the right man.

some semblance of order with the help of an in-out basket, Rolodex file, and pencil holder.

Every office supply store is heavily patronized by men. If you can skillfully initiate a conversation about staplers or printer ribbons, you just might hook up with someone who runs his own business. The business might be a multimillion-dollar enterprise with plush corporate offices or a fledgling operation that is big on ambition but short on cash flow. You may also meet a writer who was in the midst of completing the Great American Novel when he ran out of paper.

Optical Stores

Men *do* make passes at women who wear glasses . . . and sunshades and contact lenses. Be good to your eyes and get them checked on a regular basis (at least every two years). If you wear glasses, treat yourself to a new pair of frames every so often. It will give both your appearance and your morale a boost.

Most optical stores (particularly the larger chains) are quite busy at night and on the weekends. Almost without exception, the clientele is divided about 50-50 between men and women. Keep your eyes open while you're there for the perfect pair of frames and for the perfect man. He just may be there in the store, deliberating over two different styles. Help him decide by offering your opinion about what looks best on him. He may reciprocate this assistance and even ask you to join him for a cup of coffee afterward.

People who wear glasses have traditionally been stereotyped as intellectual. This is not the case in reality. You'll find the whole range of intelligence and education at an optical store, from illiterate dunces to Oxford scholars. After a few minutes of conversation, it shouldn't be difficult for you to discern where he falls on the scale.

Pet Stores

Animal owners need to shop for supplies and equipment for their pets. A large number of single men own pets, so a pet store can be an excellent place for shopping for men.

Just as parents love to talk about their children, pet owners are eager to discuss their animals. Conversation should flow easily if you notice a man who's buying supplies for the same type of pet you have. You can still talk with him if his pet is different from yours; this could be your golden opportunity to find out everything you ever wanted to know about iguanas!

Photography Stores

Shutterbugs of both sexes frequent photography stores to buy new supplies, repair old equipment, and get advice. If your camera has been sitting in the back of your closet, consider retrieving it and getting some use from it. Most salespeople at these stores are knowledgeable and helpful. They'll work with you to get you started on a hobby that can give you a great deal of satisfaction.

Technical talk about photography will be your best icebreaker with any customers (or salesmen) who grab your interest. But use discretion if the store also does film developing. Many photographers are so engrossed in looking at their prints that they may not want to engage in any conversation as they peruse them. If a man is upset with the way his photos turned out, he may not be receptive to talking with you.

Picture Framing Stores

Most works of art need to be framed to look their best. Since people are continually in the process of acquiring new art, picture framing stores do a brisk business. If you have some paintings with uninteresting frames or posters that continue to go unhung because you haven't gotten around to framing them, do your art and your walls a favor by finding just the right matting and framing for them.

Because men collect art and decorate their homes almost to the same extent as women, you're apt to find a few of them at the picture framer's. Checking out their taste in art is a great way to instantly learn something about people. Use the guide below to help you critique a man and his art.

- *Oil paintings of landscapes, seascapes, still lifes, portraiture:* Extremely conservative, he finds it difficult to break loose from tradition.
- *Watercolors or pastels:* He's a sensitive man who's in touch with his softer side and doesn't always feel compelled to be what's stereotypically considered "masculine."

- *Modern art/abstracts in any medium:* More intellectual than emotional, he may have some difficulty relating to women on more than a superficial level.
- *Black and white photographs:* He has the eyes and soul of a true artist, complete with temperamental bouts of anxiety and depression.
- *Color photographs:* He knows who he is and is not concerned with what anyone else thinks he should be.
- *Oriental art:* As a man who's seeking serenity in his life, he needs a woman who is centered and content with her own life.
- *Posters or crafts (fiber/ceramic/glass):* This man's sense of whimsy and humor makes him a delightful companion.

Although it's easy enough to initiate conversation in a framing shop by complimenting a man on his art, a new type of framing store is especially ideal for getting to know other customers. Do-it-yourself frame shops provide the materials, tools, and space for you to perform the work yourself and save a considerable amount of money in the process. You don't have to be a mechanical genius to do this; instruction and guidance are provided as you work. Depending on the type of framing and number of pictures you're doing, you may be in the store an hour or more—ample time to become acquainted with the man at the next table as you both complete your projects.

Plant Stores/Greenhouses/Nurseries

Even if you weren't blessed with a green thumb, you can find indoor and outdoor plants that will thrive. Outdoor landscaping or indoor plantscaping will greatly enhance your home. You can never have too much, so treat yourself on a regular basis to some new greenery. But don't simply grab any old plant from your grocery store. It may be convenient to throw some African violets into the shopping cart along with the cans of soup, but the selection and quality of the plants is inferior to that which can be found in a plant store, greenhouse, or nursery.

The men you will find there are quite special. These are men who aren't afraid of responsibility and are willing to make a commitment to another living thing. Many are quite sensitive and nurturing. They strive for a high quality of life and want their homes to be as attractive as possible. Discuss the disaster you had with a ficus or compare the merits of bromeliads over other succulents with an interesting stranger and see what grows from there.

When you decide to participate in an activity, don't set unrealistic goals for what you want to get out of it. According
to Drs. Margaret O'Connor and Jane Silverman in *Finding Love*
(New York: Crown, 1989), you should never say that your goal
for the evening is to meet someone. If you're unsuccessful,
you'll be disappointed and think you've failed. Instead, set
smaller and realistic goals such as conversing with new people,
exercising, getting out of the house, learning something, and
maybe meeting someone special.

Sporting Goods Stores

If you regularly participate in a sport or physical activity, you owe it to
yourself to be as well equipped for it as possible. Find a sporting goods
store with a first-rate selection of what you need. By browsing around, you
might discover other sports that look interesting and decide to pursue them
as well.

You'll find men in every section of sporting goods: athletic shoes,
clothes, and equipment. The type of sport a man is involved in will reveal
something about his personality. For detailed information on a variety of
sports and the men who pursue them, refer to Chapter 1, Sports and Fitness.

Sporting goods stores are one of the easiest places to meet men. If you
participate in the same sport, you'll find lots to talk about. If you don't know
much about his sport but are intrigued by it, this is a perfect opportunity to
find out more.

Video Stores

You've probably visited your local video store hundreds of times. Why not
combine your search for the right video with your man-watching and
-hunting? Walk out of the video store with the latest release *and* a date for
Saturday night. If he's looking at a film you've never heard of, ask him what
it's about and whether it's supposed to be good.

While the vast number of titles carried by most stores makes it impossible to describe what type of man would rent each individual video, the
following guide will enable you to evaluate men based on their selections.

After determining which category his choice falls under, you'll know a little more about him.

- *Comedy:* Enjoying life is one of the things he does best. Life may not go exactly as he has planned, but his sense of humor never deserts him.
- *Drama:* This is a man who hates boredom above all else. He's happiest when being challenged to overcome an obstacle in his life or striving to achieve a new goal.
- *Action:* He's restless physically but not intellectually. He would like to have more excitement in his life but lacks the determination and initiative to make any changes.
- *Horror/slasher:* Caution: This is a man with questionable feelings about women. Whether buried deep within him or overtly expressed in his words and actions, his misogynist tendencies make him a man to avoid.
- *Foreign:* He's open-minded and sophisticated. He needs a woman who isn't afraid of new experiences, so be sure you're ready for adventure if you get involved with him.

RESTAURANTS

At the end of a busy day, a single man doesn't feel like cooking any more than you do. That's why you both often end up eating out. By carefully choosing your restaurant, you could get more than just a decent dinner. The following guidelines will help you select a place for its male customers as well as its menu.

Fast Food

Many men go solo to grab a quick bite at a burger, chicken, fish, or pizza joint. Fast-food outlets are patronized by all types of men (even those in the upper income brackets who simply want a tasty meal on the run). As a general rule, fast-fooders lack some of the depth and sensuality found in men at other eateries. But if a straightforward, no-nonsense relationship is what you're looking for, you may be very satisfied with someone you meet at McDonald's.

Chinese

There's no question that singles of both sexes love Chinese food. But don't be deluded into thinking that by lingering over your moo shu pork, you'll connect with someone interesting. The dining room of a Chinese restaurant is more likely to be filled with families than with single men. *Takeout* is what's popular with the type of person you're looking for. Find a restaurant with an active takeout business and see if anyone waiting for his own order catches your fancy. Szechuan eateries usually attract more adventurous, sophisticated, better-educated types than Cantonese/Chinese-American restaurants.

Deli

You don't have to be a Jewish New Yorker to love pastrami on rye with a kosher dill. People on both coasts (and everywhere between) and of all religious and ethnic persuasions enjoy a good delicatessen. The type of man you *won't* find here, however, is a fitness fanatic. There's too much cholesterol served up in this type of eatery to attract someone who's into taking care of his body.

Steak/Prime Rib

Thirty years ago, men who favored this type of restaurant were considered to be masculine and self-assured. Today they're likely to be viewed in a less favorable light. They tend to have difficulty accepting women as equals and want to call all the shots in both their business and personal lives. Patronize these restaurants only if you want a very traditional male who doesn't keep up with the times.

Seafood

Good seafood is irresistible. The trouble is that the best seafood restaurants are located in coastal areas, which doesn't help those of us who live inland. Nonetheless, landlocked seafood restaurants do have a loyal following. The man you'll find here tries hard to enjoy life and make the most of it. He'll grab the gusto any way he can, and you'll probably enjoy coming along for the ride.

Southern/Barbecue

Restaurants that specialize in down-home cooking (such as country-fried steak, collard greens, sweet potato pie) or barbecue attract a certain type of man. He's frequently Southern (although men north of the Mason-Dixon line have also been known to enjoy this food), unpretentious, and satisfied with himself and his world. He may not have a college education, but he has street smarts and good common sense.

Health Food/Vegetarian

Whole men eat whole food. Natural foods eateries are favored by a certain type of man: well-read, intellectual, and somewhat nonconformist. If you're a highly emotional type who often acts without thinking, one of these cerebral men could be just what you need for a calmer, more balanced (and indisputably, healthier) life.

Italian

The Italian restaurant customer is the exact antithesis of the health food/ vegetarian patron. Whereas the latter is extremely intellectual and often a little aloof, the former is warm, outgoing, and very sensual. Highly passion-ate, he'll make your life pleasurable in every way.

French

Here's your chance to find out whether a gourmet eater makes a gourmet mate. The single man who treats himself to a good French restaurant most likely is a connoisseur of all the finer things in life. This man will keep you on your toes because he expects nothing less than perfection in everything (including his woman). In return he'll show you how to enjoy the elegant lifestyle you've always dreamed of.

Mexican

Men with well-rounded personalities are what you'll find at your local cantina. Mexican food seems to draw active males who are able to slow down long enough to catch their breath before rushing on with their busy lives. They're secure, well-adjusted, and cheerful. You could do far worse than to hook up with a burrito lover.

Exotic Ethnic

Thai, Vietnamese, Japanese, Korean, Moroccan, Lebanese, Ethiopian, Greek, and Indian . . . although these cuisines are all very different from each other, there's a certain type of man who can be found at any one of them. He likes to set himself apart from the crowd and express his unique personality. Because he becomes restless and bored easily, he needs a woman who can challenge him and keep him guessing from time to time. If this sounds like you, you'll want to consider having tandoori chicken or falafel for your next meal out.

As for making contact with a man in a restaurant, there are several ways to go about it. Salad bars provide a great opportunity to mingle with other customers. Conversation may naturally start as you both reach for the croutons. If the restaurant is crowded, you may automatically be placed in the vicinity of other solo diners. You can also try to time it so that you both walk out of the restaurant at the same time. The obvious opening line is a comment or question about the food, since that's all the two of you have in common at this point. If you've caught each other's eye on several occasions during the meal and you sense a mutual interest, be daring and arrange to have the waiter bring a drink or dessert to him with your compliments. He's guaranteed to be extremely flattered by this gesture.

OTHER COMMUNITY RESOURCES

Don't overlook these other opportunities to meet men.

Accounting/Tax Firms

No one enjoys paying taxes, but it's an inevitable part of life. Instead of panicking as April 15 draws closer, consider seeing an accountant or tax specialist *before* the end of the year to plan. Working on your taxes year round is financially prudent. It will give you the benefit of professional expertise under more relaxed circumstances than during the last two weeks of tax season. You'll be able to incorporate tax-saving strategies into 365 days of the year and very possibly wind up owing less in taxes than you would otherwise have paid.

As many men as women utilize these experts for personal and business tax planning. It may be that you meet a fellow taxpayer right in the accounting/tax firm's waiting room. Open up lines of communication by voicing your dissatisfaction with the tax system. Whether he's an owner of a successful business or just another working person, he probably shares your feelings about inequities and unreasonable rules and will be only too happy to ventilate them.

Airports

If you're a frequent flyer for business, you already know that airports are filled with all types of men. Young and old, businessmen and students, all-American and exotically foreign, thousands of male travelers pass through an airport's doors every day.

But what if your job doesn't require any out-of-town travel? You can still visit your local airport. Whenever you're expecting guests who are flying in, insist on picking them up rather than asking them to take a taxi or rent a car. Arrive early so you have lots of time to scout out the terminal and waiting room for someone who looks promising.

You can also offer to pick up your friends' and coworkers' guests up at the airport as a favor. Or you can trade services with each other (you'll pick up their guests if they'll do your grocery shopping for you) or charge a fee and begin what could blossom into a lucrative part-time business. Meeting someone else's guests whom you've never met has its advantages. If you're carrying a sign with their name or your name on it, you may attract the attention of other people as well. A single male will probably be very willing to help you find your party.

Experts agree that there are more singles-oriented activities in Los Angeles than anywhere else in the country, according to an article in the February 1990 *Los Angeles* magazine. Could there be a move to L.A. in *your* future?

In addition to the waiting areas, man-meeting opportunities are also available in the newspaper stands, gift shops, restaurants, airline-run membership lounges, and even in lines to use the telephone or automatic banking machine.

Banks

If you conduct all your financial business at the drive-through teller, you need to change your habits. Why not do your banking the old-fashioned way and *walk* into the bank? The exercise couldn't hurt and you'll have more of an opportunity to meet men while you're waiting in line. Lines are notoriously long on Fridays during lunchtime since it's payday for many people. Join everyone else and see if anything develops. Virtually every man has some transactions to take care of, so you stand a chance of meeting all types.

Waiting in line to use an automated teller machine is another possibility. But the atmosphere can be a little less congenial than the inside of a bank. If the weather is unpleasant, most people's minds are on getting to the machine as quickly as possible so they can jump back into their cars; making contact with a stranger is the last thing they're concerned about. If it's dark outside, eyes are averted and people carefully guard their personal space, wary of anyone who may be a threat. For the best results, you'll need to choose bright, sunny days to utilize ATMs.

Car Repair Shops

Waiting to have your car serviced is far from fun, but learn to make the most of it. Choose an automotive repair shop with a decent waiting room. Many provide free coffee, magazines, and television. Instead of having a friend pick you up at the shop when you drop off the car and bring you back later, use this time to unwind. Or, if you must, catch up on paperwork from the office.

Chances are you won't be alone in the waiting room. The one thing all cars have in common is that they need to be regularly serviced, both for preventive maintenance as well as actual repairs. Your fellow customers, also stranded and bored, will usually be eager to kill some time by talking. Sit near a man who looks promising and exchange your opinions about cars

In the July 16, 1984, *People* magazine, Jonathan Roberts, author of *How to California*, recommended the stoplight pickup as a dating option. All you need to do is roll down your window and ask the guy next to you to join you at the do-it-yourself car wash. He also notes that getting traffic tickets doesn't have to be a problem: "The traffic school pickup is also a very good technique."

(American vs. foreign, new models, and so on). It's possible to meet men of all types here, so keep your eyes, ears, and mind open.

Car Wash

Do your car a favor and your love life may profit as well. Since approximately half of all automobiles are owned by men and their cars get just as dirty as women's, a car wash can be a fruitful place for connecting with a member of the opposite sex.

But not just any car wash will do. The ones many gas stations provide free with a fill-up usually require you to remain inside your car as you go through them. This doesn't afford you any opportunities to meet men.

Spring for a few extra dollars and choose a car wash where you actually get out of your vehicle. While you're waiting for your car to be washed by the attendants, you can strike up a conversation with someone who's also waiting. Conversational openers can include comments or questions about your car or his. If you've always wondered whether a Volvo is as reliable as they say or a Porsche is as much fun to drive as it looks, now's your chance to find out. Or, if you're feeling energetic, consider taking your car to a do-it-yourself coin-operated car wash. While you're waxing or rinsing, you might catch the eye of the man in the next bay.

Since all types of men drive cars, the entire spectrum of the male of our species frequents car washes. In general, the men who take their cars to an attended car wash may be a little more upscale than those who hose down their own cars (although some men take their most prized possession to a do-it-yourself place not to save money but because they don't trust anyone else with it). If status or income level isn't important to you, you may be more comfortable with a man who takes care of himself (and his car) without expecting anyone else to do it for him.

Chiropractors

Some people swear by 'em; others are convinced that they're quacks. If you suffer from aches and pains, particularly in your neck and back, maybe you should try one and make up your own mind about chiropractic. Chances are you won't find a deserted waiting room. Your doctor probably has hundreds of other patients . . . and a few of them may be men you'd find interesting.

You'll find a variety of men seeking chiropractic treatment. Some will be auto accident victims; others will have been injured on the job (such as construction workers). There will also be some white-collar workers who are experiencing discomfort after hunching over a computer day in and day out. Most people will be fairly relaxed while waiting to see the doctor since they know that some relief will be forthcoming; hence, it's easy to start up a conversation.

Churches/Synagogues

If you feel you want to add a little spirituality to your life, church or synagogue is one way to start. It's also a way to meet men who have beliefs similar to your own. You can meet them at services, during educational seminars, on committees for church business and fund-raisers, as well as church-sponsored singles groups.

If you've outgrown the religion you were raised in, you can investigate other religions. Most medium-size cities have a variety of denominations. Check out a few to discover which one best suits you.

Advent Christian	Church of God in Christ
African Methodist Episcopal	Church of Jesus Christ of
Anglican-Episcopal	Latter-Day Saints (Mormon)
Apostolic	Eastern Orthodox
Baptist	Episcopal
Buddhist	Ethical Culture
Catholic	Evangelical
Charismatic	Friends (Quakers)
Christian Science	Gospel
Church of Christ	Greek Orthodox
Church of God	Holiness

Hindu	Methodist
Islamic	Orthodox
Jehovah's Witnesses	Pentecostal
Judaism	Presbyterian
Krishna Consciousness	Primitive Baptist
Lutheran	Religious Science
Mennonite	Seventh-Day Adventist
Metaphysical Science	Unity

Since each belief attracts certain types of people, it's impossible to list the specific characteristics of churchgoers in general. The common denominator in a broad sense would be the desire to focus on something beyond the mundane and materialistic concerns of the everyday world. Because all religions stress ethical ways of relating to others, most churchgoers attempt to live ethically.

You may be convinced that you don't belong in any organized religion. This may be true. But before you write off all religion, you may want to investigate two of the most liberal and untraditional denominations. Chances are they're entirely different from other religions you've experienced. These are the Baha'i and the Unitarian Universalist denominations. Most communities have fellowships or churches in these unique denominations.

Baha'i. Although you may not be familiar with it personally, the Baha'i faith has over 4 million followers in more than 200 countries and territories. The central principles are the oneness of God, the oneness of religion, and the oneness of mankind. In Baha'i teachings, God has revealed himself through messengers such as Abraham, Moses, Buddha, Jesus, and Muhammad. The Baha'i community promotes the unity of mankind and the establishment of peace in the world. They try to eradicate prejudices of race, creed, class, nationality, and sex. This is a very nonsexist religion that truly believes in the complete equality of men and women.

Many Baha'i communities hold devotional services (reciting the scriptures of all religions as well as unique Baha'i readings), study classes, and discussions in private homes rather than churches. There is no clergy, nor are there any initiation services or sacraments. Every Baha'i is under the spiritual obligation to pray daily; to fast 19 days a year, going without food or drink from sunrise to sunset; to abstain from narcotics and alcohol; and to practice monogamy.

There are 110,000 Baha'is in the United States in 1,700 local spiritual assemblies. South Carolina, California, Texas, Georgia, and Illinois have the largest Baha'i populations. There's an equal number of men and women. You'll find sensitive, caring men in this faith. Their interests and backgrounds are eclectic. One thing that should be of interest to you is their commitment to treating women as equals and the importance of marriage and family life.

**National Spiritual Assembly of the
Baha'is of the United States**
536 Sheridan Road
Wilmette, IL 60091
(708) 698-9039

Unitarian Universalist. Unitarian Universalist churches emphasize spiritual growth through liberal religion. Instead of a churchwide creed, members are encouraged to develop an open, growing faith of their own based on truths found in every branch of religion and all areas of thought, such as science, philosophy, and the arts. Members strive to live up to the wisest teachers of all humanity regardless of the era or religious environment in which they are found. They cherish Jesus, but also Moses, Buddha, and other great prophets and teachers. Jesus is considered an inspired religious leader rather than a supernatural being. The Bible is viewed as a priceless part of their religious heritage which contains some truths, not as the infallible or exclusive word of God. Earthly life is stressed rather than an afterlife. Since members believe that God is unknowable, some consider themselves to be agnostics, humanists, and atheists.

There are about 180,000 members who belong to the 1,000 congregations in every state. Most members live in the suburbs or the city rather than the country. The gender ratio is about equal. The median income is $42,000. Over three-quarters have graduated from college. The median age is 53. A little over half are married.

Unitarian Universalist men are usually liberal, nonsexist, and tolerant of individual beliefs and practices. They're highly articulate and enjoy discussing ideas and philosophies. Most are open to and encourage growth in themselves and others.

You can find Unitarian Universalist congregations in the Yellow Pages of the phone book or contact:

Unitarian Universalist Association
25 Beacon Street
Boston, MA 02108
(617) 742-2100

Copying Centers

Instead of using the photocopying machine at work for your personal needs (which is probably frowned upon), pay a visit to one of your neighborhood copy centers.

You won't meet a corporate executive here (his secretary takes care of his photocopying), but you just might come across a writer who's duplicating his manuscript or a budding entrepreneur who doesn't yet have a machine of his own.

If it's a do-it-yourself place and you like the looks of someone who has a large amount of copying to do, offer to help and see what progresses from there.

Employment Agencies

If you're actively looking to change jobs, an employment counselor can make all the difference in your search. Even if you've only been toying with the idea of moving on and are just curious about what might be available, it still can be worthwhile to visit an employment agency or recruitment firm. Since just as many men as women use these services, you may walk out of there with a date as well as some possibilities for a career move.

If you lack confidence in yourself and feel that no man will want you because of a few extra pounds or clothes that aren't as trendy or expensive as you might like, consider this from Bob Berkowitz's book *What Men Won't Tell You But Women Need to Know* (New York: Morrow, 1990): "I've interviewed dozens of men who said that some of their most satisfying relationships had been with women who weren't conventionally beautiful or well dressed."

It's simple enough to initiate a conversation in the waiting room. Career issues are on the minds of everyone there, so most people are willing to talk about where they've been working and what they're looking for. The type of man you can meet depends on the specific agency. Some are geared toward sales and marketing positions, while others deal primarily with management, accounting, or computer positions. Most men will be a little on edge since they're in the process of a career change, but they may still be receptive to getting acquainted.

Fitness/Health/Athletic Clubs

There's no escaping the need for exercise to stay in shape. You can try to adhere to a fitness routine on your own (running around your neighborhood; using a stationary bicycle at home), but many people find that they exercise more regularly and enjoy it more when they belong to a health club. Since many of these facilities require a sizable amount of money up front or on a monthly basis, choose yours wisely. Look for clean, modern facilities with a variety of fitness opportunities. Interview members to make sure they're satisfied with the club.

If you'd like your health club to tone up your romantic life as well as your muscles, make sure you don't sign up with a fitness club that caters more to women than men. If the emphasis is on aerobics classes and child care, it's likely that the membership will be predominantly female. If, on the other hand, the club features racquetball, handball, and squash, you'll find many men there. Ideally, it will offer free weights, Lifecycles, Stairmasters, Nautilus machines, indoor track and pool, basketball, massage therapy, whirlpools, saunas, and steam rooms. A juice bar, restaurant, or lounge enables you to meet people on a more social and relaxed basis than when you're busy working out.

The men you'll meet here vary widely in age, occupation, and motivation for exercising. Ages can range from high school through senior citizen status. Occupations can range from truck driver to corporate lawyer and everything in between. As for the reasons for their participation, most simply want to be as physically fit as possible to get the most out of their business and personal lives. Some are obsessed with developing and maintaining a perfect physique; most of these men are in their teens and twenties. A small percentage of the older men may have been ordered by their physicians to get into shape after some heart trouble. Most of the men at a health club are fairly social and outgoing, as demonstrated by their preference for exercising with other people rather than alone.

Gas Stations

Self-service gas stations are a fertile meeting ground: Just about all men (except the very poorest, who don't own cars, or the very wealthiest, who insist on going to full-service or have their own drivers) patronize them. Meeting a man amid the exhaust fumes may not sound like the most romantic setting in the world, but since you can't escape a weekly or biweekly trip to the gas pumps, you might as well make the best of it.

Linger a little longer and check your oil, water, and tire pressure. Not only will you be ensuring your car's safety and longevity, you may also be noticed by another motorist. He's apt to be impressed with your conscientiousness and ashamed that he's been neglecting to do the same. If he asks to borrow your tire pressure gauge, it could be the start of a meaningful friendship.

Hair Salons

If you're the type of woman who hates the thought of a man seeing her at less than her absolute best, this one's not for you. But if you don't mind being seen with your hair wet or with permanent solution or a color rinse on it, you can look for a mate while your hair is being cut, curled, or colored.

Most of us wish that we were better-looking. We often convince ourselves that we'll have difficulty finding love because we're not beautiful enough to attract men. But take heart; things aren't perfect even for those whose looks we envy. A San Francisco group called the Good-Looking People's Network meets on a monthly basis to discuss the problems and prejudices that attractive men and women encounter. Fifty or so people, age 25 to 55, usually attend. Maybe this would be a good way for *you* to meet and extend your sympathies to one of these hunks.

Obviously you'll need to go to a salon that has a sizable male clientele. A beauty parlor that caters predominantly or exclusively to women (telltale signs include body waxing, pedicures, or makeup/fashions/jewelry for sale) will not be productive.

You can find virtually all types of men in most unisex salons, with the possible exception of very traditional and conservative ones (who feel more comfortable in a barber shop). The relaxed atmosphere makes it easy to meet someone. If he's in a nearby chair, you can comment on something you heard on the radio station piped into the salon. Between him and his hairdresser and you and your hairdresser, lively four-way conversations can often develop.

Investment Firms

Do you throw your extra dollars into a savings account, even though the interest it pays may be puny? Worse yet, do you not save any money at all? Get your financial affairs in order and start saving and investing wisely. Not only will you have more security now and in the future, but you can have fun in the process as well!

Careful investing will do wonders for your financial health and it just may give you an opportunity to hook up with the man of your dreams. Your friendly neighborhood stockbroker sells a wide variety of investment vehicles: stocks, bonds, CDs (certificates of deposit), mutual funds, partnerships, and more. The more frequently you visit him or her, the greater your chances of meeting other clients at the brokerage firm. Considering that the majority of clients are men (since many women still haven't taken charge of their financial futures), the odds of meeting a man at a brokerage firm are very good.

And you won't find just any man here, either. The overwhelming majority of brokerage clients have substantial net worths and salaries that offer enough disposable income for investing. Typically they're well-educated professionals who take a responsible approach to their lives. Those who invest in speculative issues such as turbulent stocks and futures enjoy a little more risk and uncertainty than the men who prefer to play it safe and buy bonds and certificates of deposit. But both types have experienced success in making money and consequently are optimistic and confident about their futures.

It isn't difficult to start up a conversation with someone who's also waiting in the lobby to consult with his broker. Asking which direction he feels the stock market is headed is always a safe bet. You can also prevail upon your broker to hold some group educational sessions; these will enable you to increase both your investing knowledge and your opportunities to meet men.

Laundries

Believe it or not, doing your laundry doesn't have to be a dreaded chore. If you go to the right laundromat, you can relax, enjoy yourself while your clothes get cleaned, and meet members of the opposite sex. Look in your Yellow Pages for ads that proclaim big-screen televisions, bars, delis, and games such as pool, tennis, video games, and so on. There really are laundromats that sell cappuccino, croissants, soup, and salad, as well as beer and wine by the glass. Instead of heating up yet another microwave dinner, you can feast while you do your clothes. A few laundromats even offer aerobics classes, fitness equipment, and live bands. Any time after work is appropriate for going, but Sunday afternoons or Monday nights during football season can be especially productive for meeting men since many of them come to watch the game on big-screen TV.

A cross-section of men utilize laundromats. Most are working-class and live in apartments that don't have laundering facilities. Some are middle-class professionals who prefer not to devote any space in their homes to a washer and dryer. A few own washers and dryers that are on the blink and are using a laundromat until they get them repaired. In any case, man-watching at a laundromat affords you a perfect opportunity to check out someone's personal habits and wardrobe. Use this quick guide to the contents of a man's laundry basket as well as your own insights to learn more about the men you'll find in a laundromat.

- *Sweatshirts, T-shirts, shorts with college emblems, comic book heroes, or other popular characters on them:* He's afraid that his best days are behind him and prefers to live in the past. There may be a streak of immaturity in him which results in his refusal to completely grow up.
- *Bikini underwear:* This is a man who's extremely proud of himself and his body. If the underwear is especially flashy, his ego may be so strong that he's more interested in his own physique than yours.

- *Status polo shirts (such as Izod or Polo) and designer jeans:* He's a follower who doesn't have many original thoughts of his own. On the positive side, he does believe in enjoying life and going after what he wants.
- *Worn jeans and flannel shirts:* Here's a man who prizes comfort above all else. If you want someone with whom you can relax and whom you don't always have to try to impress, he'd be a good one to start with.
- *Sweats, shorts, athletic socks:* He's committed to keeping himself in shape. Make sure you're okay in the fitness department if you're interested in a relationship with this man.
- *White undershirts and briefs or boxer shorts:* He's conservative and not very original, but he's also dependable and down-to-earth.
- *Polyester or nylon shirts and pants:* He may be great with kids and animals, but his fashion taste leaves a lot to be desired. If you're not concerned about these things, try to learn more about the man who owns the green and orange flowered shirt. If public image is important to you, be honest about it and look at another's man washload.
- *Women's clothes:* Not a good sign at all. He either lives with his mother, with another woman, or has transvestite proclivities.

Make sure your own laundry basket doesn't reveal anything about you that you'd rather keep to yourself. If you still sleep in flannel nightgowns with pink bunnies on them or own underwear that you wore in high school, hand wash these at home instead of bringing them for show-and-tell at the laundromat.

There are numerous ways to initiate communication at a laundromat. If all the machines are being used, you can ask someone in the process of loading his machine if you can combine your loads. If you've forgotten your fabric softener, ask to borrow that. If he's folding an attractive shirt, let him know you admire his taste.

Dry cleaners present more limited opportunities for meeting men. While they certainly patronize these establishments, they tend to run in and run out to drop their cleaning off and pick it up. Making it even more difficult is the trend toward drive-through windows. But if you can think quickly and find an opening line within a minute or two, you may be able to connect with someone worthwhile. The vast majority of men found here are in business or professions that require wool suits and starched shirts.

Libraries

If you haven't been to your local public library in ages, you may be surprised to find that it no longer resembles the slightly musty, dreary, and somber mausoleum you remember from your youth. Today's libraries are bright, cheerful, and bustling with action. Computerization makes reference a breeze, and there's an incredible variety of books and magazines. Videos, records, and compact disks can be rented as well. Lively seminars cover topics ranging from investing in the stock market to planning vegetarian diets.

The men who use libraries are as varied as the volumes on the shelves. A unique advantage of libraries as a place to meet men is the opportunities it affords for instantly finding out something about a man through what he is reading. Here, then, is a brief guide to what various reading materials reveal about the person perusing them.

- *Business section of the newspaper, business or financial magazine:* He's extremely career-oriented and may not have many other interests besides work.

- *Classified section of the newspaper:* Not a good prospect. A truly ambitious job hunter would buy his own paper rather than reading it at the library. If it's an out-of-state paper, he's dissatisfied with his life and is planning to move away.

- *People magazine:* He may be more interested in fantasy females and outward appearances than in getting to know a real woman.

- *News magazine or front section of newspaper:* He has a healthy interest in the world around him . . . and may be happy to learn more about you, too.

- *Consumer Reports:* Cautious and sensible, he's someone you can count on.

- *Mystery novel:* Although sophisticated in many ways, he's also down-to-earth.

- *Literary novel:* He may genuinely like the writing style, but it's just as likely that he is trying to cultivate an intellectual and trendy image.

- *Cookbook:* Don't let him get away! He's sensual and dynamic. At the very least you'll be sure to get a decent home-cooked meal if you hook up with him.

- *Psychology/self-help:* He's vulnerable and open to making a change in his life (such as starting a relationship with you).

A study was conducted at Texas A & M University in which college males viewed videotapes of conversations between a young man and woman. In half the conversations, the woman asked the man to go to a movie; in the others, she did not. The woman who asked for a date was rated as kinder, warmer, and less selfish than the woman who did not ask for a date. Since you don't want to be viewed as mean, cold, or selfish, it appears that you need to ask men out! It does take some courage, but research shows that men are receptive to women making the first move.

Initiating a conversation in the library can be tricky. Select a few books (fairly current novels or nonfiction are best) and seat yourself in the proximity of someone you'd like to meet. After a few minutes of leafing through your books, choose one you're not sure about and ask if he's read it or knows whether it's any good.

Mass Transit

You're never going to meet anyone by driving yourself to work each day. In the solitary confinement of your car, your interaction with other people doesn't go beyond honking your horn or giving hand signals when someone cuts you off. You may be on the road for an hour or two a day, but you have nothing to show for it other than frazzled nerves.

Why not decrease your stress and leave the driving to someone else? At the very least, you'll put your time to better use, since you can read or catch up on correspondence while you ride the train, bus, or ferry. At best, you'll meet a fellow commuter who's as interested in you as you are in him. Small talk (about the weather, traffic, or articles in the newspaper) is appropriate in this situation.

In most urban areas, a variety of men use mass transit. You can find anyone from a 23-year-old student to a 45-year-old executive. What they all have in common is a desire to travel as stresslessly as possible so they can arrive in a saner frame of mind. These are men who can sort out what's important in life. To help the environment, traffic congestion, or their personal psychological/financial well-being, they're willing to sacrifice the convenience and anonymity of driving their own cars. Thus they tend to be more open-minded and caring than the men who plow down the highway in carpools of one.

Museums/Art Galleries

Have you been neglecting the museums in your city? If so, you're depriving yourself of a prime cultural experience and a wonderful opportunity for meeting men. Museums have traditionally been a way for individuals of taste and refinement to hook up with each other. Within the safety of the museum confines, you can check out the paintings as well as the single men. If you find yourself next to an interesting man while viewing a work of art, voice your feelings about the piece. Don't be afraid that you'll insult him by having negative feelings about a painting he really likes; part of the stimulation provided by the visual arts is the different emotions and thoughts they evoke in people. If you don't understand a piece, speak up and see how he interprets it.

Many museums are making it even easier for you to meet members of the opposite sex. Several art museums hold events just for singles at night or on the weekends. Gallery tours, special exhibits, and educational sessions are followed by refreshments. If your museum doesn't currently offer this, take some initiative and get something going. Museums are continually looking for new members and ways to raise funds, so most will be quite receptive to new ideas.

Art galleries provide similar opportunities. Since the majority are proprietary, many go all out and offer delectable refreshments in a festive atmosphere to launch a new show. Between openings, you can browse around just as you would at a museum. The major difference is that most galleries are considerably smaller than museums and will have fewer men within their halls. On the positive side, the atmosphere can be more intimate and conducive to chatting with strangers.

If you've been yearning for a man who's cultured and educated, museums and galleries are an ideal place for you. Most men you'll find in the modern art facilities are liberal and even a little avant-garde. The men in the more traditional settings are slightly more conservative but still very open-minded. They all appreciate beauty in its many forms and try to find beauty and fulfillment in life. See if you can add some to the life of one of these patrons of the arts.

Parks

People-watching at a nearby community, city, or state park may be nothing new to you. But how about really making the most of this resource and using it to connect with some men? Treat your dog to regular walks in the park rather than just a few minutes in the backyard. Your lovable canine will make it easy for men to start talking to you. When they stop to pet your pooch, conversation will just flow naturally. If you'd like to meet other pet lovers, think about starting a group where the dogs can play with each other while the owners mingle.

Other conversation-starters can include kites, boomerangs, Frisbees, guitars, drawing or painting supplies, and remote-controlled planes, cars, or boats. Not only will you have fun, you'll also attract interested bystanders who want to watch or get involved.

You'll find all types of men at parks. What they have in common is a love of the outdoors, a refusal to stay at home and be bored, and a commitment to enjoy all that life can offer. Sound good? If so, hurry to your nearest park!

Post Offices

Give your postage meter at work a break and go to the local post office to buy stamps for your personal use. The special commemorative stamps issued regularly by the P.O. are a lot more interesting than metered postage and will enliven your correspondence. While waiting to buy them, you just might find yourself in conversation with the man behind you in line.

What sort of man can you find at the post office? Theoretically, every sort. In actuality, top-level executives have their secretaries use the machine at work to stamp their mail, so you won't find any corporate bigwigs here. Instead, there will be a lot of men who are either unemployed or looking to change jobs and are sending off hundreds of résumés. There will also be some writers or would-be writers mailing query letters to publishers about their just-finished novels. It's possible that there will be a few fledgling entrepreneurs who don't yet own a postage meter. Expect also to find some eager philatelists (stamp collectors). And there will, of course, be men who just need stamps for a variety of personal uses . . . mailing Christmas cards, paying bills, and so on.

Recycling Centers

It's come to the point where we can't continue with our disposable society. Ecological experts advise us that there's no alternative but to recycle whatever we can. Glass, aluminum, plastic, and paper can be collected, processed, and reused instead of thrown out with all the other things we discard. The number of converts to recycling grows each day as people come to realize that it's the environmentally responsible thing to do.

Sorting, saving, and bringing materials to the nearest recycling centers will take some time and effort. But once you start, you'll feel guilty about throwing even one aluminum can away rather than saving it for recycling. So get in the habit of collecting the appropriate materials and regularly dropping them off at the designated centers. You won't be alone in doing this. In fact, there could be a man who will offer to help you carry your newspapers to the bin. If things progress from there, the two of you may be sorting your garbage together in your own (shared) home someday. You'll know that you've found a responsible, caring, environmentally aware man who is willing to put up with some inconvenience for the greater good. You do need to realize that there will be a few men who don't fit this mold and are doing it for the sole purpose of making a few cents at a recycling center that reimburses for aluminum cans and newspapers. These men are either in precarious financial condition or are extremely frugal. This won't be a problem if you enjoy counting and pinching every penny, but it could be disastrous if you have a more laid-back attitude about finances.

The ultimate idea in recycling was carried out by a group of women who initiated BYOB (Bring Your Old Boyfriend) parties, profiled in *Tales from the Front* (New York: Simon & Schuster, 1989) by Laura Kavesh and Cheryl Lavin. One woman's reject could be another woman's partner for a walk up the aisle. The parties (Sunday brunches, Tuesday evening discussion groups, Friday night get-togethers) have been very successful.

Of the original group of 25 women, all have married, at least once. Many met their husbands at these parties.

Sports Medicine Clinics

If striving to be physically fit is becoming more painful than pleasurable, consider going to a sports medicine clinic. Staffed by physical therapists, exercise physiologists, sports trainers, and physicians, these clinics can treat injuries you may have incurred in sports and fitness activities. They can also help you prevent future injuries and even provide you with techniques for improving your game.

Since repeat visits may be necessary until your condition improves, you may develop an acquaintance with your fellow patients in the waiting room or treatment areas. It's easy and natural to compare injuries and progress with someone who may be suffering from the same wrist or ankle problem you have. Obviously all the men you'll meet here are athletic, with enough intelligence and commitment to seek out help with their problems. If that describes you as well, it's quite possible that you'll connect with a compatible man in your local sports medicine clinic.

Travel Agencies

If you feel like you're getting burned out at work or simply wish you could shake the winter doldrums, escaping to a tropical island or foreign city may be just the tonic you need. Even if you don't have the time or money to get away in the foreseeable future, a visit to your travel agent can still be a lot of fun. Looking at all the glossy brochures and videos (of cruise ships, resorts, hotels) and dreaming about your ideal vacation spot can be highly therapeutic.

While browsing around a travel agency, you can converse with the other customers. Discussions and questions about vacation destinations are appropriate here. Many men who travel use professionals to make their

In his book *The Great American Man Shortage and Other Roadblocks to Romance* (New York: Rawson, 1983), William Novak describes amorophobia (the fear of romantic success). Don't allow yourself to suffer from this debilitating affliction. Do everything you can to empower yourself to achieve the romantic success you deserve.

reservations, so you'll probably have several men to talk with. Do note that there are three different types of travel and three corresponding mental attitudes. Don't automatically assume that someone is in a partying frame of mind just because he's at a travel agency. Not everyone is running off to the Caribbean.

- *Business travel:* If he's making arrangements for a business trip, he may be looking forward to seeing a new city or getting some important business accomplished. He also may be dreading the trip if he's getting tired of traveling or doesn't particularly want to meet with the client. The business traveler may be experiencing a moderate amount of tension, but usually not to the extent where he wouldn't be interested in getting to know you better.

- *Nonpleasurable personal travel:* If he's arranging a flight to Des Moines for a family reunion, he may be less than thrilled. He may also be flying home for a quick trip to check on an ailing parent or other emergency. Because he may be preoccupied with personal problems, he may be immune to your charms and unresponsive to your attempts at conversation.

- *Vacation travel:* Here's a man who's using a travel agency for the happiest of purposes. He'll be already enjoying the heady anticipation that comes with planning a vacation. His enthusiasm and relaxed state make it easy to get to know him. If things work out, you might be going back to the travel agent in the near future to arrange a romantic vacation for the two of you.

Veterinarian's Office

Pets can bring substantial joy and companionship into the lives of their owners. But as any pet owner knows, animals are as susceptible to illness and physical problems as humans are. Therefore, pet ownership entails some visits to the vet.

If you already own a pet, you've undoubtedly been to your local animal hospital. If you don't own a pet but have been thinking about buying or rescuing one from the animal shelter, stop delaying. When you next find yourself at the vet's office (as you inevitably will), make sure you're not so busy admiring the animals that you neglect to check out their owners.

The antics of animals help to break down conversational barriers. It's easy to compliment or comment on someone's pet. And, of course, *your* pet

---

Author Robert Masello in *What Do Men Want from Women?* (New York: Ballantine, 1983) explains that just as dogs can smell fear, people can sense desire or a longing for intimacy and love. He feels that the more you want to meet someone new, the less likely you'll be to pull it off because your need or loneliness will repel people. Independence and strength are the qualities that will draw people to you, so he suggests that women try to display as much confidence and contentment as possible.

---

will be so adorable that other people can't help but notice your furry pride and joy and then, by extension, you!

It's difficult to classify men according to the type of pet they own since there are so many individual breeds and types. But as a general guide, consider the following:

- *Dog owner:* He's open, honest, and active. Highly affectionate, he needs love in his life to be happy.
- *Cat owner:* He's subject to moodiness and sometimes has difficulty relating to people. He needs a lot of personal space and freedom in his life.
- *Bird owner:* He's chatty and sociable. While his conversation may lack intellectual depth, he does attempt to always keep lines of communication open.
- *Reptile owner:* He's very concerned with distinguishing himself from the crowd. He favors a highly individualistic lifestyle, not caring in the least whether other people find him odd.
- *Fish owner:* He's as sensual as any man you can find. But his hedonism can be very selfish, and he seldom looks out for anyone other than himself.

CHAPTER 7

Special Events

THERE ARE CERTAIN EVENTS THAT don't take place regularly. Some occur only once a year, while others happen even more infrequently (presidential elections; comets, meteors, and other astronomical occurrences). Because they're not available all the time, they should be appreciated and attended when they are.

These special events can become traditions in your life, helping you to mark the seasons or years as they pass. There's a comforting sense of continuity when you have certain things to look forward to each year, such as an art festival in September or your community's opera season in the spring. Even more special are other events that occur only once and never again; these should also be treasured, as their uniqueness can add some spice and unpredictability to your life. Almost every special event (other than seminars or festivals geared exclusively to women) offers man-meeting opportunities you should take advantage of. So don't procrastinate the next time one of these events rolls around. If you miss it, you won't get another chance until next year or even longer. Read your local newspaper to find out what's happening in your community, mark it on your calendar, and enjoy!

Astronomical Events

Sightings of comets, eclipses, certain meteors, and other astronomical events don't happen every day, so they can be special events indeed, particularly when they occur only once every hundred years. Don't miss the opportunity to see some spectacular sights in the sky. Go to your nearest planetarium; it will certainly be offering special programs for the occasion as well as powerful telescopes for better viewing. Many large office buildings remain open at night for public use during such occasions and this can afford a great view, too.

Stargazers come in all types. Some are hard-core astronomy nuts, while others do it only when there's something completely out of the ordinary. They can range in age from preadolescents to senior citizens. Men tend to be a little more interested in astronomical events than women.

Celebrity Appearances

Most people are intrigued by celebrities and enjoy meeting them. But your chances of running into one are almost nil unless you live in certain neighborhoods in New York and Los Angeles and frequent the hot spots. So when a celebrity makes a special public appearance for a book signing, new product launching (such as perfume, clothes, food, record albums), or just to draw a crowd in a store or restaurant, it's your golden opportunity to meet a famous person.

While you wait among the throng of fellow admirers, you can mingle and see if there's anyone in the crowd who interests you. You'll have at least one thing in common: you're both fans of the celebrity. The type of men you'll meet depends on the particular celebrity. An offbeat, artsy novelist will draw similar types of people; a fashion designer will attract people who are interested in clothes; a rock star can bring anyone from a preteen to a middle-aged baby boomer, depending on the star's past or current popularity.

Charity Events

All communities have special fund-raisers for a variety of charities and causes. Some are gala black-tie events, while others are more casual. All of

In *Marrying Again (The Art of Attracting a New Man and Winning His Heart)* (Chicago: Contemporary, 1988), Teddi Sanford and Mickie Padorr Silverstein note that attracting a man involves selling yourself. The basic sales techniques to "make the sale" are: get attention, spark interest, create desire, motivate a decision, and stimulate action.

them draw numbers of people who want to participate because they either care deeply about the charity or they enjoy the social aspects of the ball, dinner, or party. Either way, such events provide you with an opportunity to meet and mingle with some of the more prominent members of your community. Tickets can be expensive, but you might be able to write off some of it from your income taxes as a charitable contribution.

Obviously, the more costly functions will be attended by wealthy individuals who use such occasions to further their business/professional interests. The less formal and cheaper events are more likely to be populated with people who truly care about the charity or cause.

Festivals

Who doesn't love a festival? The upbeat mood, crowds of people, food, and music guarantee a fun time. Most festivals are outdoors, but the indoor ones can be enjoyable, too. Almost every community has its own unique festival (for example, the Winterfest in Buffalo, the Gaspirilla Festival in Tampa, the Dogwood Festival in Atlanta). These festivals are a great source of civic pride and draw many members of the community. Other types of festivals include those dedicated to the arts, books, food, Renaissance era, and a variety of ethnic heritages.

You can find out about these festivals by reading your local newspaper. Most are well attended by males and females of all ages. It's possible to meet someone anywhere or anytime at a festival . . . while waiting in line to buy a lemonade or looking over a photographic display. Just go with a lighthearted attitude, be friendly, and make it your business to enjoy yourself!

Arts Festivals.   Most communities have outdoor art festivals in the spring or fall where artists and craftspeople from far and near exhibit and sell their work. Usually paintings, drawings, photographs, ceramics, stained glass, jewelry, woven objects, and wooden pieces are available. Sometimes the performing arts (music, dance, mime, theater) are featured as well. These festivals offer you a wonderful opportunity to view and possibly acquire quality handcrafted items. Many types of people attend these festivals, but most share a genuine interest in and love for art.

Book Festivals.   Book festivals are a relatively new event, but large cities are beginning to hold them annually. Authors and publishers display their wares in a festival atmosphere. Readings, book signings, lectures, discussion circles, and entertainment are offered. If you're a book lover, you'll be in heaven browsing through the publications and perhaps even meeting your favorite writer. These festivals attract true bibliophiles. The men you'll meet here really appreciate literature and are voracious readers. Some are also writers (or would-be writers) who are interested in connecting with a publisher.

Ethnic Festivals.   Most ethnic groups hold annual festivals to celebrate their heritage. Greek, Hispanic, German, and Italian festivals are the most common, but there are also Irish, Scottish, English, Indian, Japanese, Chinese, Vietnamese, Thai, Scandinavian, African, French, Caribbean, Lebanese, and Israeli festivals. Regardless of whether the celebration is for the Chinese New Year, Israeli Independence Day, or the German Oktoberfest, there are elements common to all: music, food, dance, handicrafts, and fun. You don't have to share the same nationality as the festival's sponsors to attend; every festival is open to the general public and the sponsors will welcome anyone who is interested in learning about their culture. Many in the crowd are members of the sponsoring ethnic group, but many others are not. Those who are part of the particular ethnic group are proud of their heritage and see it as a significant part of their identity. The men who are nonaffiliated visitors tend to be adventurous and receptive to new ideas. Keep an open mind while attending the festival. Some of the customs or foods may seem strange to you, but you're there to broaden your horizons, so try to experience all you can.

Food Festivals.   Most of us love to eat, so food festivals are very appealing. Usually a number of restaurants offer small portions of their food at reasonable prices. This allows participants to graze around and sample a variety of foods. (Specialty food festivals may focus just on Oriental dishes, chocolate, seafood, and so on.) If your community holds such a festival, be sure to go. You'll be able to try many different types of food, some of which you may never have had an opportunity to taste before. You might discover some excellent restaurants in the process. Music and other entertainment add to the fun. The majority of those attending are not gluttons by any means (usually the portions are too small for major pigging out). They just enjoy trying new flavors and textures. A man with such interests generally tends to be very sensual in all aspects of his life and can be an enjoyable partner, both at and away from the dining table.

Renaissance Festivals. Renaissance festivals are held in many locations (typically a large wooded field) across the country. A group of Renaissance devotees stages the festival and attempts to offer participants an authentic experience of what England, Italy, or France was like during those times. Actors dress in period costumes and use Olde English in interacting with each other and participants (who are encouraged to do the same). Crafts and food are sold. Special offerings include music, jousting, and theater, all of which are based on that which occurred during the Renaissance. If you attend one of these festivals, get into the spirit by putting together a costume. Buy a garland of flowers for your hair. Attempt to talk in Olde English. You just might attract a man who enjoys the fantasy and has some creativity and imagination of his own.

Live Performances

Because concerts and plays are held throughout the year, most really can't be considered anything out of the ordinary. But a select few truly do qualify as special events. Concerts that feature musicians who seldom tour or combine two or more talents who usually don't perform together can be included in this category, as can major plays that are either opening or closing in your city. Possibilities for man-meeting include waiting in line to buy the tickets or to enter the theater, patronizing a refreshment/souvenir stand during intermission, or sitting by someone interesting. The type of men you meet will vary according to the performance. A country music star will draw one type of crowd, whereas Peter, Paul, & Mary attract a different following. A few performances may be so universally appealing (such as a Beatles reunion) that they attract a broad variety of people.

Presidential Elections

It may have been years since you took civics in high school, but presumably you've been convinced ever since that it's your duty to vote. Take an active part in the democratic process by voting every chance you get. Presidential elections come around every four years but they attract the biggest numbers of voters. Many polling places get flooded with more people than they can efficiently handle, resulting in long lines with waits of an hour or more.

It's absolutely not true that "you're nobody till somebody loves you." But having someone to love and being loved in return makes a nice addition to your life and your self-esteem. Choose a number of suggestions from this book and put them into action!

Don't get discouraged or leave! Stand in line and make conversation with those around you. If one of them is an attractive and interesting man, so much the better. (You may want to volunteer at the polls. That way you'll meet *every* man who comes to vote.)

Protests/Demonstrations/Rallies

During the '60s, protest demonstrations were a fertile meeting ground for young adults. Many a romance blossomed as individuals got to know each other while protesting the Vietnam War. More recently, some people managed to connect during demonstrations for and against the Persian Gulf war. Times have changed and demonstrations aren't quite as prevalent, but it still can be worth your while to participate in a cause you care about. You may not be able to change the world, but you can at least speak up and take a stand on one of the controversial issues that society is currently dealing with.

It's also very possible that you'll become acquainted with some of the men there. The type of man you can meet will be a reflection of the specific issue. Liberal, less traditional men can be found at demonstrations for animal rights (against furriers, vivisection, and so on), environmental concerns (especially antinuclear), pro-choice, AIDS support, gay rights, women's rights, freedom of speech and expression, and against hate/ultra-right-wing groups. Conservative men are found at prolife or anti–gun control/pro-NRA demonstrations. You'll also find both types at political rallies featuring the candidates of their choice.

Sporting Events

There are lots of sporting events held on a regular basis, but only one Super Bowl, Indianapolis 500, NCAA Final Four, and Kentucky Derby each year.

If you're interested in any of these sports or other annual championships and tournaments, ranging from surfing to polo, you may want to treat yourself to tickets. You'll need to decide months ahead of time, since tickets go fast.

The type of men you can meet varies according to the sport. Refer to Chapter 1, Sports and Fitness, for the specifics.

Trade Shows

Manufacturers, distributors, and retailers participate in exhibits and shows that travel through major American cities. These shows, which are frequently open to the public, allow consumers to preview new products and see other items which may not be available at the stores where you shop. Each type of show has a personality all its own and attracts a certain type of person. For example, a boat show is entirely different from a New Age Expo. Pick some that interest you and check out the men who attend. Some of the better possibilities include antiques, computers, food, garden/flower, New Age (books, services, products), outdoor and sports, and toys for adults (sports cars, electronics, hot tubs).

One good reason to use the suggestions in this book instead of resorting to a dating service is the lawsuit against a Manhattan dating service. Although the operator, Helena Amram, claims that she has been responsible for more than 8,000 weddings over her 23-year career, there have been 50 complaints that her fees were exorbitant and that she wasn't living up to the terms of her contracts. Dissatisfied customers could not get their money refunded. The state of New York is suing her for exceeding the statutory limit of $250 on dating-service fees. Customers were overcharged up to $20,000 and matched with married men and convicts. Of course, most dating services are perfectly legitimate.

Still, you will save money and hassles by finding a man through your own creative efforts. This book shows you where the men are and issues an open invitation to enrich your life by becoming involved with some of the suggested activities and experiences. Empowered by this information, you can meet the kind of men who are right for *you*.

INDEX